LITURGICAL YEAR

The Worship of God

Supplemental Liturgical Resource 7

Prepared by

The Ministry Unit on Theology and Worship
for the
Presbyterian Church (U.S.A.)
and the
Cumberland Presbyterian Church

Published by
Westminster/John Knox Press
Louisville, Kentucky

For acknowledgments, see pages 427–428.

Published by Westminster/John Knox Press
Louisville, Kentucky

PRINTED IN THE UNITED STATES OF AMERICA
2 4 6 8 9 7 5 3 1

Library of Congress Cataloging-in-Publication Data

Presbyterian Church (U.S.A.)
  Liturgical year : the worship of God / prepared by the Ministry Unit on Theology and Worship for the Presbyterian Church (U.S.A.) and the Cumberland Presbyterian Church.
      p.   cm. — (Supplemental liturgical resource ; 7)
  Includes bibliographical references.
  ISBN 0-664-25350-4

  1. Church year.   2. Presbyterian Church (U.S.A.) — Liturgy — Texts. 3. Cumberland Presbyterian Church — Liturgy—Texts.   4. Presbyterian Church—United States—Liturgy—Texts.   I. Presbyterian Church (U.S.A.). Ministry Unit on Theology and Worship. II. Cumberland Presbyterian Church.   III. Title.   IV. Series: Presbyterian Church (U.S.A.). Supplemental liturgical resource ; 7.
BX8969.5.P74 1991
264′.05137013—dc20   91-37587

CONTENTS

PREFACE   7

INTRODUCTION TO THE LITURGICAL CALENDAR
    Liturgical Time   19
    The Shape of the Liturgical Calendar   22
    The Easter Cycle: From the Ashes of Death to the
        Fire of the Spirit   26
    The Christmas Cycle: From the Darkness of the
        World to the Light of Christ   41
    Ordinary Time   49
    Liturgical Color   55

CHRISTMAS CYCLE
    Advent   61
    Christmas   73
    Epiphany   85

ORDINARY TIME BETWEEN EPIPHANY AND ASH WEDNESDAY
    Baptism of the Lord   93
    Sundays between Baptism of the Lord and
        Transfiguration of the Lord   98
    Transfiguration of the Lord 108

EASTER CYCLE
    Ash Wednesday 115
    Lent 127

Passion/Palm Sunday 139
Tenebrae 152
Maundy Thursday 159
Good Friday 171
The Great Vigil of Easter 184
Easter Sunday through Sixth Sunday of Easter 204
Ascension of the Lord and Seventh Sunday of Easter 216
Day of Pentecost 220

ORDINARY TIME BETWEEN DAY OF PENTECOST
AND FIRST SUNDAY OF ADVENT
Trinity Sunday 231
Other Sundays between Trinity Sunday and
    Christ the King 236
All Saints' Day 261
Christ the King 266

COMMENTARY ON THE LITURGICAL RESOURCES
How to Use This Resource 275
The Christmas Cycle 280
The Easter Cycle 291

MUSIC 325

NOTES 415

SOURCES OF THE LITURGICAL TEXTS 419

FOR FURTHER READING 422

ACKNOWLEDGMENTS 427

PREFACE

One of the most significant aspects of liturgical renewal in twentieth-century ecumenism is the reform of the liturgical calendar. The past twenty-five years have witnessed a remarkable convergence among the churches in the way they keep time. There is a new appreciation of the evangelical dimensions of the calendar and the ability its use has in building people up in the faith.

This is particularly significant among American Presbyterians, whose ethos was initially shaped by forces for whom the liturgical calendar had no useful purpose. In order to appreciate this shift in American Presbyterianism, it will be helpful to review some of the history of worship in the Reformed tradition, especially those forces that shaped American Presbyterian worship.

By the close of the Middle Ages, the church's calendar had badly deteriorated. It had become so overburdened with so many feast days and fast days that it had lost its primary focus upon the Lord's Day as the essential feast day. The primary structure of the annual cycle of days and seasons was obscured. Furthermore, the degeneration of the feast day celebrations into times of general revelry seriously distracted the people from genuine faith. Reform of the calendar was crucial.

In order to recover a focus upon the saving events of the gospel, the Reformers purged the calendar of everything that detracted from the proclamation of the fullness of the gospel on the Lord's Day. The annual calendar was reduced to what were called the "evangelical feasts," celebrations rooted in the biblical witness. The Lord's Day was restored as the primary biblical symbol in the way Christians keep time. The "evangelical feasts" that were preserved were: Christmas, Good Friday, Easter, Ascension, and Pentecost. Advent and Lent were cast aside. Saints' days were also cast aside, for among other reasons they obscured the primacy of the Lord's Day. However, it was suggested that preachers could profitably commend the saints as worthy examples for the people. The criteria by which the Reformed judged the acceptability of a liturgical form or practice was whether it was faithful to the New Testament witness to the gospel.

The Second Helvetic Confession (1566) is a fitting description of what the early Reformed sought to preserve in the calendar: "If in Christian liberty the churches religiously celebrate the memory of the Lord's nativity, circumcision, passion, resurrection, and of his ascension into heaven, and the sending of the Holy Spirit upon his disciples, we approve it highly."[1]

As the Reformed faith extended to England and Scotland the Reformation was forced to take root in a context much different from that on the continent. On the continent, entire political entities were Reformed. This enabled the Reformed to prepare their own books of services without interference. In English-speaking lands, those seeking to carry the reform from the continent were faced with the difficult task of reforming within a state church hostile to Genevan-inspired reform. Whereas the Scottish kirk was reformed under John Knox, the kirk continued to endure English political and religious pressures. Attempts to bring further reform within the English church led to bitter conflict with the English crown.

The political context, therefore, forced different answers to liturgical questions from those on the continent. The relentless pressures of the royal and episcopal party in the seventeenth century resulted in a gradual and significant shift in the nature of the reform sought in the English church. In the conflicts, a Puritan party emerged within the English church. As the contending party in a state church, the Puritans knew well the vulnerability of the reform they sought. The liberty of the church to order its life and worship in harmony with the Word of God was threatened. They felt under attack by both church and nation, and worship was where the conflict raged.

The struggles ultimately drove the Puritans to join forces with the separatists. The result was that both the English Puritans and the Scots were forced into a more radical liturgical position than the reform on the continent, which did not have to face such issues.

The Puritans' struggle for liberty put them in direct conflict with those who had power to legislate the content of the prayer book and to require its use. The Puritan conflict was initially not opposition to the propriety and use of a prayer book, but rather against a prayer book that did not reflect the concerns of the Puritans. Since the liturgical calendar is inseparable from the scripture readings that are read and the prayers that are said in worship (which together form the substance of a prayer book), their opposition to the prayer book being foisted upon them was in effect an opposition to the liturgical calendar the prayer book embodied. The unfortunate result was that the liturgical calendar was lost. Even the evangelical festivals the sixteenth-century Reformers found useful in building up the people in faith were cast aside. Voluntary or noncoercive adoption of a schedule of feasts and seasons was inconceivable at the time. Therefore, whereas the Reformers were in a position to *reform* the existing liturgical calendar, the political and ecclesiastical situation compelled the Puritans to *reject* the calendar for the sake of liberty. It was in such a context that the Westminster *Directory for the Publique Worship of God*, void of liturgical text, was created in 1644.

The extent to which this perspective shaped the Scottish kirk is illustrated by the fact that when the Scots adopted the Second Helvetic Confession, they excised from the text the paragraph cited above. The Scottish *Book of Discipline* (1560) furthermore condemned, among others, all "feasts of Christmas, Circumcision, Epiphany, Purification." While the Reformed on the continent could examine days and seasons according to their potential to celebrate the gospel, the Puritans and Scots were forced to direct their primary concern toward the political and liturgical expressions of a state church.

It was at this moment in history that the Puritans and the Scots settled in the New World. They formed the nucleus that initially shaped American Presbyterianism. Thus Puritan views dominated the way the church took root in American soil. The result was that no Christian festivals were celebrated among seventeenth-century American Presbyterians. In fact, those who observed Christmas were locked in the stocks.

The Directory for Worship adopted by the first General Assembly in 1789, like its 1644 predecessor, made no reference to a liturgical calendar.

Opposition to prayer books and the liturgical calendar continued even though the Puritans were no longer engaged in a struggle for liberty. The agenda remained, even though the context had changed.

American Presbyterians soon forgot why they opposed prayer books and the calendar. What began as a struggle for liberty turned into a new legalism.

In the period after the Civil War, forces in American Protestantism began to break down the legalism. The dominant forces were the Sunday school movement and revivalism. Christmas and Easter first appeared in Sunday school literature, and began to spread in the last decade of the nineteenth century. The Sunday school movement also reintroduced historic forms such as the Creed, the Lord's Prayer, and the responsive reading of the Psalms. Revivalism softened the legalism, and also reintroduced some corporate worship rituals. A romanticism also stimulated among a few an appreciation of early liturgies of the Reformed tradition and a recognition of the need for liturgical reform.

However, it was not until the end of the nineteenth century before calls to restore any of the Christian festivals were heard with any significance. The remarkable recovery of the church's liturgical calendar among American Presbyterians is thus a phenomenon unique to the twentieth century.

From the outset of the twentieth century, a restored calendar began to take shape. The 1906 edition of *The Book of Common Worship* included prayers for Good Friday, Easter, Advent and Christmas, mingled with prayers for civil observances. This merging perhaps indicates a reluctance to regard these days as liturgical festivals, but rather to view them as civil holidays.

In the 1932 edition of *The Book of Common Worship,* more serious attention was devoted to the liturgical calendar. In this edition, it is significant that prayers for church festivals and seasons were separated from prayers for civil observances. The order in the list of the church's festivals was in accord with the Western Christian tradition. Beginning with Advent, the year moved through Christmas, Lent (which was entitled "Preparation for Easter"), Palm Sunday, Good Friday, Easter, Ascension Day, Pentecost and All Saints' Day. A rudimentary lectionary was included, providing a variety of readings for the festivals and seasons. The foundation was thus laid for the future development of the church's liturgical calendar.

Growing acceptance of the liturgical year among American Presbyterians is evidenced in the 1946 edition of *The Book of Common Prayer.* In this edition, resources for Maundy Thursday (called: Thursday before Easter) and Trinity Sunday were added to those of the previous edition. A well-developed two-year lectionary was incorporated for the first time. This calendar and lectionary drew upon solid liturgical scholarship in the Church of Scotland that had shaped the Scottish *Book of Common Order* (1940).

The increased attention given to the church's liturgical calendar was soon incorporated into the Presbyterian constitution. In 1961, The United Presbyterian Church in the U.S.A. adopted a new Directory for Worship. In contrast to the previous directory (which had changed little from its adoption in 1789), the new directory gave prominence to the church's liturgical calendar. In 1963, the Presbyterian Church in the U.S. adopted its Directory for the Worship and Work of the Church. While the Lord's Day was emphasized, there was no reference to the annual liturgical calendar in this directory. Among southern Presbyterians, Puritanism continued with such force that those on the committee who favored inclusion of the church's liturgical calendar were defeated.

The Worshipbook—Services (1970; a joint publication of the United Presbyterian Church in the U.S.A., the Presbyterian Church in the U.S., and the Cumberland Presbyterian Church) included a larger treasury of resources for celebrating the church's liturgical calendar than its predecessor edition of *The Book of Common Worship. The Worshipbook* introduced collects for each Sunday in the year, as well as seasonal and festival suggestions that included scriptural calls to worship, prayers of confession, a listing of psalms for use as responsive readings, and prayers of thanksgiving. This evidenced the growing acceptance of the liturgical calendar. Liturgical colors for the days and seasons were also suggested. Its inclusion of the newly prepared Roman lectionary, adapted for Presbyterian usage, has been a major influence in the growing acceptance of the lectionary among Presbyterians. Since the liturgical calendar and lectionary are intimately related, the increase in lectionary use and the celebration of the liturgical year have been parallel developments.

The story of liturgical reform among Protestants in the twentieth century is not complete without a recognition of the way liturgical reform in the Roman Catholic Church has influenced other churches. It is one of the remarkable evidences of the work of the Holy Spirit in our time. The Second Vatican Council (1962–1965) led to profound changes in the way Catholics worship. Many of the reforms are remarkably similar to the reforms the sixteenth-century Reformers sought. The Council indirectly changed the way other churches go about their task of shaping liturgical life.

In reforming the calendar, the Roman Catholic Church made much use of ecumenical liturgical scholarship. Flowing from this new spirit of collegiality, church leaders and liturgical scholars of a variety of traditions began to work cooperatively on liturgical projects. While this has international dimensions, in North America one result was the formation of the Consultation on Common Texts (C.C.T.). From the beginning of the Consultation, Presbyterians have taken an active role in its work. In 1978 the Consultation introduced a liturgical calendar agreed upon by the denominational representatives. This common calendar has historical roots with early Christians, and has been incorporated into the service books of various denominations. The Consultation on Common Texts is also responsible for the preparation of the Common Lectionary published in 1983, and for the revised Common Lectionary to be completed by the end of 1991.

In the two decades since the publication of *The Worshipbook*, the liturgical calendar available to Presbyterians has steadily moved toward the ecumenical consensus. In 1981 the United Presbyterian General Assembly approved a List of Special Days and Seasons for 1983–84 that reflected the common calendar. The Presbyterian action included for the first time Baptism of the Lord, Transfiguration of the Lord, and Christ the King. It also restored All Saints' Day, which was inadvertently omitted in *The Worshipbook* but was included in the revisions proposed to the General Assembly in 1974. All Saints' Day had been included in both of the trial-use publications that preceded *The Worshipbook* as well as *The Book of Common Worship* (1932 and 1946). Furthermore, the lectionaries Presbyterians have been using since 1970 have included the readings for Baptism of the Lord, Transfiguration of the Lord, and Christ the King, even though the titles of the days were previously not used.

In 1983, the Cumberland Presbyterian Church adopted a new directory that admonished congregations to use the liturgical year, recognizing it as an instrument to help insure that worship would reflect the whole of the gospel.

In 1989 a new Directory for Worship was adopted by the Presbyterian Church (U.S.A.). This Directory moves beyond its predecessors and outlines the full liturgical year (*Book of Order*, W-3.2001–3.2002) in keeping with ecumenical agreements.

The calendar that is the basis of this book is, therefore, the calendar that has evolved from very cautious first steps in the 1906 *Book of Common Worship* to a calendar that is shared in common with other Christian churches.

Liturgical Year contains a rich collection of prayers and other liturgical texts that will be useful in planning worship for each Sunday and festival throughout the year. Of special significance is the inclusion for the first time in an American Presbyterian liturgical resource the full services for Holy Week (Passion/Palm Sunday, Maundy Thursday, Good Friday, and the Easter Vigil). The recovery of these services in the contemporary liturgical movement is a significant aspect of the reforming of the church in the twentieth century. The paschal mystery these services celebrate is at the heart of the Christian faith and, therefore, is to be at the center of the church's liturgical calendar. When carefully planned and led, these services can root the faithful more firmly in the paschal mystery, the death and resurrection of Jesus Christ.

It is the intent of those who prepared *Liturgical Year* that it will be used creatively. Its rich treasury of prayers and liturgies are commended for those who plan and lead worship. Some of the material is drawn from or based upon a long and venerable tradition within the Christian church. These texts contribute to a sense of unity with that great continuum of Christians from every time and place. We are enriched in ways others before us have been strengthened in the faith. Some of the material is drawn from other churches, Roman and Orthodox, as well as other Protestant traditions. These texts remind us that the church is one, sharing one faith and one baptism. Some of the material is written for this resource, and seeks to meet particular needs unmet in available materials. All of the resources are in harmony with the directories for worship of the Presbyterian Church (U.S.A.), and of the Cumberland Presbyterian Church. More importantly, great care was taken in the development of *Liturgical Year* that it be a faithful witness to the gospel of Jesus Christ. This resource is provided with the conviction that it can be an instrument of renewal of the church at the center of its life togther, and can deepen the faith of the people.

Practical help is included to suggest ways congregations can creatively appropriate the resources into their life together. Each congregation will need to use the resource in ways that are most appropriate for the local situation, adapting the material in a manner that is pastorally responsible.

Liturgical Year is the seventh in the series of Supplemental Liturgical Resources. This series has its origins in actions taken in 1980 by the churches that formed the present Presbyterian Church (U.S.A.) and by the Cumberland Presbyterian Church. These churches acted to begin the process of developing "a new book of services for corporate worship" and expressed the hope that the new book would be "an instrument for the renewal of the church at its life-giving center." The process called for a series of volumes for trial use before the publication of the book of services. This volume and those Supplemental Liturgical Resources that have preceded it are the response to that action. *Liturgical Year* is the last volume in the series that will be the basis for the new service book, now scheduled for availability in 1993. However, other Supplemental Liturgical Resources are anticipated to supplement the service book.

Liturgical Year is the work of a task force appointed in 1984 by the Administrative Committee of the former Office of Worship of the Presbyterian Church (U.S.A.) to prepare a resource for celebrating the liturgical year. The progress of the task force over the five years of its labor was monitored by the Administrative Committee through 1987, and then by the Theology and Worship Ministry Unit of the Presbyterian Church (U.S.A.), which absorbed the functions of the former Office of Worship.

Those who served on the task force for some portion of its life were: William R. Forbes (chair), Peter C. Bower, Judith Kolwicz, David Lancaster, Barbara Miller, Juan Trevino, and Karmen Van Dyke; and Harold M. Daniels (staff).

The assistance of others not on the task force, whose work was solicited by the task force, was particularly helpful: Donald W. Stake provided some of the prayer texts; Stanley R. Hall gave valuable counsel in shaping the historical summary in this preface; Hal H. Hopson suggested the tones for singing the seasonal refrains and the lines from hymns to sing as responses; and John Weaver graciously accepted the invitation of the task force to provide musical settings for texts given him by the task force.

In 1990, the work of the task force was tested and extensive evaluations and suggestions for its revision were received. The manuscript was carefully and thoroughly revised in response to the testing and was subsequently approved for publication by the Theology and Worship Ministry Unit.

Those who served on the Administrative Committee of the Office of Worship that appointed the task force and monitored its early work were Melva W. Costen; Helen Hamilton; Collier S. Harvey, Jr.; Robert H. Kempes; James G. Kirk; Wynn McGregor; Ray A. Meester; Robert D. Miller; David C. Partington (chairperson); Robert Stigall;

D. Leandor Swann; John Weaver; Harold M. Daniels, Director of the Office of Worship; and Marion L. Liebert, Administrative Associate of the Office of Worship.

Those who served on the Theology and Worship Ministry Unit Committee at the time of the completion of the work of the task force were José H. Bibiloni; Muriel Brown; Sandra Hanna Charles; Harland Collins; Melva W. Costen; Margery Curtiss; Donna Frey de Cou; Joseph G. Dempsey; Gershon B. Fiawoo; Richard Fiete (chairperson); Daniell C. Hamby; Daniel W. Martin; William McIvor; Lewis Mudge; Deborah F. Mullen; Peter Ota; Heath K. Rada; Joan SalmonCampbell; James C. Spalding; R. David Steele; May Murakami Nakagawa (Presbyterian Association of Musicians representative); Gordon Turnbull (Theological Institute Advisory Member). Staff of the worship function of the Theology and Worship Ministry Unit were Harold M. Daniels and Nalini Jayasuriya. Those serving on the Worship Subunit were Melva W. Costen; Donna Frey de Cou; Gershon B. Fiawoo; Daniell C. Hamby (chair); Robert T. Henderson; Fred Holper; May Murakami Nakagawa; Donald W. Stake; R. David Steele; staff: Harold M. Daniels and Nalini Jayasuriya. George B. Telford, Director of the Theology and Worship Ministry Unit, and Joseph D. Small, Associate Director, as well as other members of the Unit's staff, have provided valuable guidance. The care given to details by Cindy Ohlmann Stairs, former worship administrative assistant, and Regina J. Noel, first as worship secretary and then as worship administrative assistant, greatly helped to facilitate a smooth moving from the work of the task force actions to the completed book.

We invite your evaluation of this resource presented to the church for trial use as it anticipates a new book of services which is scheduled for release in 1993. Send your comments to the Theology and Worship Ministry Unit, Room 3408, 100 Witherspoon St., Louisville, KY 40202-1396.

HAROLD M. DANIELS
Associate for Liturgical Resources

INTRODUCTION TO THE LITURGICAL CALENDAR

LITURGICAL TIME

It all began with the proclamation of the Word. The proclamation of the Word shaped the faith of the church concerning what God had done and was now doing in Christ.

The Inseparable Link Between Story and Time

Throughout the church's history, hearing the stories of God's past freed people to have faith in God's future, and, therefore, to live in the present. "Faith comes from what is heard," writes Paul (Rom. 10:17). By continually hearing the stories of God's faithfulness in the past and God's promises for the future, people know to whom they belong and to what they are called in the present. God's unfinished story today inevitably moves toward God's promised future. From the very beginning, story and time had been inseparable.

That Jewish and Christian worship have instinctively linked story and time is no surprise. God's purpose directs the people of God toward an end. Jews annually retell, in the context of a communal meal, the exodus story about God redeeming them from bondage. The *Haggadah* (narrative story) for the *Seder* (order of service) at *Pesach* (Passover) is an all-encompassing, identity-shaping, direction-giving story of how God liberates from slavery. By telling their children year after year the story of the exodus—affliction, suffering, sorrow, and struggle—Jews lay claim to a promise in a living word that lies at the heart of their faith. The more they relive the story, the more it becomes a part of their present and future lives. Without the exodus story there is no people called Israel.

Likewise, the Easter Vigil shaped the people called Christians. The great saving acts of the Lord not only recorded in scripture but read, contemplated, proclaimed, and lived over and over again provide a reality that lies at the heart of Christ's church.

Both Jewish and Christian worship include constantly retelling the memories from God's faithfulness in the past (story) and ritually enacting those memories (liturgical practice) in order to kindle hope in God's promised future and, thereby, be enabled to live freely in the present. Telling the story of God-with-us, and naming that presence in daily, weekly, monthly, seasonal, and annual cycles (ordered time) always have been and still are crucial to both Jewish and Christian worship.[1]

The gospel story proclaimed over a period of time spawned the church's liturgical practices. That period of time—permeated by the proclamation of the Word and by the people's response to the Word—has come to be known as the liturgical calendar.

The major factor in shaping the liturgical year has been the inseparable link between story and time. Thomas Talley writes that the annual festivals and seasons grew out of the proclamation of the gospel in one locale after another over time. The drawing together of these "local customs" into one creates the complex calendar called the "liturgical year." It all began with the proclamation of the Word.[2]

The Redeeming Work of Christ

What we hear in the Gospel stories of God-with-us is the redeeming work of Christ: incarnation-crucifixion-resurrection-outpouring of the Spirit:

Christ was born.
Christ taught.
Christ was crucified.
Christ was raised up.
And the Spirit was poured out on us.

The saving work of Christ is the story behind the story of Jesus' life.

The liturgical calendar, therefore, commemorates not the historical life of Christ but the redeeming work of Christ. Liturgy may be dramatic but it does not reproduce history. We are called not to reenact what Christ said and did, but to proclaim what Christ said and did.

Therefore, in our worship, extreme caution must be exercised with the fascination for re-living historical moments in the life of Christ.

Reenacting the life of Jesus historicizes a mystery which transcends time and place. Mimicking details of events in Jesus' life domesticates if not trivializes the holy awe of incarnation-crucifixion-resurrection-outpouring of the Spirit. We do not reproduce the Last Supper; rather, we celebrate the Lord's Supper. We do not perform Christmas liturgies that duplicate past events; rather, we rejoice in the present reality of Christmas. The festive liturgies throughout the liturgical calendar are not reenacted historical dramas of the past but contemporary encounters with Christ.

In the retelling and commemorating of the stories of God-with-us, the Spirit draws us into the mystery of the saving work of Christ. The liturgical calendar offers a series of celebrations that confront us with who we are in Christ and present us with a pattern for growth in Christ. The liturgical calendar permeates us with the mystery of Christ's redeeming work so we may conform our lives to Christ. It opens to us now the fulfillment of our lives for a future which is already with us in Christ and for which we were created.[3]

THE SHAPE OF THE LITURGICAL CALENDAR

The nature and fullness of God's time is so radically different from our natural and arbitrary understanding of time that at best we can say: "Now we see in a mirror, dimly, but then we will see face to face. Now I know only in part; then I will know fully, even as I have been fully known" (1 Cor. 13:12). The liturgical calendar gives us a glimpse of the way God's time breaks into our time.

The Lord's Day

From earliest times, Christians have gathered on Sunday (the Lord's Day): "On the first day of the week, when we met to break bread, Paul was holding a discussion with them" (Acts 20:7). By the end of the first century, a church manual called the *Didache* instructed Christians to come together every Lord's Day for giving thanks and breaking of bread.[4] Justin Martyr, in the mid-second century, writes of worship on Sunday as the common time to celebrate the resurrection and the transformation of creation.[5] Sunday was and is the normal day for celebrating the fact that "everything has become new" (2 Cor. 5:17).

The reason the early Christians gathered for public worship on Sunday is found in the New Testament focus on the "first day of the week"—the day of Jesus' resurrection. All four Gospels affirm the first day of the week as the day of Christ's resurrection (Matt. 28:1ff.; Mark 16:2; Luke 24:1; John 20:1, 19). The risen and victorious Christ triumphed over the power of death. The Lord of life reigned. To honor God's work in raising Jesus from the dead, Christians gathered on the first day of the week to break bread and encounter the risen Lord. Sunday derives its meaning from Christ's resurrection, and it became a thankful celebration of being raised together with Christ.[6]

As they recalled the creation stories of Genesis, the first Christians (primarily Jews) remembered how God completed the work of creation in six days and rested on the seventh. On the eighth day of creation ("the first day of the week," according to all four Gospels), God continued the work of creation by raising Christ from the dead. This eighth day of creation/first day of the week is what became commonly known as the Lord's Day (Rev. 1:10), the day of resurrection.

The Lord's Day was characterized by recollecting Jesus' words and deeds, and celebrating the presence of the risen Christ among them in the bread and cup of the Lord's Supper. A story and a meal formed the heart of worship each Sunday. Sunday was and is a festival in its own right.

On Sunday, the church's worship focused on the presence of the risen Lord. And, since the church's definitive celebration and experience of the resurrection of the Lord is the Lord's Supper, the Lord's Day of resurrection, Sunday, is inseparably linked to the Lord's Supper.[7]

The weekly cycle of Sundays also looks ahead to a final future fulfillment. The *Epistle of Barnabas*, written by a late-first-century Christian of Alexandria, urged rejoicing on the eighth day of creation/ the first day of the week as "the beginning of a new world, because that was when Jesus rose from the dead."[8] Every Lord's Day (of resurrection) celebrates the unfolding presence of the new creation revealed in the risen Christ. In hearing the scriptures and breaking bread each first day of the week, Christians celebrate the age to come.

Thus Sunday, the "original feast day," not only shaped the church's calendar but transforms all days. The standard or "ordinary" time for worship—the Lord's Day—reveals that which is becoming all creation's ordinary time. Sunday proclaims that all of time has been redeemed in Christ. The Lord's Day is the foundation of the way Christians keep time.

The Annual Calendar

While the whole gospel is celebrated on each Lord's Day, it is not surprising that early Christians found meaning in celebrating particular days that centered on a major event or aspect of the saving story. Gradually an annual calendar emerged. By the fourth century its major features were in place. That basic shape remains today. Whenever it has focused on the saving events of Christ it has played a major role in forming the faith of the people.

What we can faintly discern of God's time in our present calendar may be portrayed as two recurring cycles of *extra*ordinary time undergirded by periods of ordinary time. Each cycle of extraordinary time commences with a period of preparation and anticipation, and culminates in a season of celebration. One cycle spirals around incarnation, and the other around resurrection. Together they lead us through God's time.

An outline of the calendar that is the basis of this book follows. There is wide ecumenical concurrence on its major features.

The Christmas (Incarnation) Cycle
Four weeks of Advent
Twelve days of Christmas
The Epiphany of the Lord

Ordinary Time
(January 7 through Tuesday before Ash Wednesday)

The Easter (Resurrection) Cycle
"Forty days" of Lent
Fifty days of Easter
The Day of Pentecost

Ordinary Time
(Monday after the Day of Pentecost through
Saturday before the First Sunday of Advent)

Particular days in and out of season offer a special focus or special occasions on which to begin or conclude a cycle:

The Baptism of the Lord (begins Ordinary Time)
The Transfiguration of the Lord (concludes Ordinary Time)
Ash Wednesday (begins Lent)
Passion/Palm Sunday
Maundy Thursday
Good Friday
Saturday of Holy Week (concludes Lent)
The Ascension of the Lord
Trinity Sunday (begins Ordinary Time)
All Saints' Day
Christ the King (ends Ordinary Time)

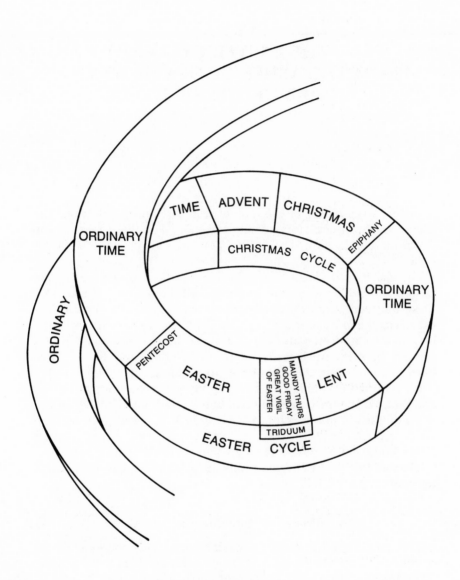

THE LITURGICAL YEAR

THE EASTER CYCLE:
FROM THE ASHES OF DEATH TO THE
FIRE OF THE SPIRIT

Easter is the oldest of the annual festivals, and it celebrates the central event of the story of our salvation. For these reasons the description of the annual calendar that follows begins with the Easter cycle.

The Easter cycle consists of six Sundays in Lent, seven Sundays of Easter, and one Sunday of Pentecost ("the fiftieth day"). Throughout these fourteen Sundays, the emphasis upon cross *and* resurrection expresses the unity of the cycle. Cross and resurrection are inseparable, both in the Christian faith and in our liturgical celebration. We observe Lent in anticipation of the resurrection, and we celebrate Easter remembering the cost of the cross's life-giving victory.

We will first examine the nature of the resurrection joy of Easter, and then turn to the Lenten preparation for such joy. Finally, we will focus on the gift of the Spirit to the church at Pentecost, setting it on fire to witness to the crucified and risen Christ. We begin with Easter rather than Lent because it is only when we understand what Easter is all about that we can begin to consider appropriate ways to prepare for celebrating it.

Easter *(Pascha):* Celebrating the New Order

The early church's annual calendar began and ended with the celebration of *Pascha* (Easter)—a "big Sunday." *Pascha* is the English transliteration of both the Greek and Hebrew words for "Passover," the central festival for Jews. The early Christians appropriated this term for the annual celebration of the death and resurrection of

Christ. *Pascha* signified the great deliverance accomplished in the Lord's new Passover.

For Christians, *Pascha* was initially a feast that included everything from the incarnation, through the death and resurrection of Christ, to the gift of the Spirit. The Lord's life-giving victories were proclaimed and celebrated each year in a fast and vigil near the time of Passover. Jewish Christians, particularly in Asia Minor, observed this annual festival of *Pascha* on the actual date of Passover (14 Nisan), which had now been transformed by Christ's resurrection. Gentile Christians throughout the Roman Empire gathered for this yearly celebration on a Sunday—the day of the Lord's resurrection. The annual Paschal Vigil was celebrated on these two different dates until the Council of Nicaea (A.D. 325) declared the Sunday *Pascha* as the official day.[9]

As the principal service of the year, since at least the second century, the Paschal Vigil celebrated the promise of new life, of forgiveness of sins, and of victory over death. Lighting of the fire and the paschal candle symbolized Christ passing through darkness into light. This was followed by singing the Exsultet, the great hymn in praise of the redemption. On this night of nights, stories were recalled—of creation, of Israel passing through the waters from oppression to liberation, of God preparing the world for the coming of Christ, and of Christ's bursting the bonds of death and rising victorious from the grave.

It was furthermore the occasion for baptism. "What time is more appropriate for baptism," wrote St. Basil of Caesarea, "than this day of the Pasch. It is the memorial day of the resurrection. Baptism implants in us the seed of resurrection. Let us then receive the grace of resurrection on the day of the resurrection."[10] On this night of nights, new converts to the faith were baptized into Christ Jesus, and so into his death and resurrection: "We have been buried with him by baptism into death, so that just as Christ was raised from the dead by the glory of the Father, so we too might walk in newness of life" (Rom. 6:4).

The Paschal Vigil concluded in the early hours of Sunday morning, the great resurrection day, as the community of faith gathered at the table of the Lord to celebrate the Lord's Supper.

Pascha is the central event, the time of transformation, of becoming a resurrected people, God's new people. On this Sunday of all Sundays, *Pascha*, we celebrate our transformation as a new people.

When Christ rose from the grave, death and all other "principalities and powers" that seek to entomb God's will were forever defeated.

Easter is not simply the miracle of a dead person raised from a grave, but a celebration of power that can shatter death in order that people can freely serve the God of life. In the resurrection of Christ, God's awesome purposes were on display, revealing a radically new world—of peace and harmony and equality and mutuality—about which we can only dream. The Lord of the future has been disclosed to us. Both the incarnation at Christmas and the resurrection at Easter testify to the Lordship of the Christ.

Resurrection Faith

Resurrection shouts "no" to everything in our world that works against God's will, and "yes" to God's victory. At the same time, Easter draws us toward a future salvation for which we wait with patience. History is marching to a final end. What Christ accomplished on Easter is a glorious revelation of the future, for resurrection implies a totally new order. "We will be changed," writes Paul (1 Cor. 15:52). The new age will transform the old age. "If anyone is in Christ, there is a new creation: everything old has passed away; see, everything has become new!" (2 Cor. 5:17). The scriptures offer confidence in the power of God who raised up Jesus, and an invitation to trust God's grace for life and for death.

God reversed the judgment upon us by raising Christ from the dead. The great hymn in Ephesians (2:14–16) tells of Christ breaking down the walls that separate us from each other and from God, to make us one people. Out of a divided humanity, Christ formed a new humanity that transcends differences in race, religion, nationality, politics, and economic class. Christ's resurrection not only absolved humanity from sin; it established a new reality. Post-Easter history is history in a new dimension. Post-Easter Christians are new people, citizens of the city without walls.

Behold the New Order

On Easter we glimpse a new landscape—the age to come—and experience a sense of holy awe at the significance of the resurrection for human life. The shape of the age to come reveals a new people of God, a new humanity.

When Christ was crucified, humanity died with him on Calvary. But on Easter morning, a new world was born—raised up with the crucified and risen Christ. Bursting the bonds of death, the first human being of a new human race, Jesus Christ, appeared among those who crucified him. In the midst of the old sin-struck world, God gave the world a new beginning, a new humanity. By faith the old guilt-ridden humanity was born again into the new forgiven humanity of Jesus Christ. Ever since, here and there, clusters of the new people of God live according to the new social order of the new age.

Therefore, Easter faith recalls the past, especially the awesome act of God in raising the crucified Christ from the grave. Easter hope looks to the promised future, to that which awaits us. Easter love celebrates the presence of the crucified and risen Christ who is now among us, reconciling us as one people. Resurrection faith asserts that by grace we are born again into the new humanity of Jesus Christ. We are called to new life for God and for neighbors. As representatives of the new humanity we walk in newness of life.

Ascension Day

The seven weeks of the Easter season include the festival of the Ascension of our Lord—Ascension Day.

Throughout the earliest centuries of the church, every Sunday celebrated the unitive festival of the paschal mystery: the passion-death-resurrection-ascension of Christ, the giving of the Spirit, and Christ's coming in glory at the end of time. Over the years, however, Christ's redeeming work was gradually separated into individual feasts on specific days. For instance, by the late fourth century, the Lord's ascension and the outpouring of the Holy Spirit were commemorated as two distinct aspects of Christ's redeeming work. Ascension Day's exaltation of Christ, however, still looks both back to Transfiguration and Easter, and forward to Christ the King.

Adhering to the Lukan sequence of events in Acts 1:1–11, Christ's ascension was celebrated on "the fortieth day" after resurrection. This custom probably originated in the Constantinople-Antioch area of Asia Minor and then spread westward to northern Italy and eastward to Jerusalem. Obviously, Ascension Day was and is observed always on the fortieth day after the resurrection (the Thursday after the sixth Sunday of Easter), or on the Sunday following.

In that John Calvin's theology placed great importance on the ascended and regnant Christ, Ascension Day is in some ways *the* Presbyterian feast day. Christ is Lord of the world and head of the church, we proclaim. Christ's ascension, therefore, concerns us not only with ecclesiastical matters but also with social and political ones. If Christ has ascended, then Christ's word rules the world as well as the church. If Christ has ascended, then there are no other rulers—all others are merely pretenders. Christ reigns supreme.

With the raising of Christ to a position above all worldly powers, the earthly ministry of Christ begun at Christmas's incarnation now concludes. The path of faithfulness obediently followed by Christ traveled through the suffering of the cross to the exaltation of the glory. From glory to suffering to glory again is the shape of Jesus' ministry as well as ours. We too are destined for the glory we share now in Christ only by faith. "It does not yet appear what we shall be, but we know that when Christ appears we shall be like him" (1 John 3:2).

Lent: The Way of the Cross to Easter (Pascha)

Pascha (Easter) quickly evolved into a cycle that we now celebrate as a day and a season of the "Great Fifty Days" ending with Pentecost and preceded by a period of preparation. Though the earliest traditions are unclear, Lent apparently evolved as a time for training, particularly as a time of final preparation of candidates for baptism at Easter. Lent also became a time for the renewal of the faithful, as well as a time for the excommunicated to prepare to return to the community of faith.

By the fourth century, Lent had developed from a two-day fast, through a week-long fast, to a biblical "forty days." Originally, though Lent contained elements of penitence, it was primarily a time devoted to preparing those who were to be baptized. The Lenten season seems to have developed as a period of learning with a focus on what it means to be a follower of Christ. Those preparing for baptism learned the Creed, the teachings of Jesus (perhaps the Sermon on the Mount), and the disciplines of the Christian faith.

The period of Lent had and still has an emphasis on reaffirming baptismal identity, of knowing and living the faith. During Lent, we have the opportunity to reaffirm who we are and always will be, in anticipation of Easter.

Commencing the Journey of the Cross to Easter (Pascha)

The Lenten journey from the ashes of death to resurrected life begins on the first day of Lent, Ash Wednesday, which signifies a time to turn around, to change directions, to repent. This first day of Lent reminds us that unless we are willing to die to our old selves, we cannot be raised to new life with Christ. The first step of this journey calls us to acknowledge and confront our mortality, individually and corporately. In many traditions this is symbolized through the imposition of ashes—placing a cross of ashes on one's forehead. During the imposition of ashes the words: "You are dust, and to dust you will return" are repeated again and again. We are to remember that we are but temporary creatures, always on the edge of death. On Ash Wednesday we begin our Lenten trek through the desert toward Easter.

Ashes on the forehead is a sign of our humanity and a reminder of our mortality. Lent is not a matter of being good, and wearing ashes is not showing off one's faith. The ashes are a reminder to us and our communities of our finite creatureliness. The ashes we wear on our Lenten journey symbolize the dust and broken debris of our lives as well as the reality that eventually each of us will die.

Trusting in the "accomplished fact" of Christ's resurrection, however, we listen for the word of God in the time-honored stories of the Church's Lenten journey. We follow Jesus into the wilderness, resist temptation, fast, and proceed "on the way" to Jerusalem, and the cross. Our Lenten journey is one of *metanoia* ("turning around"), of changing directions from self-serving toward the self-giving way of the cross.

What we hear during Lent is the power and possibility of the paschal mystery, and that the way of the cross, the way to Easter is through death. To appropriate the new life that is beyond the power of death means we must die with Christ who was raised for us. To live for Christ, we must die with him. New life requires a daily surrendering of the old life, letting go of the present order, so that we may embrace the new humanity. "I die every day," asserts Paul (1 Cor. 15:31). Resurrection necessitates death as a preceding act. The church's peculiar Lenten claim is that in dying we live, that all who are baptized into Christ are baptized into his death. To be raised with Christ means one must also die with Christ. In order to embrace the resurrection, we must experience the passion of Jesus. The way of the cross, the way to Easter, is through death of the "old self." In dying, we live.

Therefore, at the beginning of Lent, we are reminded that our possessions, our rulers, our empires, our projects, our families, and even our lives do not last forever. "You are dust, and to dust you shall return" (Gen. 3:19). The liturgies throughout Lent try to pry loose our fingers, one by one, from presumed securities and plunge us into unknown baptismal waters, waters that turn out to be not only our death tomb, but surprisingly our womb of life. Rather than falling back into nothingness, we fall back upon everlasting arms. Death? How can we fear what we've already gone through in baptism?[11]

It is the power of the resurrection on the horizon ahead that draws us in repentance toward the cross and tomb. Through the intervention of God's gracious resurrection, lifelong changes in our values and behavior become possible. By turning from the end of the "old self" in us, Lenten repentance makes it possible for us to affirm joyfully, "Death is no more!" and to aim toward the landscape of the new age. Faithfully adhering to the Lenten journey of "prayer, fasting, and almsgiving" leads to the destination of Easter.

Completing the Journey of the Cross to Easter (Pascha)

During the final week, Holy Week, we hear the fullness of Christ's passion, his death and resurrection. From Jesus' triumphal entry into Jerusalem and on to the Triduum (Maundy Thursday, Good Friday, and Holy Saturday), all of Holy Week focuses on the passion. As his followers, we travel Christ's path of servanthood through the Lord's Supper and the suffering of the cross toward the glory of Easter, all of which underscores the inseparable link between the death and resurrection of Jesus.

Passion/Palm Sunday

The service for Passion/Palm Sunday maintains the inherent tension that exists between the joyful entry of the palm processional and the somberness of the passion, the focus of Holy Week. The triumphal entry as a gateway to the week may be celebrated by a congregational procession into the sanctuary. Christ's suffering and death for all is then proclaimed through the passion narratives in Matthew, Mark, or Luke.

The question is frequently asked, "Why combine the passion and the palms?"

First, it is in accord with historical tradition. Since at least the fourth century, the focus of the first day of Holy Week, or Great Week, has been the passion of Christ. After a palm processional, a Gospel passion narrative has been read. Western churches have kept the first day of Holy Week by concentrating on both the glory and the passion of Christ, recalling both the passion and the palms. Presbyterians, Methodists, and Roman Catholics call this day "Passion/ Palm Sunday." The United Church of Christ calls it "Palm/Passion Sunday;" Lutherans and Episcopalians call it "The Sunday of the Passion: Palm Sunday." Though the name may differ, what all the churches share is the Western tradition of linking the joy of Christ's triumphal entry into Jerusalem with sober meditation on the suffering and death of Christ.

Pastoral values result from combining the passion and the palms. Many people simply do not attend worship on Good Friday. The result is that, for them, there is a distortion in the story. A story that skips from Jesus' triumphal entry into Jerusalem to Jesus' resurrection from the dead evades the question, "What happened in between?" If we leap from Palm Sunday's "Hosannas" to Easter Day's "Hallelujahs" we overlook the pivotal event of Christ's suffering and death on the cross. The journey to Jerusalem has the cross as its goal, and the cross needs to be kept in sight even during the triumphal entry into Jerusalem. Where the tradition of reading the whole passion narrative on Passion/Palm Sunday is appropriated, congregations have found the value of reading the entire passion narrative on Passion/Palm Sunday. Those who do not attend the Good Friday service hear the fullness of Christ's passion.

Combining the passion and the palms furthermore provides for a critical understanding of entire passion narratives. Instead of hearing only bits and pieces of the various Gospel accounts of the passion of Christ, congregations may hear an entire passion narrative, including differences and similarities with other accounts. The unique character of each Gospel account of the passion helps parishioners understand the theological and apologetic viewpoint present in each Gospel account, especially since the writers of each Gospel saw and understood Jesus Christ differently.

Though the passion narratives have been misused as a foundation for anti-Judaic sentiments in Christian theology and in the life of Christian churches, caution is urged in combining biblical texts into one harmonious story. Such efforts typically smooth over the different Christological emphases of each Gospel, and consequently each Evangelist's version loses its distinctive theological and apologetic contribution. If we allow the differences and similarities of the Gospels to stand, we allow the Word, through the work of the Spirit, to open to us a fresh critical understanding of each passion narrative.

The most important reason for combining the passion and the palms is the relationship between the death and the resurrection of Jesus. In order to understand the resurrection, we must contemplate the passion of Jesus. Long, careful meditation upon the mystery of the cross must precede the wonderful message of Easter.

An oversimplified theology of glory may devalue death by implying that it is merely a stepping-stone on the path to resurrection. Therefore, in order to experience resurrection, one must die, and upon death one will automatically ascend from the grave to glory. On the other hand, an oversimplified theology of the cross may overvalue death as a "work," by implying that resurrection is merely a consequence of the passion; therefore, if one suffers and dies for the faith, one will be resurrected. The cross and resurrection must be held together theologically; the extent to which we understand the resurrection of Jesus will be determined by our understanding of his passion.

Thus, the palm procession with ringing Hosannas symbolically foreshadows the Hallelujahs of God's promised future when the risen Jesus will lead his people into a new Jerusalem. Interwoven with such liturgical experiences are the stories of the passion of Christ. Thus the eight-day week from Passion/Palm Sunday to Easter Day is framed by resurrection and death on one side, and death and resurrection on the other.

The need to affirm, as Holy Week begins, the inseparable relationship between the death and the resurrection of Jesus is precisely the reason why the passion of Christ and the palms are linked together as Passion/Palm Sunday.

The Triduum ("The Three Days")

All of Holy Week points toward the passion—the death and resurrection of Christ. The week's three final days (from sunset Thursday through sunset on Easter) complete the commemoration of Christ's passion. These three days are called the *Triduum*.

The Triduum engages us from Thursday until Sunday in a unified act. What happens on Maundy Thursday, Good Friday, and the Easter Vigil forms a continuous dramatic story. These days are to be seen together rather than separately. The services of the three final days of Holy Week connect with one another and, together, comprise the oneness of the Triduum.

Because of this interrelationship of the three days, each service of the Triduum needs the others to tell the whole story. For example, resurrection is incomprehensible without Christ's self-giving in crucifixion and at the Lord's Supper. Therefore, Easter needs Good Friday and Maundy Thursday to be fully understood. The way to the triumph of Easter is through the Triduum.

All of Holy Week, and particularly its three concluding days (the Triduum), provides an opportunity to undertake a pilgrimage of renewed commitment and joy; to travel Christ's path of servanthood, through the Lord's Supper and the suffering of the cross, as we move toward Easter.

Our joy during the great festival of resurrection will be enhanced by faithful participation in worship during the preceding week, especially during the whole of the Triduum.

Maundy Thursday

The opening service of the Triduum is not inherently mournful. The penitential acts of Maundy Thursday have celebratory aspects as well: restoration through the bold declaration of pardon; the act of footwashing connoting humility and intimacy; the celebration of the Lord's Supper embodying the mystery of Christ's enduring redemptive presence. Maundy Thursday's acts provide the paradox of a celebratively somber and solemnly celebrative service.

Footwashing. A powerful symbolic response to the Word, representing the way of humility and servanthood to which we are called by Christ, is the act of footwashing, practiced within the church since at least the fifth century.

The practice of footwashing in first-century Palestine may have been as common as when today a host helps guests take off their coats, a waiter seats customers, or a driver holds the taxi door for passengers. Hospitality underlies all such welcoming gestures.

However, if the focus of footwashing today is primarily on the act itself and not its meaning, then footwashing often is perceived as a quaint rite that can become a fad to enliven worship. Churches should be cautioned to resist including footwashing for its quaintness, and rather to consider its dramatic, potent message.

The difference between yesterday's footwashing and today's common courtesy is that the person expected to wash guests' feet was at the bottom of the household pecking order. In the prevailing practice, according to the way of the world, therefore, footwashing was a lowly task performed by menials, with or without pay. What is shocking about the footwashing story in John is not the act of footwashing, but the identity of the servant who washed others' feet—Jesus, God-with-us, the least likely person. The focus is on the *person* washing feet, not on the *act*. Following the footwashing, Jesus took upon himself the humiliation of the cross, the ultimate symbol of his selfless love for others.

The life of servanthood is affirmed again and again by Jesus as the life to which he calls people. Recall such poignant sayings of Jesus as "The Son of Man came not to be served but to serve, and to give his life as a ransom for many" (Matt. 20:28; Mark 10:45); "Let the greatest among you become as the youngest, and the leader as one who serves. . . . I am among you as one who serves" (Luke 22:26, 27b). In response to the command of the gospel, footwashing is an example of the servanthood that Jesus urges on all who follow him. In essence, Jesus' act of footwashing says to us, "I have descended; you, too, descend."

In the priesthood of all believers (not hierarchies of power), *all* members of the body of Christ can "kneel" before each other and wash one another's feet as did our Lord and Savior himself—neighbor to neighbor, perhaps even stranger to stranger. More important, as the priesthood of all believers, our corporate kneeling before others for the earthy task of footwashing symbolizes our servanthood within and beyond the body of Christ.

Churches whose members dare to wash one another's feet may find themselves transformed so that they also turn toward other neighbors in service—the family next door, the single parent, the retired, the unemployed, the unwanted child, refugees, prisoners—and begin to see the image of God in the face of the world. Washing another's feet may help us minister in the church by joining other Christians in caring, not only for one another, but for the world God loves.

Therefore ask *who* is washing feet. Not a hired butler or maid, not a person paid to perform what the world views as menial tasks, but someone called to Christ's ministry of serving others. Focus on the person washing feet, for he or she symbolizes the radical nature of servanthood.

The Lord's Supper. Though on this night we remember and celebrate the final supper Jesus shared with his disciples in the context of Passover, we are neither celebrating a Seder ("order of service"), nor reenacting the Last Supper, but sharing with our risen Lord a foretaste of the heavenly banquet.

In recent years, some congregations have begun to celebrate a Maundy Thursday Eucharist in the context of a Christianized Seder (Passover meal). Before deciding to celebrate a Christian Passover, remember that seeking to experience the historical origins of the Last Supper presents an almost impenetrable path through which to walk.

1. Since no Jewish Seder texts earlier than the ninth century exist, any attempt at historical reconstruction of an authentic first-century Seder is suspect because it cannot possibly represent what Jesus did. The Gospels themselves present conflicting data regarding the day of the meal. The Eucharist was instituted either *during* the Passover meal (Matthew, Mark, and Luke) or *before* the feast of the Passover (John 13:1).

2. At a contemporary "Christian Passover Seder" the attempt is sometimes made to "Christianize" the rite by adding on the words of institution of the Lord's Supper, or by adding "through Jesus Christ our Lord" to the prayers. Both practices may be offensive to Jews.

3. The focus of the Lord's Supper is not the annual reactualization of the exodus, but the celebration of salvation in Christ. The annual liturgy of liberation for Christians is the Easter (Paschal) Vigil (cf. pages 182–203, 312–321).

4. The term *"last* supper" suggests that it was only one of many meals shared by Jesus and his disciples, and not *the* meal. The Eucharist is rooted not only in the Last Supper but also in Jesus' eating with sinners, and in his feeding the crowd with the loaves and fishes, and it foreshadows the meals after his resurrection. All together they connote the multiple meanings of the Lord's Supper. To reduce the Lord's Supper to the Last Supper is to cut off the sacrament from its eschatological significance (i.e., as it relates to the unfolding of God's purpose and in the ultimate destiny of humankind and the world).

5. What constitutes the Eucharist is a ritual meal that combines the sharing of bread and cup with the offering of a great prayer of thanksgiving. Therefore, the Eucharist as a ritual meal eliminates the need for an actual meal of multiple courses.

6. The quest to imitate Jesus' Last Supper with his disciples in the upper room is a historicism that inevitably undermines the symbols of offering of a great prayer of thanksgiving and sharing of bread and cup as effective means of conversion or nurture.

It may be far better, therefore, for Christians to participate in Jewish Seders as guests, rather than entangling themselves in the hazards of celebrating "Christian Passover" meals.

Good Friday

The Good Friday service is a penitential service, yet it is also a celebration of the good news of the cross. We should retain the paradox of the day in the form, mood, and texts of the service. Good Friday is a day in which to allow for numerous contemplative moments, and to permit the power of silence to speak for itself.

No colors, flowers, candles, or decorative materials are appropriate on Good Friday, except, perhaps, "representations of the way of the cross."

The passion narrative according to John is read on Good Friday, because at the heart of John's passion narrative is the good news of the cross—the victory of the cross. Thus, John's emphasis on crucifixion and glory corresponds to the tension and ambiguity of the day.

Easter Vigil

On the final night of this Easter journey we pause in vigil, at which time we remember stories about who we have been and are now becoming. As the community of faith we recount our centuries-long pilgrimage culminating in the renewal of baptismal promises. The Easter Vigil is akin to sitting around a campfire while listening to the stories of generations past and future. During the Easter Vigil we tell our name to ourselves and to those not of the household of faith. Our name is a very long story—of how we were made, of how God chose us from among all peoples, of how God liberated us from bondage, of how God planted us in the promised land, of how, in these last times, God has given the story a new twist in the life, death, and resurrection of Jesus. Because we have been here for so long, it takes a long time to tell who we are. We will not be hasty folk on that night.[12]

To hear Christ's teaching is one of the traditional disciplines of the season of Lent. Listen for the Word of God throughout all of Lent, and perhaps this season will become a *turning from* the mind of this age *to* that of Christ, and a renewing of baptismal identity (who we are and always will be), all in anticipation of Easter.

Pentecost: Set on Fire as Witnesses to the Crucified and Risen Christ

For seven weeks, a week of Sundays, we acclaim the resurrection of Christ by the power of God. The period of seven weeks of jubilation can be traced back to its Jewish roots of the fifty days celebrated from the day after Passover to Shavuoth (Feast of "Weeks"—Ex. 23:16). For Jews, the Feast of Weeks closed the season of harvest, which had been initiated by the Feast of Unleavened Bread. In the first century, in similar manner, Christians observed a fifty-day period of celebration from Easter to the Day of Pentecost. To underscore the uninterrupted rejoicing of these fifty days, fasting and kneeling in prayer were forbidden at least as early as the end of the second century. On the *pentēcostē* ("fiftieth") day, not only was the fifty-day period concluded, but a festival with its own proper content was celebrated. The Jews observed a feast of covenant renewal and eventually commemorated the giving of the Law. Christians celebrated the gift of the Spirit as preparing the way for the day of the Lord. What Moses and the Law did for the Jewish community, the Holy Spirit now does for the community of Christ.[13]

The Gift of the Spirit

According to the Day of Pentecost story in Acts 2:1–13, God gave the gift of Holy Spirit to empower witnesses to the resurrection. Sounds from heaven, cosmic language, the rush of a mighty *ruach* (wind, spirit, breath) invaded the house in which the apostles gathered, and appeared to them as a burning fire. Tongues of fire touched their nerve centers. A power—the unseen power of God— moved among them and gripped them. The Holy Spirit is unseen, like the wind, which is why the Old Testament calls it *ruach YHWH*, "the wind, or breath, of God" (cf. John 3:8). The Spirit is the "unseenness of God" working among us.

According to Joel (2:28–29), the *ruach* is to open everybody to God's future. People young and old will dream and will have visions of hope; they will be able to loose themselves from the way things are now, because God is establishing a whole new economy of creation. The Holy Spirit breaks us out of our preoccupation with ourselves and frees us to serve neighbors; loosens our grasp on possessions, and sets us to loving people. New creation is what Joel is talking about. Pentecost is new creation.

The book of Acts tells the story of the outcome of Pentecost's new creation: people witness in word and in deed to the risen Christ. At the outset, the newborn church immediately tumbled out into the streets to witness to God's mighty works in the languages of people all over the world. By the end of the story, a tiny, Spirit-filled community of faith that broke from its present order has spread across the continents with incredible power to bring new things into being. With the gift of the Spirit, all things are possible.

The Spirit-filled experience ignited the faithful and sent them outward, giving utterance in word and deed to the good news. "The cause of good works, we confess," states the *Scots Confession* (chapter 13) "is not our free will, but the Spirit of the Lord Jesus."[14] Our call as disciples of Christ is not only to celebrate but also to show and tell neighbors about God's new world coming in the name of the crucified and risen Christ.

The same Spirit that empowered Jesus to love enemies was the Spirit that enabled the Corinthian church to love their antagonists. A living fellowship means living as the body of Christ by preaching the Word with freedom, breaking bread together, reconciling with adversaries, and serving neighbors, near and far. What makes possible the church's witness to the resurrection of Christ is the Spirit of God.

Life Together in Christ,
Filled with the Holy Spirit

Note that the Spirit is conceived, first of all, as God's presence within the whole community of faith, rather than the private possession of solitary individuals. The essential mark of the Spirit's presence is obedience to the will of God within the context of the community of faith. Both Old and New Testament witnesses to Spirit-filled life portray an experience of new community.

Therefore, on the Day of Pentecost, we celebrate God's gift of Holy Spirit which draws us together as one people, helps us comprehend what God is doing in the world, and empowers us to proclaim, in word and in deed, God's plan of reconciling all people in the name of Christ (Eph. 1:10).

Without the gift of the Spirit, Christ's church dries up and withers away, and we are left with only our broken selves. With the gift of the Spirit, all things are possible. A spirit-filled community of faith opens eyes to needs in the world and sees its mission as God's new people. The Day of Pentecost is the climax of the Great Fifty Days of Easter, celebrating as it does the gift of the Spirit to the body of Christ—the church.

THE CHRISTMAS CYCLE:
FROM THE DARKNESS OF THE WORLD
TO THE LIGHT OF CHRIST

The Christmas cycle evolved over several hundred years and eventually developed its shape in the latter half of the fourth century. Both Western and Eastern traditions helped to decide the central dates of this cycle: Christmas (December 25) and Epiphany (January 6). Both traditions also shaped how to celebrate these days that encompass the incarnation, the visit of the magi, the baptism of Jesus, and the marriage at Cana. As Easter is preceded by a time of preparation, Lent, so Christmas/Epiphany is preceded by a time of preparation, Advent. However, Advent is far more than preparing to celebrate the first coming of Christ, the incarnate Word. Advent is a season of hope, during which we anticipate the future coming of Christ to judge, and to establish his rule over all things. In the light of Christ's first coming, we have hope for fulfillment of the realm of God in the future. The Christmas cycle focuses on preparing for and celebrating the coming of the Word, Jesus Christ, in whom God's saving purposes are realized.

In the following description of the Christmas cycle, we begin with Christmas rather than Advent because it is only when we understand what Christmas is all about that we can begin to consider appropriate ways to prepare for celebrating it.

Christmas: The Advent of the Messianic Savior

There are currently two theories concerning the origin of Christmas.

The first theory proposes that Christmas is the result of the transformation, or Christianizing, of a pagan festival. The earliest empirical evidence of the celebration of Christmas has been found in fourth-century Roman documents. The civil calendar of A.D. 354 lists December 25 as the "Birthday of the Unconquered Sun." A list of martyrs' anniversaries compiled in A.D. 336 notes: "December 25: Christ, born in Bethlehem of Judea." The reason Christians identified December 25 as the day of Christ's birth, according to this theory, is that they took over the Roman "Birthday of the Unconquered Sun" that was celebrated on the winter solstice. On December 25 the sun completed its southward journey; when reborn, it began traveling northward with the promise of more light. Thus the pagan feast of the Unconquered Sun marked the winter solstice when days began to be longer. Christians in Rome appropriated this holiday for their purposes as the day when "the sun of righteousness" (Mal. 4:2) arose, when the "Light of the world" entered (John 8:12).

The second theory, the "computation hypothesis," was proposed by Louis Duchesne in 1889 and has recently been revived by Thomas Talley.[15] As early as the third century there was interest in computing the date of Christ's birth. Calculation apparently followed a Jewish tradition of assigning the birth and death of significant people (e.g., patriarchs) to the same date, thereby signifying a wholeness to their lives. For Jesus, conception and crucifixion were the events that offered such completeness. According to the computations of a mixture of calendars (Jewish, Julian, and Gregorian), Christ's death (and therefore conception) was either March 25 (in Western churches) or April 6 (in Eastern churches). By counting nine months forward, Christ's birth was further computed to have occurred on December 25 or on January 6. In Rome, the day became fixed on December 25, which coincided with the winter solstice and the celebration of the pagan feast of the Unconquered Sun. Thus, the computation hypothesis downplays, if it does not reject, the common idea that December 25 was chosen simply as a Christian takeover of a secular holiday.

The Incarnation of God's Saving Purposes

On December 25, Christmas Day, more Christians pause in their frenzied lives to acknowledge Christ than on any other day of the year. Images of "the baby in the manger" and "peace among all on earth" fill our minds. On Christmas Day, Christians unite in celebrating the birth of the Christ child.

What is "Christmas?" It is three words: God in flesh; or four syllables: in-car-na-tion. The Gospel according to John (1:14) tells us, "The Word became flesh, and dwelt among us, full of grace and truth." Christmas proclaims that God has come in flesh, has come "to save us all from Satan's power."[16] Christmas celebrates far more than a birthday; Christmas acclaims the advent of the messianic salvation. Christ was sent among us in order to save us. Note how the biblical "sending formula" ("God sent Christ in order to . . .") always reveals Christ's saving purpose:

I must proclaim the good news of the kingdom of God to the other cities also; for I was sent for this purpose. (Luke 4:43)

God did not send the Son into the world to condemn the world, but in order that the world might be saved through him. (John 3:17)

In this is love, not that we loved God but that he loved us and sent his Son to be the atoning sacrifice for our sins. (1 John 4:10)

And we have seen and testify that the Father has sent his Son as the Savior of the world. (1 John 4:14)

Moreover, the "sending formula," with its purpose of human salvation, is combined with a reference to the birth of Christ:

But when the fullness of time had come God sent his Son, born of a woman, born under the law, in order to redeem those who were under the law, so that we might receive adoption as children. (Gal. 4:4–5, read on the First Sunday after Christmas [B] as well as on The Name of Jesus [January 1, A,B,C])

What we pay homage to at Christmas, therefore, is that the ultimate fulfillment of God's saving purpose begins with the birth of Jesus, the messianic Savior. God's only Son is born among us in order to save the world. This is the message of Christmas.

From the beginning of time God's saving purpose has been at work. God has raised up the seed of Abraham, including Moses and Gideon and Samson and John the Baptist. Through all these generations, God has been faithfully at work raising persons to bring us the Davidic Messiah, the messianic King, the Son of the Most High who will ascend the throne of David. Through all of human history, God has been bringing forth Jesus Christ. Now through the birth of the Savior, God's purpose will be fulfilled. God has acted to save God's people. The Christ child is born for the saving of the world.

The Day of Epiphany: Light to All People

A part of the joy of Christmas lies in the utter improbability of the Nativity. Because of the new possibilities and hopes in Christ given to us by the sheer grace of God, we rejoice. Throughout the twelve days of Christmas we extol the advent of Jesus, the messianic Savior, for: "The grace of God has appeared *(epephanē)* bringing salvation to all, . . . the manifestation *(epiphaneia)* of the glory of our great God and Savior Jesus Christ" (Titus 2:11, 13).

On Epiphany, the "coming down" of the Savior is manifested to the whole world. At Christmas and Epiphany we rejoice in Jesus' "cross-shaped" advent, descending and spreading, among us. We celebrate during Christmas the entrance of the true Light into the world, and on Epiphany the showing forth of the true Light to the world.

Jesus is the light to all nations, races, classes, all peoples, the whole world. At Epiphany, Christ is revealed to the "Gentile world"; God's covenant with Israel is now open to people of every place and time. All are extended an invitation to the gathering of the New Israel in the New Jerusalem.

The Origins of the Feast of Epiphany

The word "epiphany" (from the Greek *epiphaneia* or *theophaneia*) means "appearance" or "manifestation" of God, and has roots in the word for sunrise or dawn. In ancient times an epiphany meant either a visible manifestation of a god or the solemn visit of a ruler venerated as a god.

For Christians, Christmas marks the coming of God to us; Epiphany celebrates the appearance of the Lord in the midst of humanity. The Christmas stories of the birth of Immanuel declare the divine entry; Epiphany extols the revelation of God to the world in the person of Jesus of Nazareth. How did the church come to make this subtle distinction?

Epiphany probably evolved from squabble over *the* christological moment when God revealed who Jesus was. According to Adolf Adam,[17] the earliest traces of a feast of the Epiphany appear in the writings of Clement of Alexandria (Egypt), about A.D. 205. Clement reported that the followers of the Gnostic Basilides (c. A.D. 150) celebrated a feast of the *baptism* of Jesus, which they regarded as being *the* real moment of the "birth" of the Son of God into the world.

Others, however, noted that for Luke and especially Matthew, the conception and birth of Jesus are the christological moment when God revealed who Jesus was. Christ's birth marks the entrance of "the Light of the world." Therefore, presumably in reaction to the Gnostic understanding, the following took place.

First, the feast of the Epiphany (i.e., Christ's physical birth, considered the actual moment of the Son of God's entry into the world) was introduced into the church and became familiar to the churches of the East.

Shortly thereafter, the commemoration of Jesus' baptism in the Jordan was also linked with this feast of Jesus' birth. Thus, the day of the Epiphany became an important date for baptism in the East.

Also associated with this feast of the Epiphany was the commemoration of the first "sign" (or miracle) of Jesus, in which Jesus changed water into wine, once again revealing his glory (John 2:1–11).

Thus in its early stages, the feast of the Epiphany, as celebrated in the churches of the East, was a festival of the revelation of Christ's glory that united three elements: birth, baptism, and first "sign."

Churches of the West, however, accented the concept of the "sun of righteousness" (Micah 4:2) as breaking into the world in the birth of Jesus as Savior. In the fourth century, therefore, the West began to celebrate Christ's birth on December 25 (probably because of its cultural context) with the East continuing its feast of the Epiphany on January 6.

About A.D. 375, Eastern and Western churches "appropriated" each other's "birthday feast" of Jesus, and adoration by the magi, the result being:

	December 25
West celebrated:	*East celebrated:*
birth of Jesus	birth of Jesus and
	the coming of the magi

	January 6
coming of the magi	baptism of Jesus
baptism of Jesus	Jesus' miracle at Cana, and
wedding feast at Cana	reserved the day for the conferral
	of baptism

What East and West share in common, however, is Epiphany's celebration of Jesus' manifestation to the whole world. In our celebrations of Christmas and Epiphany we rejoice in the dawning and the arising of Light in darkness, stability amid chaos, assurance amid anxiety for the whole creation. Epiphany not only discloses the Savior to the world but also calls the world to show forth Christ, to be witnesses to God's true Light. The timeless mystery of the incarnation, God in flesh, leads us forth to show and tell of Christ as God's gift of grace and salvation for all persons. Some call this ongoing epiphany the "work of Christmas."

Advent: Come, Lord Jesus! Our Lord Has Come!

Since the first century, as Christians await the advent of the true Light in prayer and liturgy they have uttered the word *Maranatha*, often translated "Our Lord, come!" Maranatha is a Greek transliteration from the Aramaic in 1 Corinthians 16:22, and often printed in Greek New Testaments as one word—maranatha.

In Aramaic, as in Syriac, maranatha may be two words, with differing translations:

marana tha	=	an imperative form oriented toward the *future*, translated as: "Come, our Lord!"
maran atha	=	the perfect form expressing a completed event in the *past*, translated as: "Our Lord has come."

The two directions in these translations[18] are crucial for our Advent liturgies. The cry of maranatha and the season of Advent emphasize both our remembrance of the past and our hope for the future. In Advent, the beginning and end times meet. In fact, in mid-sixth century Rome, Advent was considered as the end of the liturgical year, while today we regard Advent as the beginning.[19] We live between *marana tha*, our prayer for the future coming of the Lord, and *maran atha*, our belief that the Lord has come as God's ultimate act in history.

In Advent we expectantly wait for the One who has already come. We anticipate the promised justice of God's new world, yet we praise God who raised the "righteous branch" to rule with justice and righteousness. We hope for the restoration of the afflicted, the tormented, and the grieving, yet we delight that healing has come in Christ. We long for the beating of swords into plowshares, yet we rejoice that the Prince of peace has appeared. We yearn for the barren deserts of our inner cities to flourish, yet we laud the desert Rose that has bloomed. We dream of the land where lions and lambs live in harmony, yet we acclaim the child born to lead us into the promised land.

Christ has come! Christ is risen! Christ will come again! In Advent, we are living between the first and the second coming of the Lord.

The dialectical tension of maranatha—placing us between memory and hope, past and future—may strengthen our Advent liturgies. Perhaps we need to cling to the ancient cry of *Maranatha!* and its paradoxical meanings so we may freely embrace "the new thing" prophesied by Isaiah (43:19) that God is doing among us right now. The tension and the paradox we find in Advent shapes our celebrations during the season.

Waiting for the One Who Has Already Come

Though at Christmas we rightly retell the story of the babe in the manger nearly two thousand years ago, Christmas ultimately focuses on the mystery of Immanuel (God is with us) breaking into our world. Though we paint pictures of the sweet baby in a manger "asleep on the hay," Christmas centers on the Christ who inaugurates God's realm of justice and peace. Though we sing of the baby with "no crib for his bed" and "no crying he makes,"[20] Christmas holds before us Jesus of Nazareth whose human life fulfills God's saving purpose by preaching, teaching, liberating, healing, and living according to the rule of God. On Christmas Day we celebrate the mystery of the incarnation.

How? We can retell the birth narratives of Matthew and Luke, display the wide-ranging artistic interpretations of the Christ child's birth, and sing the powerfully evocative hymn texts. These stories, images, and songs are all vehicles for telling the astounding story of incarnation, of a Savior breaking into our world.

Advent, however, is the time to prepare for the One who is coming to us as our judge and redeemer. During these weeks we anticipate the Second Coming of Christ, the coming peace and justice of the Lord. Our Advent call is therefore to prepare the world for Christ's coming now and in the end time.

Since we believe the Lord is coming to judge the world, then we must prepare the world for judgment. Since we believe the Christ is coming, Advent becomes a time for words and deeds that witness to Christ's new age. Our Advent witness to the coming of Christ requires caring about our world, our neighbors, our enemies—everyone. Advent is the time to care about peace and justice in the world, since we believe Christ has come and, therefore, everything that has come in Christ will be fulfilled in the world. Maranatha! Come, Lord Jesus! Maranatha! Our Lord has come!

Christmas is the time for celebration. "Joy to the world!" God has inaugurated a new realm in Jesus Christ. God has established the new age. The time of justice and peace has arrived. Clap your hands! Dance for joy! Sing a new song to the Lord, for the Lord has done marvelous things! Each year we have twelve days in which to celebrate these incredible acts of God. Twelve days in which to taste and experience Christmas.

When the church embraces an Advent season of waiting, preparing, and serving in both its worship and mission, it is natural for twelve days of Christmas joy to follow. By beginning and maintaining a tone of suspense, anticipation, and expectation regarding the coming Savior, the opportunity is present to sustain it through the four weeks and then build on it at Christmas.

For example, on the first Sunday of Advent, we begin our watch and preparation for the coming of the Lord. In the midst of human disorder, anguish, desolation, and uncertainty we hear the promises of Jeremiah (Year C of the Common Lectionary) that the days are coming when God will raise up "a righteous Branch" from David's line who will rule with "justice and righteousness" (Jer. 33:14–16). We believe God has raised up the "righteous Branch" from David's line in Jesus Christ, who rules with justice and righteousness.

We also hear Luke's (21:25–36) apocalyptic vision of the end of the world: signs in the sun and moon and stars, distress of nations, people fainting with fear, and the "Son of Man" coming. As we listen for the Word of God in these signs, we raise our heads, look up, and see that Christ's redemption is near. We do not know when, but we watch, pray, prepare, and gladly expect the coming of the Lord. Christ has come! Christ is risen! Christ will come again!

During Advent, therefore, our eyes are focused on God's future promised in Jesus Christ. At Christmas, we rejoice that it has arrived.

ORDINARY TIME

In calendar reforms following Vatican II, the periods between Epiphany and Lent, and between Pentecost and Advent, are called Ordinary Time. There are good reasons why this term should have wider acceptance.

The common practice has been to identify time after Epiphany and Pentecost as, for example, the "Fifth Sunday after Epiphany," or the "Twelfth Sunday after Pentecost." Unfortunately these are often misunderstood to be part of an "Epiphany Season" or a "Pentecost Season." Neither Epiphany nor Pentecost are seasons. Each is a single day. This misunderstanding has tended to distort the nature of these two periods in the liturgical calendar. The periods following Epiphany and Pentecost are periods that do not center upon a dominant event or theme. The practice of keeping time in reference to the immediate past festival was simply a way to keep track of time. In short, it is Ordinary Time whether or not we have called it that.

Continued use of "Sundays after Pentecost" has also resulted in a great deal of confusion in the use of the Common Lectionary and of resources based upon it.

More important, the term "Ordinary Time" can make its own unique and valuable contribution to the way we understand liturgical time. Since Ordinary Time is not a season, this period allows Sunday to be preeminent. This is in accord with the insights of the Reformed tradition, for which the Lord's Day has always had a dominant role, whether or not annual festivals were maintained.

Time Between Epiphany and Lent
and Time Between Pentecost and Advent

Ordinary Time is the norm of time kept by the church. The Sundays of Ordinary Time celebrate the good news of Christ's death and resurrection, and the unfolding presence of the new creation. Ordinary Time presents us with an ongoing opportunity to witness to the living Lord who makes all things new. The standard time of the church is Ordinary Time.

The (liturgical) term "ordinary" means that which is standard, normative, usual, or typical. For example, ordinary or invariable elements of worship (e.g., the Lord's Prayer, Doxology, the Creed, the Kyrie ["Lord, Have Mercy"], Gloria ["Glory to God in the highest"], Alleluia, Sursum Corda ["Lift up your hearts"], and so forth) are said or sung week after week. As the standard elements of worship, they are called "ordinaries." They are the elements that are common to worship every Sunday.

In like manner, week after week, Sunday "ordinarily" celebrates the resurrection and the unfolding of the new creation. The standard for worship is, therefore, the ordinary time of Sunday in the week-to-week progression of time.

Twice each year, however, Ordinary Time is heightened by the extra-ordinary time of the Christmas and Easter cycles. They are extra-ordinary in that they intensify the foundational doctrines of incarnation and resurrection. The liturgical contribution of these cycles is to supplement the "ordinaries" of worship with additional or seasonally reflective elements, the "propers," those elements that change from Sunday to Sunday (prayers, hymns, carols, rituals, etc.). Thus, the ordinary time of the church is made extra-ordinary during the Christmas and Easter cycles.[21]

This interruption of Ordinary Time by the Christmas and Easter cycles results in two segments of Ordinary Time. Thus Ordinary Time is a period of from four to nine weeks following Epiphany and a period of about one half of the year (from 23 to 28 weeks) following Pentecost.

At the beginning and end of each of these periods are transitional Sundays that move the church from what has preceded to what is to follow. The first two Sundays that follow Epiphany develop some of the emphases of Epiphany, namely, Jesus' baptism on the Sunday immediately following Epiphany, and the marriage of Cana on the Second Sunday in Ordinary Time (Cycle C). The Sunday that concludes this part of Ordinary Time, the Transfiguration of the Lord, serves as a transition to a focus upon what is to happen in Jerusalem, Christ's dying and rising. The Sunday that follows Pentecost, Trinity Sunday, underscores the trinitarian nature of the Easter cycle that preceded it. The Sundays that conclude this part of Ordinary Time, and especially the final Sunday before Advent, are eschatological in character. These Sundays move the church toward Advent with its focus on the new age that is to come.

Festivals in Ordinary Time

We turn now to a closer look at each of the festivals that begin and end the two segments of Ordinary Time, and at All Saints' Day, which is a major festival in November.[22]

The Baptism of the Lord

The Baptism of the Lord is closely related to Epiphany and should be considered in relation to that feast. Jesus' ministry to bring in God's rule was inaugurated in his baptism. As he came out of the water, the Spirit rested on Jesus, and a sign of God's approval was heard. On this day we celebrate not only Jesus' baptism, but our own as well, for our baptism is rooted in Christ. Baptism joins us to Christ and his church, and with all of the baptized we are called to share in Jesus' ministry. In the waters of baptism we are buried with Christ, cleansed of our sins, and raised to share in his resurrection. The Spirit is given to us and we are declared the children of God.

The Transfiguration of the Lord

From ancient times the Feast of the Transfiguration has been important in Eastern Orthodox traditions. In 1457 it was adopted in the Western church with its date of August 6. In recent lectionary alterations, the Transfiguration of the Lord has gained greater prominence because it is given focus on a Sunday before or at the beginning of Lent. The Sunday immediately prior to Ash Wednesday is an appropriate time to celebrate the Transfiguration of the Lord, because this event marked a transition in Jesus' ministry in which he "set his face to go to Jerusalem" (Luke 9:51), where he would die.

In Jesus' transfiguration, we are assured that Jesus is the hope of the ages. Jesus is the One who fulfilled the Law given through

Moses, the One dreamed of by the prophets, of whom Elijah is the greatest.

In celebrating this event, we rejoice in the divine majesty of Christ, whose glory shone even when confronted with the cross. It is given us for our journey through Lent toward the agony of the cross and the victory of the empty tomb. We celebrate this mystery in order that our faith may be renewed. We are transformed into the new being in Christ as we join Christ in his death and resurrection in Lent and Easter.

Trinity Sunday

Unlike other festivals in the church's liturgical calendar, Trinity Sunday centers on a *doctrine* of the church, rather than an *event*. It celebrates the unfathomable mystery of God's being as Holy Trinity. It is a day of adoration and praise of the one, eternal, incomprehensible God.

There is a sense in which Trinity Sunday synthesizes all we have celebrated over the past months which has centered upon God's mighty acts: Christmas-Epiphany celebrating God's taking flesh and dwelling among us in Jesus Christ; Easter celebrating Christ's death and resurrection for us; Pentecost, celebrating God the Holy Spirit becoming our Sanctifier, Guide and Teacher. It is therefore a fitting transition to that part of the year when Sunday by Sunday the work of God among us is unfolded in a more general way.

The triune God is the basis of all we are and do as Christians. In the name of this triune God we were baptized. As the baptized ones we bear the name of the triune God in our being. We are of the family of the triune God. We affirm this parentage when, in reciting the creeds, we say what we believe. Our discipleship is rooted in the mighty acts of this triune God who is active in redeeming the world. The triune God is the basis of all our prayers—we pray *to* God the Father, *through* Jesus Christ, *by* the Holy Spirit. The Trinity holds central place in our faith.

Earliest evidence of celebration of a Trinity feast dates from early in the eleventh century. It gained official standing in 1334.

In celebrating Trinity Sunday we should remember that every Lord's day is consecrated to the triune God. On the first day of the week God began creation. On the first day of the week, God raised Jesus from the grave. On the first day of the week, the Holy Spirit descended upon the newly born church. Every Sunday is special. Every Sunday is the day of the Holy Trinity.

All Saints' Day (November 1)

All Saints' Day is a time to rejoice in all who through the ages have faithfully served the Lord. The day reminds us that we are part of one continuing, living communion of saints. It is a time to claim our kinship with the "glorious company of apostles . . . the noble fellowship of prophets . . . the white-robed army of martyrs" (Te Deum). It is a time to express our gratitude for all who in ages of darkness kept the faith, for those who have taken the gospel to the ends of the earth, for prophetic voices who have called the church to be faithful in life and service, for all who have witnessed to God's justice and peace in every nation.

To rejoice with all the faithful of every generation expands our awareness that there is a great company of witnesses above and around us like a cloud (Heb. 12:1). It lifts us out of a preoccupation with our own immediate situation and the discouragements of the present. In the knowledge that others have persevered, we are encouraged to endure against all odds (Heb. 12:1–2). Reminded that God was with the faithful of the past, we are reassured that God is with us today, moving us and all creation toward God's end in time. In this context, it is appropriate for a congregation on All Saints' Day to commemorate the lives of those who died during the previous year.

Christ the King

The festival of Christ the King ends our marking of Ordinary Time after the Day of Pentecost, and moves us to the threshold of Advent, the season of hope for Christ's coming again at the end of time.

The day centers us upon the crucified and risen Christ, whom God exalted to rule over the whole universe. The celebration of the Lordship of Christ thus looks back to Ascension, Easter, and Transfiguration, and points ahead to the appearing in glory of the King of kings and Lord of lords. Christ reigns supreme. Christ rules in peace. Christ's truth judges falsehood. As the Alpha and Omega, the beginning and the end, Christ is the center of the universe, the ruler of all history, the judge of all people. In Christ all things began, and in Christ all things will be fulfilled. In the end, Christ will triumph over all of the forces of evil.

Such concepts as these cluster around the affirmation that Christ is King. As sovereign ruler, Christ calls us to a loyalty that transcends every earthly claim upon the human heart. To Christ alone belongs the supreme allegiance of our lives. Christ calls us to stand with those who in every age confessed, "Jesus Christ is Lord!" In every generation, demagogues emerge to claim an allegiance that belongs only to God. But Christ alone has the right to claim our highest loyalty. The blood of martyrs, past and present, witnesses to this truth.

Behold the glory of the eternal Christ! From the beginning of time to its ending, Christ rules above all earthly powers!

LITURGICAL COLOR

In recent decades it has been customary for Presbyterian congregations to vest their clergy with stoles and other vestments, and to adorn their worship spaces with paraments, banners, and other textiles in colors that are traditional to the days and seasons of the liturgical calendar. Congregations often ask, "What are the *correct* colors?" To help congregations, the *Presbyterian Planning Calendar* of the Presbyterian Church (U.S.A.) has for several years displayed the colors that are most commonly used.[23]

A brief examination of the use of liturgical colors throughout church history quickly leads to the conclusion that no pattern of liturgical color is "correct" in and of itself. For over a thousand years the church gave little attention to the use of color. White vestments predominated. It was not until the twelfth century that schemes assigning colors to seasons and festivals began to appear in wealthier cathedrals, abbeys, and churches. Local custom predominated, practice varying from place to place with great freedom in the use of color. It was common, for example, to reserve the newest and most beautiful vestments, regardless of their color, for the great festivals, and to use the older ones for the rest of the year.

In 1570, the Roman Catholic Church for the first time defined a sequence of color usage. Local differences still continued until the nineteenth century, when attempts were made to standardize practice. Since Vatican II, the Catholic Church has been less prescriptive in the use of liturgical color, resulting in a new sense of freedom and spontaneity.

Calvinists in the sixteenth century saw no value in the use of colored vestments, so they abolished them. Black vestments predominated. In the nineteenth and twentieth centuries, however, Protestants began to recognize the value of involving people's eyes as well as their ears in worship. The result is that liturgical colors are now widely used. It ought to be stated, however, that their use is attributed more to the influence of church supply houses promoting matching sets of vestments and paraments in the "correct" colors, than it is from ecclesiastical pressures. Furthermore, their use often reflects little more than an aesthetic concern or desire for variety.

The traditional liturgical color schema is fairly simple. *White* and *gold* are used for festivals of great joy that focus on the work of our Lord. *Red* is the color for the festival of Holy Spirit and the commemoration of the lives of the martyrs. *Purple* marks seasons of penitence or preparation. *Green* is used at all other times. Recently, *blue* has often been used instead of purple during the season of Advent. Blue is expressive of hope (expectation, anticipation), which is the dominant mood of Advent. Light shades of blue should be used rather than dark blue.

The use of the seasonal color is ordinarily not affected by baptisms, Holy Communion, or marriage services. For funerals, however, white is the standard color. Red is sometimes used for ordinations and installations (since ordained ministry enriches the life of the whole church), and for church dedications and anniversaries.

While the use of liturgical colors does not have the antiquity of the liturgical calendar itself, there is value in displaying the colors presently associated with festivals and seasons. The colors are helpful in teaching, prompt within us responses appropriate to the season, unite us ecumenically with the whole church past and present, and add beauty to our worship. These values, inherent in the traditional liturgical colors, ought to be kept clearly in mind. We should use them, however, with an informed and creative freedom, rather than simply adhering to what is considered correct.

We are also free to use other colors in ways that enhance the celebration of the saving work of our Lord. Sensitivity to the psychology of color, and the emotions each color prompts, can help us to use effectively more of the full range of color in worship. It is also important to understand the different moods that hues can evoke. Before choosing the color(s), ask: "What mood, tone, affect is intended?" "What color(s) will fulfill that intention?" For example, the color associations of the warm and sometimes hot colors of red, orange, and yellow are suitable for fast-paced, upbeat, active, exciting experiences. On the other hand, the cool colors of blue and violet are more appropriate for passive, calming, subdued, meditative, pensive times. While a light or medium blue may speak of hope, a dark blue may speak of despair. It is also helpful to be aware of what is communicated by the texture of a fabric. A rich piece of silk says something far different from a piece of monk's cloth or burlap, even though they are dyed the same color. Colors and textures do prompt various moods and, therefore, consistency with such moods is important.

Also, consider the many ways in which color(s) may be displayed throughout worship: vestments, paraments, choir robes, banners, bulletin covers, vessels (of metal, wood, stone, etc.). When based on an adequate understanding of the nature and meaning of the season and festivals, fabric and color can be used in fresh ways to enhance the meanings and mood of the time being celebrated. The depth of our involvement in the mighty acts of God, which we celebrate in the liturgical calendar, will thus be enriched.

Following is the predominant practice concerning use of liturgical color:

Christmas Cycle:
Advent—purple or blue.
Christmas (12 days)—white and gold.
The Epiphany of the Lord (January 6)—white and gold.

Ordinary Time:
January 7 through the Tuesday before Ash Wednesday—green, except for:
Baptism of the Lord—white.
Transfiguration of the Lord—white.

Lent:
Ash Wednesday through first five weeks—purple.
Passion/Palm Sunday—red and/or purple.
Monday, Tuesday, and Wednesday of Holy Week—purple.
Maundy Thursday—purple (until church is stripped bare).
Good Friday and *Saturday in Holy Week*—No color since the church remains stripped bare.

Easter Cycle:
Easter Season (including *Ascension of the Lord*)—white and gold.
Day of Pentecost—red.

Ordinary Time:
Monday after Day of Pentecost
through Saturday before the First Sunday of Advent—green, except
   for:
Trinity Sunday—white.
All Saints' Day (or First Sunday in November)—white.
Christ the King—white.

CHRISTMAS CYCLE

ADVENT

On each successive lighting of the Advent candles, all texts from the preceding lightings are read in addition to the text introduced that day.

On the First Sunday of Advent and following Sundays:

We light this candle as a sign of the coming light of Christ.

Advent means coming.

We are preparing ourselves for the days

when the nations shall beat their swords into plowshares,
and their spears into pruning hooks;
nation shall not lift up sword against nation,
neither shall they learn war any more. *Isa. 2:4*

And, on the Second Sunday of Advent, and successive lightings:

The wolf shall live with the lamb,
the leopard shall lie down with the kid,
the calf and the lion and the fatling together,
and a little child shall lead them. *Isa. 11:6*

And, on the Third Sunday of Advent, and successive lightings:

The wilderness and the dry land shall be glad,
the desert shall rejoice and blossom;
like the rose it shall blossom abundantly,
and rejoice with joy and singing. *Isa. 35:1*

And, on the Fourth Sunday of Advent, and successive lightings:

The Lord will give you a sign.
Look, the young woman is with child
and shall bear a son,
and shall name him Immanuel (God is with us). *Isa. 7:14b*

And, on the eve of Christmas, or Christmas Day:

The people who walked in darkness have seen a great light;
those who lived in a land of deep darkness,
on them light has shined.   *Isa. 9:2*

Each lighting is concluded with these words:

Let us walk in the light of the Lord.

PRAYER OF CONFESSION

God of the future,
you are coming in power
to bring all nations under your rule.
We confess that we have not expected your kingdom.

Lord, have mercy.

Lord, have mercy.

We have lived casual lives,
and ignored your promised judgment.

Christ, have mercy.

Christ, have mercy.

We have been slow to serve you and our neighbors.

Lord, have mercy.

Lord, have mercy.

Forgive us for the sake of Christ, our Savior,
whose coming we await.[1]

Amen.

GREAT PRAYER OF THANKSGIVING

The Lord be with you.

And also with you.

Lift up your hearts.

We lift them to the Lord.

Let us give thanks to the Lord our God.

It is right to give our thanks and praise.

It is truly right and our greatest joy
to praise you, O Lord our God,
creator and ruler of the universe.
You formed us in your image
and breathed into us the breath of life.
You set us in this world to love and serve you,
and to live in peace with all that you have made.

When we turned from you,
you did not turn from us.
When we were captives in slavery,
you delivered us to freedom,
and made covenant to be our sovereign God.
When we were stubborn and stiff-necked,
you spoke to us through prophets
who looked for that day
when justice shall triumph
and peace shall reign over all the earth.

Therefore, we praise you,
joining our voices with all the inhabitants of heaven,
and with the faithful of every time and place,
who forever sing to the glory of your name:

**Holy, holy, holy Lord, God of power and might,
heaven and earth are full of your glory.**
  Hosanna in the highest.

Blessed is he who comes in the name of the Lord.
  Hosanna in the highest.

You are holy, O God of majesty,
and blessed is Jesus Christ, your Son, our Lord.
You sent him into this world
to satisfy the longings of your people for a Savior,
to bring freedom to the captives of sin,
and to establish justice for the oppressed.
He came among us as one of us
taking the lot of the poor,
sharing human suffering.
We rejoice that in his death and rising again,
you set before us the sure promises of new life,
the certain hope of a heavenly home,
where we will sit at table with Christ our host.

The words of institution may be said here, or in relation to the breaking of the bread.

[We give you thanks that on the night before he died,
Jesus took bread.
After giving thanks to you, he broke it,
and gave it to his disciples, saying,
"Take, eat.
This is my body, given for you.
Do this in remembrance of me."

In the same way he took the cup, saying,
"This cup is the new covenant sealed in my blood,
shed for you for the forgiveness of sins.
Do this in remembrance of me."]

In remembrance of your acts of mercy in Jesus Christ,
we take this bread and this wine
and celebrate his dying and rising,
as we await the day of his coming.
With thanksgiving we offer our very selves to you
to be a living and holy sacrifice,
dedicated to your service.

So we proclaim the mystery of faith:

Christ has died,
Christ is risen,
Christ will come again.

Gracious God,
pour out your Holy Spirit
upon us and upon these your gifts of bread and wine,
that the bread we break and the cup we bless
may be the communion of the body and blood of Christ,
a foretaste of Christ's heavenly banquet.

By your Spirit make us one with Christ,
that we may be one with all who share this feast,
united in ministry throughout the world,
until Christ comes in final victory.

Through Christ, with Christ, in Christ,
in the unity of the Holy Spirit,
all glory and honor are yours, almighty God,
now and forever.[2]

Amen.

Prayer of Thanks

For use when the Eucharist is not celebrated.

Let us give thanks to the Lord our God.

It is right to give our thanks and praise.

Eternal God,
as you led your people in ages past,
you go before us into your future.
We give you thanks that
you came to us in Jesus Christ,
and we eagerly await his coming again
that his rule may be complete
and your righteousness reign over all the world.
Then we will feast at his royal banquet,
and sing his praises with the choirs of heaven.
By your Spirit,
open our eyes to the generosity of your hand,
and alert our souls to all spiritual gifts.
Fill us with gratitude overflowing
that we may share life and love in praise to you,
God of all the ages,

in the gracious name of Jesus Christ, your Son,
by the power of your Holy Spirit.[3]

Amen.

CALL TO WORSHIP AND
PRAYER OF THE DAY

FIRST SUNDAY OF ADVENT

Call to Worship

Salvation is nearer to us now than when we became believers;
the night is far gone,
the day is near.

**Let us then lay aside the works of darkness
and put on the armor of light.** *Rom. 13:11*

Or

The days are surely coming, says the Lord,
when I will fulfill the promise:
I will cause a righteous Branch to spring up for David;
and he shall execute justice and righteousness. *Jer. 33:14a, 15*

Prayer of the Day

Faithful God,
your promises stand unshaken through all generations.
Renew us in hope,
that we may be awake and alert
watching for the glorious return of Jesus Christ,
our judge and savior,
who lives and reigns with you
in the unity of the Holy Spirit,
one God, forever and ever.[4]

Amen.

Or

Eternal God,
through long generations you prepared a way
for the coming of your Son,
and by your Spirit
you still bring light to darkened lives.
Renew us in faith and hope
that we may welcome Christ to rule our thoughts
and claim our love,
as Lord of lords and King of kings,
to whom be glory always.[5]

Amen.

SECOND SUNDAY OF ADVENT

Call to Worship

A voice cries:
In the wilderness prepare the way of the Lord,
make straight in the desert a highway for our God.   *Isa. 40:3*

Or

As it is written in the book of the words of the prophet Isaiah,
"The voice of one crying out in the wilderness:
Prepare the way of the Lord,

make his paths straight.

Every valley shall be filled,

and every hill shall be made low,

the crooked shall be made straight,

the rough ways made smooth;
and all flesh shall see the salvation of God."   *Luke 3:4–6*

Or

Get you up to a high mountain,
O Zion, herald of good tidings;
lift up your voice with strength,
O Jerusalem, herald of good tidings,
lift it up, fear not;
say to the cities of Judah:

Behold your God.   *Isa. 40:9*

Or

In accordance with God's promise
we wait for new heavens and a new earth
where righteousness is at home.   *2 Peter 3:13*

Prayer of the Day

God of all peoples,
your servant John came baptizing
and calling for repentance.
Help us to hear his voice of judgment
that we may also rejoice in his word of promise.
So may we receive the Prince of Peace
and be found pure and blameless in his glorious Day.
We pray in his own strong name.[6]

Amen.

Or

Stir up our hearts, O Lord,
to prepare the way for your only Son.
By his coming give us strength in our conflicts
and shed light on our path through the darkness of this world;
through your Son, Jesus Christ our Lord,
who lives and reigns with you and the Holy Spirit,
one God, now and forever.[7]

Amen.

THIRD SUNDAY OF ADVENT

Call to Worship

Rejoice in the Lord always;
again I will say, Rejoice.

Let your gentleness be known to everyone.
The Lord is near.   *Phil. 4:4*

Or

The Spirit of the Lord God is upon me,
because the Lord has anointed me
to bring good news to the oppressed.   *Isa. 61:1*

Prayer of the Day

Almighty God,
you have made us and all things to serve you;
now prepare the world for your rule.
Come quickly to save us,
so that violence and crying may end,
and your children may live in peace,
honoring one another with justice and love;
through Jesus Christ, who lives in power with you,
and the Holy Spirit,
one God, now and forever.[8]

Amen.

Or

Eternal God,
you once called John the Baptist
to witness to the coming of your Son
and to prepare his way.
Give us wisdom to see your purpose today
and openness to hear your will,
that we may witness to Christ's coming
and so prepare his way;
through Jesus Christ our Lord,

who lives and reigns with you and the Holy Spirit,
one God now and forever.[9]

Amen.

FOURTH SUNDAY OF ADVENT

Call to Worship

Then Mary said, "Here am I,
the servant of the Lord;
let it be with me according to your word."   *Luke 1:38*

          Or

You, the Almighty, have done great things for me,
and holy is your name.   *Luke 1:49*

Prayer of the Day

God of grace,
you chose the Virgin Mary, full of grace,
to be the mother of our Lord and Savior.
Now fill us with your grace,
that in all things we may embrace your will
and with her rejoice in your salvation;
through Jesus Christ our Lord,
who lives and reigns with you and the Holy Spirit,
one God, now and forever.[10]

Amen.

          Or

God of grace,
your eternal Word took flesh among us
when Mary placed her life
at the service of your will.
By the power of your Spirit,
prepare our hearts for his coming again.
Keep us faithful in doing your will,

and steadfast to watch with hope,
that we may receive the coming of his kingdom,
for the sake of Jesus Christ the ruler of all.[11]

Amen.

LITANY FOR ADVENT
O ANTIPHONS

May be used from December 17 through 23.

O Wisdom,
coming forth from the mouth of the Most High,
pervading and permeating all creation,
you order all things with strength and gentleness:
come now and teach us the way to salvation.

Come, Lord Jesus.

O Adonai,
Ruler of the house of Israel,
you appeared in the burning bush to Moses
and gave him the Law on Sinai:
come with outstretched arm to save us.

Come, Lord Jesus.

O Root of Jesse,
rising as a sign for all the peoples,
before you earthly rulers will keep silent,
and nations give you honor:
come quickly to deliver us.

Come, Lord Jesus.

O Key of David,
Scepter over the house of Israel,
you open and no one can close,
you close and no one can open:
come to set free the prisoners
who live in darkness and the shadow of death.

Come, Lord Jesus.

O Radiant Dawn,
splendor of eternal light,
Sun of justice:
come, shine on those who live in darkness
and in the shadow of death.

Come, Lord Jesus.

O Ruler of the nations,
Monarch for whom the people long,
you are the Cornerstone uniting all humanity:
come, save us all,
whom you formed out of clay.

Come, Lord Jesus.

O Immanuel,
our Sovereign and Lawgiver,
desire of the nations and Savior of all:
come and save us, O Lord our God.

Come, Lord Jesus.

After a brief silence, the leader concludes the litany:

God of grace,
ever faithful to your promises,
the earth rejoices in hope of our Savior's coming
and looks forward with longing
to his return at the end of time.
Prepare our hearts to receive him when he comes,
for he is Lord forever and ever.[12]

Amen.

CHRISTMAS

Prayer of Adoration

Glory to you, almighty God,
for you sent your only-begotten Son,
that we might have new life.

Glory to you, Lord Jesus Christ,
for you became flesh and dwelt among us
that we might become your people.

Glory to you, Holy Spirit,
for you direct and rule our lives.

Glory to you, almighty God,
and to your Son, Jesus Christ,
and to the Holy Spirit,
now and forever.[13]

Amen.

Prayer of Confession

**Holy God, you sent a star
to guide wise men to the child Jesus.
We confess that we have not followed the light of your word.
We have not searched for signs of your love in the world,
or trusted your good news to be good.
We have failed to praise your Son's birth,
and refused his peace on earth.
We have expected little,
and hoped for less.
Forgive our doubt,
and renew in us all fine desires,
that we may watch and wait
and once more hear the glad story of our Savior,
Jesus Christ the Lord.[14]**

The Lord be with you.

And also with you.

Lift up your hearts.

We lift them to the Lord.

Let us give thanks to the Lord our God.

It is right to give our thanks and praise.

It is truly right and our greatest joy to praise you,
O holy God, creator and ruler of the universe.
You created light out of darkness
and brought forth life on the earth.
You formed us in your image
and called us to love and to serve you.
When we were unfaithful to you
and turned from your ways,
you did not forsake us,
your love remained steadfast.
You delivered us from captivity,
made covenant to be our sovereign God,
and sent prophets to call us to return to your ways.

In the fullness of time
you sent your only Son Jesus Christ to be our Savior.
In him, your Word, dwelling with you from all eternity,
became flesh and dwelt among us, full of grace and truth,
and we beheld your glory.

Therefore, we praise you,
joining our voices with the celestial choirs,
and with all the faithful of every time and place,
who forever sing to the glory of your name:

**Holy, holy, holy Lord, God of power and might,
heaven and earth are full of your glory.**
   Hosanna in the highest.

Blessed is he who comes in the name of the Lord.
   Hosanna in the highest.

You are holy, O God of majesty,
and blessed is Jesus Christ, your Son, our Lord.
Born in humility,
he came to rule over all.
Helpless as an infant,
he showed the power of your love.
Poor in things of the world,
he brought the wealth of your grace.

In his dying and rising
you gave birth to your church,
delivered us from slavery to sin and death,
and made with us a new covenant by water and the Spirit.

> *The words of institution may be said here, or in relation to the breaking of the bread.*

[We give you thanks that on the night before he died,
Jesus took bread.
After giving thanks to you, he broke it,
and gave it to his disciples, saying,
"Take, eat.
This is my body, given for you.
Do this in remembrance of me."

In the same way he took the cup, saying,
"This cup is the new covenant sealed in my blood,
shed for you for the forgiveness of sins.
Do this in remembrance of me."]

In remembrance of your mighty acts in Jesus Christ,
we take this bread and this wine
and celebrate this holy sacrament.
With thanksgiving we offer our very selves to you
to be a living and holy sacrifice,
dedicated to your service.

So we proclaim the mystery of faith:

**Christ has died,
Christ is risen,
Christ will come again.**

Gracious God,
pour out your Holy Spirit
upon us and upon these your gifts of bread and wine,
that the bread we break and the cup we bless
may be the communion of the body and blood of Christ,
our Immanuel, God-with-us.

By your Spirit make us one with Christ,
that we may be one with all who share this feast,
united in ministry throughout the world,
until Christ comes in final victory
and we feast with him in his eternal kingdom.

Through Christ, with Christ, in Christ,
in the unity of the Holy Spirit,
all glory and honor are yours, almighty God,
now and forever.[15]

Amen.

PRAYER OF THANKS

For use when the Eucharist is not celebrated.

Let us give thanks to the Lord our God.

It is right to give our thanks and praise.

God of mystery and might,
we praise and worship you,
for you came in the silence of light
to enter our world as a child of humble birth.
We thank you for your Son, Jesus Christ,
born of your handmaid Mary.
In his face we beheld your glory,
for in his life as in his death
was your gift of salvation.
By your Spirit,
make our hearts burn with thanksgiving,
that we may give as we have received.
Let our whole lives be gifts of praise to you,
God of love and peace,

in the gracious name of Jesus Christ, your Son,
by the power of your Holy Spirit.[16]

Amen.

Or

Let us give thanks to the Lord our God.

It is right to give our thanks and praise.

Great God of power,
we praise you for Jesus Christ
who came to save us from our sins.
We thank you for the hope of the prophets,
the song of the angels,
and the birth of Jesus in Bethlehem.
We thank you that in Jesus you became flesh and dwelt among us,
sharing human hurts and pleasures.
Glory to you for your grace-filled love.
Glory to you, eternal God;
through Jesus Christ, Lord of lords,
and King of kings, forever.[17]

Amen.

CALL TO WORSHIP
PRAYER OF THE DAY

CHRISTMAS EVE

Call to Worship

For a child has been born for us,

a son given to us;

authority rests upon his shoulder,
and he is named:

**Wonderful Counselor,
Mighty God,
Everlasting Father,
Prince of Peace.**

Isa. 9:6

Or

The people who walked in darkness have seen a great light;
those who lived in a land of deep darkness—
on them light has shined.   *Isa. 9:2*

Prayer of the Day

Eternal God,
this holy night is radiant
with the brilliance of your one true light.
As we have known the revelation of that light on earth,
bring us to see the splendor of your heavenly glory;
through Jesus Christ our Lord,
who is alive and reigns with you the Holy Spirit,
one God, now and forever.[18]

Amen.

Or

Give us, O God, such love and wonder,
that with shepherds and wise men,
and pilgrims unknown,
we may come to adore the holy child, the promised King;
and with our gifts worship him,
our Lord and Savior Jesus Christ.[19]

Amen.

Or

Great God,
as you came in the stillness of night,
enter our lives this night.
Overcome darkness with the light of Christ's presence,
that we may clearly see the way to walk,
the truth to speak,
and the life to live for him,
our Lord Jesus Christ.[20]

Amen.

CHRISTMAS DAY

Call to Worship

I bring you good news of a great joy
which will come to all the people;
for to you is born this day a Savior,
who is Christ the Lord.

Luke 2:10, 11

Prayer of the Day

All glory to you, great God,
for the gift of your Son,
light in darkness and hope of the world,
whom you sent to save us.
With singing angels,
let us praise your name,
and tell the earth his story,
that all may believe, rejoice, and bow down,
acknowledging your love;
through Jesus Christ our Lord.[21]

Amen.

Or

Holy God,
you brought peace and good will to earth
when Christ was born.
Fill us with such gladness
that, hearing again the news of his birth,
we may come to worship him,
who is King of kings, and Lord of lords,
Jesus Christ our Savior.[22]

Amen.

FIRST SUNDAY AFTER CHRISTMAS DAY

Call to Worship

Let the peace of Christ rule in your hearts;
let the word of Christ dwell in you richly.

Col. 3:15, 16

Prayer of the Day

Almighty God,
you wonderfully created
and yet more wonderfully restored
the dignity of human nature.
In your mercy,
let us share the divine life of Jesus Christ
who came to share our humanity,
and who now lives and reigns with you and the Holy Spirit,
one God, now and forever.[23]

Amen.

Or

Almighty God,
you have shed upon us
the new light of your incarnate Word.
May this light, enkindled in our hearts,
shine forth in our lives;
through Jesus Christ our Lord,
who lives and reigns with you,
in the unity of the Holy Spirit,
one God, now and forever.[24]

Amen.

SECOND SUNDAY AFTER CHRISTMAS DAY

Call to Worship

The Word became flesh and dwelt among us,
full of grace and truth.

We have beheld his glory. Alleluia!   *John 1:14*

Or

Glory to Christ
who is proclaimed among the nations,
and believed in throughout the world.   *Based on 1 Tim. 3:16*

Prayer of the Day

Almighty God,
you have filled us with the new light of the Word
who became flesh and lived among us.
Let the light of faith shine in all that we do;
through Jesus Christ our Lord,
who lives and reigns with you and the Holy Spirit,
one God, now and forever.[25]

Amen.

Or

Eternal God,
a thousand years in your sight
are like a watch in the night.
You have led us in days past;
guide us now and always,
that our hearts may turn to choose your will,
and new resolves may be strengthened;
through Jesus Christ our Lord.[26]

Amen.

OUTLINE OF
A FESTIVAL OF LESSONS AND CAROLS

Processional Hymn
Greeting and Prayer

First Lesson—Genesis 3:8–15
Christmas Carol, Hymn, Canticle, or Anthem

Second Lesson—Genesis 22:15–18
Christmas Carol, Hymn, Canticle, or Anthem

Third Lesson—Isaiah 9:2, 6–7
Christmas Carol, Hymn, Canticle, or Anthem

Fourth Lesson—Micah 5:2–4
Christmas Carol, Hymn, Canticle, or Anthem

Fifth Lesson—Luke 1:26–35, 38
Christmas Carol, Hymn, Canticle, or Anthem

Sixth Lesson—Matthew 1:18–21
Christmas Carol, Hymn, Canticle, or Anthem

Seventh Lesson—Luke 2:8–20
Christmas Carol, Hymn, Canticle, or Anthem

Eighth Lesson—Matthew 2:1–11
Christmas Carol, Hymn, Canticle, or Anthem

Ninth Lesson—John 1:1–14
Christmas Carol, Hymn, Canticle, or Anthem

Prayer
Hymn
Blessing

A FESTIVAL OF LESSONS AND CAROLS

PROCESSIONAL HYMN

GREETING AND PRAYER

Friends in Christ, in this Christmas season we delight to hear again the message of the angels, to go to Bethlehem and see the Son of God lying in a manger.

Let us therefore open the Holy Scriptures and read the story of the loving purpose of God from the time of our rebellion against God until the glorious redemption brought to us by this holy child, and let us make this place glad with carols of praise.

But first, let us pray for the needs of the whole world:

for peace and justice on earth . . .

for the unity and mission of the church for which Christ died. . . .

And because Christ particularly loves them, let us remember in his name:

the poor and helpless . . .

the cold, the hungry and the oppressed . . .

the sick and those who mourn . . .

the lonely and unloved . . .

the aged and little children . . .

and all who do not know and love the Lord Jesus Christ. . . .

Finally, let us remember before God that multitude which no one can number, whose hope was in the Word made flesh, and with whom, in Jesus, we are one for evermore. . . .

And now, to sum up all these petitions, let us pray in the words which Christ himself has taught us, saying:

Our Father. . . .

Here shall follow the reading of the nine lessons. When possible, each lesson is read by a different person.

Christmas carols, hymns, canticles, and anthems are sung by the congregation or choir between the readings. For suggestions see pp. 288–290.

At the beginning of each lesson, the words given below are said.

FIRST LESSON   Genesis 3:8–15

God announces in the Garden of Eden that the offspring of woman shall strike the serpent's head.

SECOND LESSON   Genesis 22:15–18

God promises to faithful Abraham that by his offspring, all the nations of the earth shall be blessed.

THIRD LESSON   Isaiah 9:2, 6–7

Christ's birth and kingdom are foretold by Isaiah.

FOURTH LESSON   Micah 5:2–4

The prophet Micah foretells the glory of Bethlehem.

FIFTH LESSON   Luke 1:26–35, 38

The angel Gabriel visits the blessed Virgin Mary.

SIXTH LESSON   Matthew 1:18–21

St. Matthew tells of the birth of Jesus.

SEVENTH LESSON   Luke 2:8–20

The shepherds go to the manger.

EIGHTH LESSON   Matthew 2:1–11

The wise men are led by the star to Jesus.

NINTH LESSON   John 1:1–14

St. John unfolds the mystery of the incarnation.

PRAYER

A prayer appropriate to the season, such as one of the Prayers of the Day from pp. 78–81, is said.

HYMN

BLESSING

EPIPHANY—JANUARY 6 (or First Sunday in January)

Arise, shine: for your light has come,

and the glory of the Lord has risen upon you.

Nations shall come to your light

and rulers to the brightness of your rising.   *Isa. 60:1–3*

> *Or*

The grace of God has dawned upon the world
with healing for all humankind.   *Titus 2:11*

PRAYER OF THE DAY

Lord God,
you revealed your Son to the nations by the leading of a star.
Lead us now by faith
to know your presence in our lives,
and bring us at last to the full vision of your glory;
through Jesus Christ our Lord,
who lives and reigns with you and the Holy Spirit,
one God, now and forever.[27]

Amen.

> *Or*

Eternal God,
who by a star led wise men to the worship of your Son,
guide by your light the nations of the earth,
that the whole world may know your glory;
through Jesus Christ our Lord,
who lives and reigns with you and the Holy Spirit,
one God, now and forever.[28]

Amen.

PRAYER OF CONFESSION

**God of grace,
you have given us Jesus, the light of the world,
but we choose darkness
and cling to sins that hide the brightness of your love.
Immersed in ourselves, we have not risen to new life.
Baptize us with your Spirit,
that, forgiven and renewed,
we may preach your word to the nations
and tell of your glory shining in the face of Jesus Christ,
our Lord and our Light forever.**[29]

GREAT PRAYER OF THANKSGIVING

The Lord be with you.

And also with you.

Lift up your hearts.

We lift them to the Lord.

Let us give thanks to the Lord our God.

It is right to give our thanks and praise.

It is truly right and our greatest joy
to give you praise, God of majesty and splendor.
By your power you created all that is,
making a universe out of chaos,
and ruling over all things in love.
Throughout the ages you called your people
to love and to serve you,
and to be your light among the nations.
When we failed you,
you did not fail us
but sent prophets to call us to return to your ways.

We praise you that in the fullness of time,
you revealed your love for the world
by sending your Son Jesus
to be the Light of the world.
He came to heal our brokenness
and to set before us the way of truth,
of peace and love.

Therefore, we praise you,
joining our voices with angels and archangels,
and all the faithful of every time and place,
who forever sing to the glory of your name:

**Holy, holy, holy Lord, God of power and might,
heaven and earth are full of your glory.
Hosanna in the highest.**

**Blessed is he who comes in the name of the Lord.
Hosanna in the highest.**

You are holy, O God of majesty,
and blessed is Jesus Christ, your Son, our Lord,
in whom we have seen your glory.
In his birth,
he became one with us.
In his death,
he overcame death.
In his rising from the tomb,
he raised us to eternal life,
and made with us a new covenant
by water and the Spirit.

> *The words of institution may be said here, or in relation to the
> breaking of the bread.*

[We give you thanks that on the night before he died,
Jesus took bread.
After giving thanks to you, he broke it,
and gave it to his disciples, saying,
"Take, eat.
This is my body, given for you.
Do this in remembrance of me."

In the same way he took the cup, saying,
"This cup is the new covenant sealed in my blood,
shed for you for the forgiveness of sins.
Do this in remembrance of me."]

In remembrance of your mighty acts in Jesus Christ,
we take this bread and this wine
and celebrate this holy sacrament.
With thanksgiving we offer our very selves to you
to be a living and holy sacrifice,
dedicated to your service.

So we proclaim the mystery of faith:

Christ has died,
Christ is risen,
Christ will come again.

Gracious God,
pour out your Holy Spirit
upon us and upon these your gifts of bread and wine,
that the bread we break and the cup we bless
may be the communion of the body and blood of Christ.

Illumine our hearts with the radiance of your presence,
that our lives may show forth his love in this weary world.

By your Spirit make us one with Christ,
that we may be one with all who share this feast,
united in ministry throughout the world,
until Christ comes in final victory
and we feast with him in his eternal kingdom.

Through Christ, with Christ, in Christ,
in the unity of the Holy Spirit,
all glory and honor are yours, almighty God,
now and forever.[30]

Amen.

Prayer of Thanks

For use when the Eucharist is not celebrated.

Let us give thanks to the Lord our God.

It is right to give our thanks and praise.

God of majesty and light,
you hold the whole world in your hand.
So we give you our great praise
that in Jesus Christ all people may see your glory.
We thank you for revealing Jesus to be your Son,
and for claiming our lives in baptism
to be his glad disciples.
By your Spirit,
may peace descend upon us
that we may follow him with grateful hearts.
Take us and all we have to be useful in your service,
God of all nations,
in the gracious name of Jesus Christ, your Son,
by the power of your Holy Spirit.[31]

Amen.

ORDINARY TIME
BETWEEN EPIPHANY AND
ASH WEDNESDAY

BAPTISM OF THE LORD

Sunday between January 7 and 13 inclusive

CALL TO WORSHIP

A voice came out of the cloud, saying,
"This is my Son, my Chosen; listen to him!" *Luke 9:35*

>   *Or*

Sing to the Lord, bless God's name;

proclaim God's salvation from day to day.

Declare the Lord's glory among the nations,

the Lord's marvelous works among all the peoples! *Ps. 96:2–3*

PRAYER OF THE DAY

Eternal God,
at the baptism of Jesus
you revealed him to be your Son,
anointing him with the Holy Spirit.
Keep your children, born of water and the Spirit,
faithful to their calling;
through Jesus Christ our Lord,
who lives and reigns with you and the Holy Spirit,
one God, now and forever.[32]

Amen.

>   *Or*

Holy God,
you sent your Son to be baptized among sinners,
to seek and save the lost.
May we, who have been baptized in his name,
never turn away from the world,
but reach out in love to rescue the wayward;
by the mercy of Christ our Lord.[33]

Amen.

Prayer of Confession

Merciful God,
in baptism you grafted us into the body of Christ,
promising us forgiveness of sin and newness of life.
But we fail to live as forgiven people.
We keep destructive habits and hold grudges,
We allow our past to hold us hostage,
and are reluctant to welcome newness.

In your loving kindness, have mercy on us,
and free us from sin.
Remind us of the promises you have made to us in baptism
so that we may live as your people,
claimed in the waters of promise.[34]

Great Prayer of Thanksgiving

The Lord be with you.

And also with you.

Lift up your hearts.

We lift them to the Lord.

Let us give thanks to the Lord our God.

It is right to give our thanks and praise.

It is truly right and our greatest joy
to give you praise, God of mercy and might.
In your wisdom, you made all things
and sustain them by your power.
You have called forth men and women in every age
to be your servants and speak your word.
When we rebelled against your call
and turned from your ways,
in your love you called us to return to you.
You delivered us from captivity,
and made covenant to be our sovereign God.
You sent prophets to call us to justice and compassion.

Therefore, we praise you,
joining our voices with the choirs of heaven,
and with all the faithful of every time and place,
who forever sing to the glory of your name:

**Holy, holy, holy Lord, God of power and might,
heaven and earth are full of your glory.
  Hosanna in the highest.**

**Blessed is he who comes in the name of the Lord.
  Hosanna in the highest.**

You are holy, O God of majesty,
and blessed is Jesus Christ, your Son, our Lord,
in whom you have revealed yourself,
our light and our salvation.

In his baptism in Jordan's waters,
Jesus took his place with sinners
and your voice proclaimed him as your beloved.
Your Spirit anointed him
to bring good news to the poor,
to proclaim release to captives,
to restore sight to the blind,
to free the oppressed.
He lived among us in power and grace,
touching broken lives with your healing peace.

By the baptism of his suffering, death, and resurrection
you made with us a new covenant
by water and the Spirit.

> *The words of institution may be said here, or in relation to the
> breaking of the bread.*

[We give you thanks that on the night before he died,
Jesus took bread.
After giving thanks to you, he broke it,
and gave it to his disciples, saying,
"Take, eat.
This is my body, given for you.
Do this in remembrance of me."

In the same way he took the cup, saying,
"This cup is the new covenant sealed in my blood,
shed for you for the forgiveness of sins.
Do this in remembrance of me."]

In remembrance of your mighty self-giving in Jesus Christ,
we take this bread and this wine
and celebrate his dying and rising,
as we await the day of his coming.
With thanksgiving we offer our very selves to you
to be a living and holy sacrifice,
dedicated to your service.

So we proclaim the mystery of faith:

Christ has died,
Christ is risen,
Christ will come again.

Gracious God,
pour out your Holy Spirit
upon us and upon these your gifts of bread and wine,
that the bread we break and the cup we bless
may be the communion of the body and blood of Christ,
and that we may be his body, the church.

By your Spirit make us one with Christ,
that we may be one with all who share this feast,
united in ministry throughout all the world,
until Christ comes in final victory
and we feast with him in eternity.

Through Christ, with Christ, in Christ,
in the unity of the Holy Spirit,
all glory and honor are yours, almighty God,
now and forever.[35]

Amen.

PRAYER OF THANKS

For use when the Eucharist is not celebrated.

Let us give thanks to the Lord our God.

It is right to give our thanks and praise.

God of heaven and earth,
you call us to come in humility before you,
bringing the offering of our very selves.
As you revealed Jesus to be your Son
in his baptism at the hand of John,
so you claimed our lives in baptism,
that we might die to sin
and be raised with him to new life.
By your Spirit,
confirm in our hearts the witness
that Christ is Savior of the world
and our Lord.
Accept all we have and are, O God,
in the service of Jesus Christ,
and strengthen us with your Spirit's power.[36]

Amen.

SUNDAYS BETWEEN
BAPTISM OF THE LORD
AND TRANSFIGURATION OF THE LORD

SECOND SUNDAY IN ORDINARY TIME

Sunday between January 14 and 20 inclusive

Call to Worship

The Word became flesh and lived among us,

and we have seen his glory.

To all who received him,

he gave power to become children of God.   *John 1:14, 12*

Or

B
We have found the Messiah,
Jesus Christ, who brings us truth and grace.   *Based on John 1:41, 16*

Or

C
Jesus revealed his glory;
and his disciples believed in him.   *John 2:11*

Prayer of the Day

Almighty God,
your Son our Savior Jesus Christ
is the light of the world.
May your people,
illumined by your word and sacraments,
shine with the radiance of his glory,
that he may be known, worshiped, and obeyed
to the ends of the earth;

who lives and reigns with you and the Holy Spirit,
one God, now and forever.[37]

Amen.

Or

C
Great God,
your mercy is an unexpected miracle.
Help us to believe and obey,
that we may be free from the worry of sin,
and be filled with the wine of new life,
promised in the power of Jesus Christ our Savior.[38]

Amen.

THIRD SUNDAY IN ORDINARY TIME

Sunday between January 21 and 27 inclusive

Call to Worship

A
Jesus proclaimed the good news of the kingdom
and healed every sickness among the people.   *Matt. 4:23*

Or

B
The time is fulfilled
and the kingdom of God has come near;
repent, and believe the good news.   *Mark 1:15*

Or

C
The Spirit of the Lord has anointed me
to preach good news to the poor
and release to the captives.   *Luke 4:18*

Prayer of the Day

AB
Almighty God,
by grace alone you call us
and accept us in your service.
Strengthen us by your Spirit,
and make us worthy of your call;
through Jesus Christ our Lord,
who lives and reigns with you and the Holy Spirit,
one God, now and forever.[39]

Amen.

Or

B
Loving God,
through your Son you have called us to repent of our sin,
to believe the good news,
and to celebrate the coming of your kingdom.
Like Christ's first apostles,
may we hear his call to discipleship,
and, forsaking old ways,
proclaim the gospel of new life to a broken world,
through our Lord and Savior Jesus Christ.[40]

Amen.

Or

C
Almighty God,
you sent Jesus to proclaim your kingdom
and to teach with authority.
Anoint us with your Spirit,
that we, too, may bring good news to the afflicted,
bind up the brokenhearted,
and proclaim liberty to the captive;
through Jesus Christ our Lord.[41]

Amen.

FOURTH SUNDAY IN ORDINARY TIME

Sunday between January 28 and February 3 inclusive

Call to Worship

A
Rejoice and be glad,
for your reward is great in heaven.   *Matt. 5:12*

Or

B
Jesus went throughout Galilee,
teaching, proclaiming the good news,
and healing every sickness among the people.   *Matt. 4:23*

Or

C
The Spirit of the Lord has anointed me
to preach good news to the poor
and release to the captives.   *Luke 4:18*

Prayer of the Day

Living God,
in Christ you make all things new.
Transform the poverty of our nature
by the riches of your grace,
and in the renewal of our lives
make known your glory;
through Jesus Christ our Lord,
who is alive and reigns with you and the Holy Spirit,
one God, now and forever.[42]

Amen.

Or

A
Holy God,
you challenge the ruling powers of this world

and show favor to the lowly.
Make us to hunger and thirst for righteousness,
and keep us steady in seeking peace,
that we may be your faithful children
and know the blessedness of your kingdom,
through Jesus Christ.[43]

Amen.

Or

C
God of compassion,
you have shown us in Christ
that your love for us is never-ending.
Enable us to love you with all our hearts
and to love one another as Christ loved us.
Grant this through our Lord Jesus Christ,
who lives and reigns with you and the Holy Spirit,
one God, forever and ever.[44]

Amen.

FIFTH SUNDAY IN ORDINARY TIME

Sunday between February 4 and 10 inclusive

Call to Worship

A
You are the light of the world.
Let your light shine before others,
so that they may see your good works
and give glory to your Father in heaven.   *Matt. 5:14, 16*

Or

B
He took our infirmities
and bore our diseases.   *Matt. 8:17*

Or

C

I am the light of the world.
Whoever follows me will never walk in darkness
but will have the light of life.   *John 8:12*

Prayer of the Day

Faithful God,
you have appointed us your witnesses,
to be a light that shines in the world.
Let us not hide the bright hope you have given us,
but tell everyone your love,
revealed in Jesus Christ the Lord.[45]

Amen.

Or

O God,
in the folly of the cross
you reveal how great is the distance
between your wisdom and human understanding.
Open our minds to the simplicity of the gospel,
that, fervent in faith and tireless in love,
we may become light and salt for the world,
for the sake of Jesus Christ, your Son,
who lives and reigns with you
in the unity of the Holy Spirit,
one God, forever and ever.[46]

Amen.

SIXTH SUNDAY IN ORDINARY TIME

Sunday between February 11 and 17 inclusive
(Except when this Sunday is the Transfiguration of the Lord)

Call to Worship

A

Happy are those whose way is blameless,

who walk in the law of the Lord.

Happy are those who keep the Lord's decrees,

who seek the Lord with their whole heart. *Ps. 119:1, 2*

Or

C
Rejoice and leap for joy,
for surely your reward is great in heaven. *Luke 6:23*

Prayer of the Day

A
Almighty God,
you gave the law as a good guide for our lives.
May we never shrink from your commandments,
but, as we are taught by your Son Jesus,
fulfill the law in perfect love;
through Christ our Lord and Master.[47]

Amen.

Or

B
Almighty and everliving God,
whose Son Jesus Christ healed the sick
and restored them to wholeness of life,
look with compassion on the anguish of the world,
and by your power make whole all peoples and nations;
through Jesus Christ our Lord,
who lives and reigns with you and the Holy Spirit,
one God, now and forever.[48]

Amen.

Or

C
Holy God,
you challenge the powers that rule this world
and show favor to the oppressed.
Give us a true sense of your justice,

that we may know the marks of your kingdom
and join the struggle that right may prevail
for the sake of Jesus Christ our Lord.[49]

Amen.

SEVENTH SUNDAY IN ORDINARY TIME

Sunday between February 18 and 24 inclusive
(Except when this Sunday is the Transfiguration of the Lord)

Call to Worship

A
Love of God is perfected
in those who obey the word of Christ.   *Based on 1 John 2:5*

      Or

B
The Spirit of the Lord has anointed me
to preach good news to the poor
and release to the captives.   *Luke 4:18*

      Or

C
I give you a new commandment,
that you love one another.
As I have loved you,
you also should love one another.   *John 13:34*

Prayer of the Day

Almighty God,
your Son revealed in signs and miracles
the wonder of your saving love.
Renew your people with your heavenly grace,
and in all our weakness
sustain us by your mighty power;
through Jesus Christ our Lord,
who is alive and reigns with you and the Holy Spirit,
one God, now and forever.[50]

Amen.

EIGHTH SUNDAY IN ORDINARY TIME

Sunday between February 25 and 29 inclusive
(Except when this Sunday is the Transfiguration of the Lord)

Call to Worship

A
The word of God is living and active.
It is able to judge
the thoughts and intentions of the heart.   *Heb. 4:12*

     Or

B
God gave us birth by the word of truth,
that we might be a kind of first fruits of God's creatures. *James 1:18*

     Or

C
Shine like stars in the world,
holding fast to the word of life.   *Phil. 2:15, 16*

Prayer of the Day

Almighty God,
grant us the Spirit to think and do always
those things that are right,
that we, who can do nothing good without you,
may live according to your holy will;
through Jesus Christ our Lord,
who lives and reigns with you and the Holy Spirit,
one God, now and forever.[51]

Amen.

     Or

A
O God,
in the suffering and death of your Son
you revealed your limitless love to the world.

Renew us by the power of Christ's cross
and break the chains of hatred and violence,
so that, in the victory of good over evil,
we may bear witness to your gospel of reconciliation,
in the name of Jesus Christ,
who lives and reigns with you and the Holy Spirit,
one God, forever and ever.[52]

Amen.

TRANSFIGURATION OF THE LORD

CALL TO WORSHIP AND
PRAYER OF THE DAY

Call to Worship

Beloved, we are God's children now;
what we will be has not yet been revealed.
What we do know is this:
when he is revealed,
we will be like him,
for we will see him as he is.   *1 John 3:2*

    Or

This is my Son, the Beloved,
with whom I am well pleased.
Listen to him!   *Matt. 17:5*

Prayer of the Day

O God,
in the transfiguration of your Son
you confirmed the mysteries of the faith
by the witness of Moses and Elijah.
In the voice from the cloud
you foreshadowed our adoption as your children.
Make us, with Christ, heirs of your glory,
and bring us to enjoy its fullness,
through Jesus Christ our Lord,
who lives and reigns with you and the Holy Spirit,
one God, now and forever.[53]

Amen.

    Or

Almighty God,
whose Son was revealed in majesty
before he suffered death upon the cross,
give us faith to perceive his glory,

that, being strengthened by his grace,
we may be changed into his likeness, from glory to glory;
who lives and reigns with you and the Holy Spirit,
one God, now and forever.[54]

Amen.

PRAYER OF CONFESSION

God of compassion,
in Jesus Christ we behold your transforming light,
yet we continue to live in darkness.
Preoccupied with ourselves,
we fail to see your work in the world.
We speak when we should listen,
we act when we should reflect.
Empower us to live in your light
and to walk in your ways,
for the sake of him who is the light of the world,
Jesus Christ, our Lord and Savior.[55]

GREAT PRAYER OF THANKSGIVING

The Lord be with you.

And also with you.

Lift up your hearts.

We lift them to the Lord.

Let us give thanks to the Lord our God.

It is right to give our thanks and praise.

It is right to give you thanks and praise,
eternal God our Creator,
for you brought light out of darkness
and set the sun to brighten the day
and the moon and stars to illumine the night.
Your glory blinds the eyes of our sinful souls,
and yet your radiance warms our needy hearts.
So you lead us by the light of your truth
into the way of righteousness and peace.

Therefore, we praise you,
singing with all the inhabitants of heaven,
and with the faithful of every time and place,
to the glory of your mighty name:

**Holy, holy, holy Lord, God of power and might,
heaven and earth are full of your glory.
   Hosanna in the highest.**

**Blessed is he who comes in the name of the Lord.
   Hosanna in the highest.**

You are holy, O God of majesty,
and blessed is Jesus Christ, your Son, our Lord.
On a lonely mountain
his human frame was transfigured by your divine splendor.
In his face, we have glimpsed your glory;
in his life, we have seen the dazzling brightness of your love.
For your image is untarnished in him,
and the burden of human sorrow and suffering
could not diminish his reflection of your holiness.
The world was dark at his death,
but the light of his life could not be extinguished.
From the grave he rose like the sun,
with blinding power and radiant peace.

> *The words of institution may be said here, or in relation to the
> breaking of the bread.*

[We give you thanks that on the night before he died,
Jesus took bread.
After giving thanks to you, he broke it,
and gave it to his disciples, saying,
"Take, eat.
This is my body, given for you.
Do this in remembrance of me."

In the same way he took the cup, saying,
"This cup is the new covenant sealed in my blood,
shed for you for the forgiveness of sins.
Do this in remembrance of me."]

Remembering your glory in Jesus Christ,
we take this bread and this wine
and celebrate this holy sacrament.
With thanksgiving we offer our very selves to you
to be a living and holy sacrifice,
dedicated to your service.

So we proclaim the mystery of faith:

Christ has died,
Christ is risen,
Christ will come again.

Gracious God, by your Holy Spirit,
may the bread we break and the cup we share
be for us communion in the body and blood of Christ.
Illumine our lives with the radiance of his love,
and inspire us to shine in faith and witness
as his holy disciples.

By your Spirit make us one with Christ,
that we may be one with all who share this feast,
united in ministry throughout the world,
until Christ comes in final victory
and we feast with him in eternity.

Through Christ, with Christ, in Christ,
in the unity of the Holy Spirit,
all glory and honor, praise and adoration are yours,
now and forever.[56]

Amen.

PRAYER OF THANKS

For use when the Eucharist is not celebrated.

Let us give thanks to the Lord our God.

It is right to give our thanks and praise.

O Lord our God, you are great indeed,
clothed in majesty and splendor,
wrapped in light as with a robe.

In the solitude of a mountain height
you revealed your glory in Jesus Christ,
even as he faced his crucifixion.
We praise you for this glimpse of the mystery of our redemption.

You loved the world so much
that you sent your beloved Son
to dwell with us.
He who bears your very image,
the firstborn of all creation,
through whom all things have been created,
took our flesh and suffered death
that we might be made whole.
By his death he conquered death,
and by his rising he gives eternal life.
We praise you for your saving grace.

Transfigure us by your Spirit,
and let your love shine in all we do and say,
that all the world may see the radiant light of God
guiding all creation, Jesus Christ our Lord.[57]

Amen.

EASTER CYCLE:
LENT, EASTER, AND
DAY OF PENTECOST

OUTLINE OF
THE SERVICE FOR ASH WEDNESDAY

GATHERING

Call to Worship
Prayer of the Day
Hymn

LITURGY OF THE WORD

Prayer for Illumination
First Lesson
Second Lesson
[Anthem]
Gospel Lesson
Sermon
Invitation to Observance of the Lenten Discipline
Imposition of Ashes
    Prayer
    Imposition
Psalm 51

*If the Eucharist
is not celebrated:*

THE EUCHARIST

Invitation to the Lord's Table
Great Prayer of Thanksgiving,
    followed by the Lord's Prayer
Breaking of the Bread
Communion of the People
Prayer

Prayer of Thanks,
    followed by the
    Lord's Prayer

SENDING

Psalm, Hymn, or Spiritual
Benediction

ASH WEDNESDAY

The community gathers in silence. Any procession should be in silence.

GATHERING

CALL TO WORSHIP

Let us worship God

God sent the Son into the world,
not to condemn the world,
but that the world might be saved through him.   *John 3:17*

God's love endures forever.

God is our refuge and strength,
a present help in trouble,
Therefore we will not fear
though the earth should change,
though the mountains shake in the heart of the sea;
though the waters roar and foam,
though the mountains tremble with its tumult.   *Ps. 46:1–3*

God's love endures forever.

PRAYER OF THE DAY

Let us pray.

Silence.

Gracious God:
Out of your love and mercy,
you breathed into dust the breath of life,
creating us to serve you and our neighbors.
Call forth our prayers and acts of tenderness,
and strengthen us to face our mortality;
that we may reach with confidence for your mercy;
in Jesus Christ our Lord.[58]

Amen.

Or

Almighty God,
you despise nothing you have made,
and you forgive the sins of all who are penitent.
Create in us new and contrite hearts,
that, truly repenting of our sins,
and acknowledging our brokenness,
we may obtain from you, the God of all mercy,
full pardon and forgiveness;
through your Son, Jesus Christ our Lord,
who lives and reigns with you and the Holy Spirit,
one God, now and forever.[59]

Amen.

Or

Renew us, O God of grace,
through prayer, fasting, and works of compassion,
that we may be true signs of the way of the cross;
through Jesus Christ our Lord and Savior.[60]

Amen.

A hymn may be sung.

LITURGY OF THE WORD

A prayer for illumination is said.

FIRST LESSON: Joel 2:1–2, 12–17
                          or Isaiah 58:1–12

SECOND LESSON: 2 Corinthians 5:20b—6:10

An anthem may be sung.

GOSPEL LESSON: Matthew 6:1–6, 16–21

SERMON

INVITATION TO THE OBSERVANCE OF THE LENTEN DISCIPLINE

The following or similar words may be spoken:

Friends in Christ,
every year at the time of the Christian Passover
we celebrate our redemption
through the death and resurrection
of our Lord Jesus Christ.
Lent is a time to prepare for this celebration
and to renew our life in the paschal mystery.
We begin this holy season
by remembering our need for repentance,
and for the mercy and forgiveness
proclaimed in the gospel of Jesus Christ.

If ashes are used, the following may be said.

We begin our journey to Easter with the sign of ashes,
an ancient sign,
that speaks of the frailty and uncertainty of human life,
and marks the penitence of this community.

The minister continues:

I invite you therefore, in the name of the Lord,
to observe a holy Lent
by self-examination, penitence, prayer,
fasting, and almsgiving,
and by reading and meditating on the word of God.
Let us bow before our creator and redeemer.[61]

A brief silence is observed.

IMPOSITION OF ASHES

Let us pray.

Almighty God,
you have created us out of the dust of the earth.

May these ashes be to us
a sign of our mortality and penitence,
so we may remember that only by your gracious gift
are we given everlasting life;
through Jesus Christ our Savior.[62]

Amen.

People are invited to come forward to receive the imposition of ashes.

During the imposition, suitable hymns or psalms may be sung, or silence may be kept.

The ashes are imposed by a worship leader with the following words:

Remember that you are dust,
and to dust you will return. *Gen. 3:19*

PSALM *Psalm 51 is sung or said.*

THE EUCHARIST

If the Eucharist is not to be celebrated, the service concludes with the prayer on page 126.

INVITATION TO THE LORD'S TABLE

Hear the gracious words of our Savior Jesus Christ:

Come to me, all you who labor and are heavily burdened,
and I will give you rest.
Take my yoke upon you, and learn from me;
for I am gentle and lowly in heart,
and you will find rest for your souls. *Matt. 11:28, 29*

I am the bread of life.
Those who come to me shall not hunger,
and those who believe in me shall never thirst.
No one who comes to me will I cast out. *John 6:35, 37*

Blessed are those who hunger and thirst for righteousness,
for they will be filled. *Matt. 5:6*

GREAT PRAYER OF THANKSGIVING

The minister leads the people in the great prayer.

The Lord be with you.

And also with you.

Lift up your hearts.

We lift them to the Lord.

Let us give thanks to the Lord our God.

It is right to give our thanks and praise.

It is truly right and our greatest joy
to give you praise,
eternal God, creator and ruler of the universe.

You are our God,
and we are the creatures of your hand.
You made us from the dust of the earth,
breathed into us the breath of life,
and set us in your world to love and to serve you.

When we rejected your love and ignored your wisdom,
you did not reject us.
You still loved us
and called us to turn again to you
in obedience and in love.

Therefore, we praise you,
joining our voices with the heavenly choirs,
and with the faithful of every time and place,
who forever sing to the glory of your name:

The following may be sung or said:

Holy, holy, holy Lord, God of power and might,
Heaven and earth are full of your glory.
  Hosanna in the highest.

Blessed is he who comes in the name of the Lord.
  Hosanna in the highest.

You are holy, O God of majesty,
and blessed is Jesus Christ, your Son, our Lord.
Out of your great love for the world,
you sent Jesus among us
to set us free from the tyranny of evil.
He lived as one of us,
sharing our joys and sorrows.
By his dying and rising,
he frees us from the bondage of sin
and releases us from the dominion of death.

> *The words of institution may be said here or in relation to the breaking of the bread.*

[We give you thanks that on the night before he died,
Jesus took bread.
After giving thanks to you, he broke it,
and gave it to his disciples, saying,
"Take, eat.
This is my body, given for you.
Do this in remembrance of me."

In the same way he took the cup, saying,
"This cup is the new covenant sealed in my blood,
shed for you for the forgiveness of sins.
Do this in remembrance of me."]

In remembrance of your acts of mercy in Jesus Christ,
we take from your creation this bread and this wine
and celebrate his dying and rising,
as we await the day of his coming.
With thanksgiving we offer our very selves to you
to be a living and holy sacrifice,
dedicated to your service.

So we proclaim the mystery of faith.

> *The following may be sung or said:*

**Dying you destroyed our death,
rising you restored our life.
Lord Jesus, come in glory.**

Gracious God,
pour out your Holy Spirit
upon us and upon these your gifts of bread and wine,
that the bread we break and the cup we bless
may be the communion of the body and blood of Christ.

By your Spirit make us one with Christ,
that we may be one with all who share in this feast,
united in ministry throughout the world.

Keep our eyes fixed on Jesus Christ
until this mortal life is ended,
and all that is earthly returns to dust.
Then with the redeemed of all the ages,
bring us to the joy of resurrection.

Through Christ, with Christ, in Christ,
in the unity of the Holy Spirit,
all glory and honor are yours, almighty God,
now and forever.[63]

Amen.

The Lord's Prayer is sung or said.

Or

Our Father in heaven,	**Our Father, who art in heaven,**
hallowed be your name,	**hallowed be thy name,**
your kingdom come,	**thy kingdom come,**
your will be done,	**thy will be done,**
on earth as in heaven.	**on earth as it is in heaven.**
Give us today our daily bread.	**Give us this day our daily bread;**
Forgive us our sins	**and forgive us our debts,**
as we forgive those who sin against us.	**as we forgive our debtors;**
Save us from the time of trial	**and lead us not into temptation,**
and deliver us from evil.	**but deliver us from evil.**
For the kingdom, the power, and the glory are yours, now and forever. Amen.	**For thine is the kingdom, and the power, and the glory, forever. Amen.**

BREAKING OF THE BREAD

Or

If the words of institution were included in the great prayer, the minister breaks the bread in silence and in full view of the people.

If the words of institution were not included in the great prayer, the minister breaks the bread in full view of the people saying:

The Lord Jesus, on the night of
    his arrest, took bread,
and after giving thanks to God,
he broke it and said,
"This is my body, given for you.
Do this in remembrance of me."

The minister lifts the cup, saying:

In the same way, he took the
cup after supper, saying,
"This cup is the new covenant
    sealed in my blood.
Whenever you drink it,
do it in remembrance of me."

Every time you eat this bread and
    drink this cup,
you proclaim the death of the
    Lord,
until he comes.

(1 Cor. 11:23–26; Luke 22:19–20)

Holding out both the bread and the cup to the people, the minister says:

The gifts of God
for the people of God.

The following, or another version of "Jesus, Lamb of God," may be sung or said.

Jesus, Lamb of God:

have mercy on us.

Jesus, bearer of our sins:

have mercy on us.

Jesus, redeemer of the world:

give us peace.

COMMUNION OF THE PEOPLE

As the bread and wine are given, the following words may be said:

The body of Christ given for you.

Amen.

The blood of Christ shed for you.

Amen.

PRAYER AFTER COMMUNION

After all are served, the following prayer may be offered by the minister or by all:

God of compassion,
through your Son Jesus Christ
you reconciled your people to yourself.
Following his example of prayer and fasting,
may we obey you with willing hearts
and serve one another in holy love;
through Jesus Christ our Lord.[64]

Amen.

SENDING

A psalm, hymn of praise, or spiritual is sung.

The people are dismissed with these or other words of scripture:

May the God of peace
make you holy in every way
and keep your whole being—
spirit, soul, and body—
free from every fault
at the coming of our Lord Jesus Christ.   *1 Thess. 5:23*

Amen.

Go in peace to love and serve the Lord.

Thanks be to God.

All may depart in quietness.

If the Eucharist is not celebrated, the service continues here from page 119.

PRAYER

The following prayer may be offered by the minister or by all:

God of compassion,
through your Son Jesus Christ
you reconciled your people to yourself.
Following his example of prayer and fasting,
may we obey you with willing hearts
and serve one another in holy love;
through Jesus Christ our Lord.[65]

Amen.

SENDING

A psalm of praise, or spiritual is sung.

The people are dismissed with these or other words of scripture:

May the God of peace
make you holy in every way
and keep your whole being—
spirit, soul, and body—
free from every fault
at the coming of our Lord Jesus Christ.   *1 Thess. 5:23*

Amen.

Go in peace to love and serve the Lord.

Thanks be to God.

All depart in quietness.

LENT

Almighty God, you alone are good and holy.
Purify our lives and make us brave disciples.
We do not ask you to keep us safe,
but to keep us loyal,
so we may serve Jesus Christ,
who, tempted in every way as we are,
was faithful to you.

Amen.

From lack of reverence for truth and beauty;
from a calculating or sentimental mind;
from going along with mean and ugly things;

O God, deliver us.

From cowardice that dares not face truth;
laziness content with half-truth;
or arrogance that thinks we know it all;

O God, deliver us.

From artificial life and worship;
from all that is hollow or insincere;

O God, deliver us.

From trite ideals and cheap pleasures;
from mistaking hard vulgarity for humor;

O God, deliver us.

From being dull, pompous, or rude;
from putting down our neighbors;

O God, deliver us.

From cynicism about others;
from intolerance or cruel indifference;

O God, deliver us.

From being satisfied with things as they are,
in the church or in the world;
from failing to share your indignation about injustice,

O God, deliver us.

From selfishness, self-indulgence, or self-pity;

O God, deliver us.

From token concern for the poor,
for lonely or loveless people;
from confusing faith with good feeling,
or love with wanting to be loved;

O God, deliver us.

For everything in us that may hide your light,

O God, light of life, forgive us.[66]

Or

**God of mercy,
you sent Jesus Christ to seek and save the lost.
We confess that we have strayed from your truth
and from your holy will.
We have failed in love,
forgotten to be just,
and have turned away from your wisdom.
Forgive us our sin and restore us to your ways,
for the sake of your Son,
our only Savior, Jesus Christ the Lord.**[67]

GREAT PRAYER OF THANKSGIVING

It is suggested that text no. 181 or 182 in The Service for the
Lord's Day *(Supplemental Liturgical Resource 1) be used as the
invitation to the table. Since the Words of Institution are not included
in the prayer, they are said in relation to the breaking of the bread
(text no. 209 in* The Service for the Lord's Day).

The Lord be with you.

And also with you.

Lift up your hearts.

We lift them to the Lord.

Let us give thanks to the Lord our God.

It is right to give our thanks and praise.

It is truly right and our greatest joy
to give you praise, O God our creator and redeemer.
In your wisdom, you made all things
and sustain them by your power.
You formed us in your image
to love and to serve you,
but we forgot your promises
and abandoned your commandments.
In your mercy, you did not reject us
but still claimed us as your own.

When we were slaves in Egypt you freed us
and led us through the waters of the sea.
You fed us with heavenly food in the wilderness,
and satisfied our thirst from desert springs.
On the holy mountain you gave us your law
to guide us in your way.
Through the waters of the Jordan
you led us into the land of your promise,
and sustained us in times of trial.
You spoke through prophets
calling us to turn from our willful ways
to new obedience and righteousness.
You sent your only Son
to be the way to eternal life.

Therefore, we praise you,
joining our voices with choirs of angels,
and with all the faithful of every time and place,
who forever sing to the glory of your mighty name:

Holy, holy, holy Lord, God of power and might,
Heaven and earth are full of your glory.
   Hosanna in the highest.

Blessed is he who comes in the name of the Lord.
   Hosanna in the highest.

You are holy, O God of majesty,
and blessed is Jesus Christ, your Son, our Lord.
He took upon himself the weight of our sin,
and carried the burden of our guilt.
He shared our life in every way,
and though tempted, was sinless to the end.
By his dying and rising,
Christ frees us from sin and heals our brokenness.

Christ is the life of the world,
light to dispel our darkness,
living water to satisfy our thirsting spirits.

In remembrance of your great self-giving in Jesus Christ,
we take from your creation this bread and this wine
and celebrate his dying and rising,
as we await the day of his coming.
With thanksgiving we offer our very selves to you
to be a living and holy sacrifice,
dedicated to your service.

So we proclaim the mystery of faith.

**Dying you destroyed our death,
rising you restored our life.
Lord Jesus, come in glory.**

Gracious God,
pour out your Holy Spirit
upon us and upon these your gifts of bread and wine,
that in broken bread and shared cup
we may know Christ's redemptive love
and have new life in him.

By your Spirit make us one with Christ,
that we may be one with all who share this feast,
united in ministry throughout the world,
until Christ comes in final victory.

Strengthen us to be faithful in obeying your call
to love all your children,
to do justice and show mercy,
and to live in peace with your whole creation.
Guide us through the desert of life;

quench our thirst with the living waters;
satisfy our hunger with the bread of heaven.
Bring us to that promised day of resurrection
when you will gather us with the saints of all the ages
to feast with you at your table in glory.

Through Christ, with Christ, in Christ,
in the unity of the Holy Spirit,
all glory and honor are yours, God of all ages,
now and forever.[68]

Amen.

PRAYER OF THANKS

For use when the Eucharist is not celebrated.

Let us give thanks to the Lord our God.

It is right to give our thanks and praise.

God of mercy,
we praise you that in love
you have reached across the abyss of our sin
and brought us into your embrace.
We thank you for the sacrifice of your Son on the cross,
for the breaking of his body for our sakes,
and for the spilling of his blood
to seal us in the covenant of your love.
By your Spirit,
give us the grace of repentance,
and guide us in ways of righteousness.
Take our humble offerings
as tokens of our commitment
to follow our crucified and risen Lord.[69]

Amen.

Or

Let us give thanks to the Lord our God.

It is right to give our thanks and praise.

God of compassion,
we praise you that you look upon our frail lives
with love and understanding,
and that you desire for us all
new life in Jesus Christ.
We are overwhelmed by your love
which goes to the cross for us,
endures the grave,
and leads us to new life.
By your Spirit,
strengthen our souls
to be brave and bold in Christ's service.
Take our offerings,
and use them and us for your purposes
in the name of the crucified and risen Lord.[70]

Amen.

CALL TO WORSHIP AND PRAYER OF THE DAY

FIRST SUNDAY IN LENT

Call to Worship

One does not live by bread alone,
but by every word that comes from the mouth of God.   *Matt. 4:4*

Or

If any want to become my followers,
let them deny themselves
and take up their cross daily
and follow me.   *Luke 9:23*

Or

Have mercy on me, O God, according to your loving kindness;

in your great compassion blot out my offenses.

Wash me thoroughly from my wickedness,

and cleanse me from my sin!   *Ps. 51:1–2*

Or

We do not have a high priest
who is unable to sympathize with our weaknesses,
but we have one who in every respect
has been tested as we are, yet without sin.
Let us therefore approach the throne of grace with boldness,
so that we may receive mercy
and find grace to help in time of need.   *Heb. 4:15, 16*

Prayer of the Day

Almighty God,
whose Son fasted forty days in the wilderness,
and was tempted as we are but did not sin:
Give us grace to discipline ourselves
in submission to your Spirit,
that as you know our weakness,
so we may know your power to save;
through Jesus Christ our Lord,
who lives and reigns with you and the Holy Spirit,
one God, now and forever.[71]

Amen.

Or

O Lord God,
you led your people through the wilderness
and brought them to the promised land.
So guide us,
that, following our Savior,
we may walk through the wilderness of this world
toward the glory of the world to come;
through your Son, Jesus Christ our Lord,
who lives and reigns with you and the Holy Spirit,
one God, now and forever.[72]

Amen.

SECOND SUNDAY IN LENT

Call to Worship

Mercy and forgiveness belong to the Lord our God,
though we have rebelled against God.   *Dan. 9:9*

Or

Is not this the fast I choose:
to loose the bonds of injustice;

to share your bread with the hungry;

to bring the homeless poor into your house;

when you see the naked to clothe them?

Then your light shall break forth like the dawn,

And your healing shall spring up quickly.   *Isa. 58:7, 8*

Or

The Son of Man must be lifted up,
that whoever believes in him may have eternal life.   *John 3:14, 15*

Prayer of the Day

God of mercy,
you are full of tenderness and compassion,
slow to anger, rich in graciousness,
and always ready to forgive.
Grant us grace to renounce all evil
and to cling to Christ,
that in every way we may prove to be your loving children;
through Jesus Christ our Lord,
who lives and reigns with you and the Holy Spirit,
one God, forever and ever.[73]

Amen.

Or

God of all times and places,
in Jesus Christ, lifted up on the cross,
you opened for us the path to eternal life.
Grant that we, being born again of water and the Spirit,
may joyfully serve you in newness of life
and faithfully walk in your holy ways;
through Jesus Christ our Lord.[74]

Amen.

THIRD SUNDAY IN LENT

Call to Worship

The Lord God said:
I will give you a new heart and a new mind.
I will take away your stubborn heart of stone
and give you an obedient heart.   *Ezek. 36:26*

Or

All flesh is grass,

but the word of our God endures forever.

Its beauty is like the flower of the field

but the word of our God endures forever.

When the breath of the Lord blows upon it the grass withers,

but the word of our God endures forever.

The grass withers, and the flower fades,

but the word of our God endures forever.   *Isa. 40:6b–8*

Prayer of the Day

ABC
Eternal Lord, your kingdom has broken into our troubled world
through the life, death, and resurrection of your Son.
Help us to hear your Word and obey it,

that we may become instruments of your saving love;
through Jesus Christ our Lord,
who lives and reigns with you and the Holy Spirit,
one God, now and forever.[75]

Amen.

Or

C
Almighty God,
whose Son Jesus Christ gives the water of eternal life,
may we always thirst for you,
the spring of life and source of goodness;
through him who lives and reigns with you
and the Holy Spirit,
one God, now and forever.[76]

Amen.

FOURTH SUNDAY IN LENT

Call to Worship

A
I am the light of the world.
Whoever follows me will never walk in darkness
but will have the light of life.   *John 8:12*

Or

B
By grace you have been saved through faith,
and this is not your own doing;
it is the gift of God.   *Eph. 2:8*

C
Jesus said:
Come to me, all who labor and are heavily burdened,
and I will give you rest.
Take my yoke upon you,
and learn from me;

for I am gentle and lowly in heart,
and you will find rest for your souls.
For my yoke is easy,
and my burden is light.   *Matt. 11:28*

Prayer of the Day

Almighty God,
through the waters of baptism
Christ has made us children of light.
May we always walk in his light
and show forth your glory in the world;
through Jesus Christ our Lord,
who is alive and reigns with you and the Holy Spirit,
one God, now and forever.[77]

Amen.

FIFTH SUNDAY IN LENT

A
I am the resurrection and the life, says the Lord;
Everyone who lives and believes in me will never die.   *John 11:25, 26*

> *Or*

B
Whoever serves me must follow me, says the Lord,
and where I am, there will my servant be also.   *John 12:26*

> *Or*

C
Forgetting what lies behind
and straining forward to what lies ahead,
I press on toward the goal
for the prize of the heavenly call of God in Christ Jesus.   *Phil. 3:13, 14*

Prayer of the Day

Almighty God, our redeemer,
in our weakness we have failed

to be your messengers of forgiveness and hope in the world.
Renew us by your Holy Spirit,
that we may follow your commands
and proclaim your reign of love;
through Jesus Christ our Lord,
who lives and reigns with you and the Holy Spirit,
one God, now and forever.[78]

Amen.

Or

Almighty God,
your Son came into the world
to free us all from sin and death.
Breathe upon us with the power of your Spirit,
that we may be raised to new life in Christ,
and serve you in holiness and righteousness all our days;
through the same Jesus Christ, our Lord.[79]

Amen.

AN OUTLINE OF
THE SERVICE FOR PASSION/PALM SUNDAY

GATHERING
Call to Worship
Prayer
Proclamation of the Entrance into Jerusalem
Procession into the Church [Hymn or psalm]
[Prayer of the Day]

LITURGY OF THE WORD
[Prayer for Illumination]
Old Testament Lesson
Psalm
Epistle Lesson
Gospel Lesson
Silent Reflection/Sermon
Hymn of the Passion
Creed or Affirmation of Faith (optional)
Prayers of Intercession
    [or Solemn Reproaches of the Cross]
Offering
The Peace

*If the Eucharist
is not celebrated:*

THE EUCHARIST
Invitation to the Lord's Table
Great Prayer of Thanksgiving,   Prayer of Thanks,
    concluding with the Lord's   concluding with the
    Prayer   Lord's Prayer
Breaking of the Bread
Communion of the People
Prayer after Communion

SENDING
Hymn, Spiritual, or Psalm (optional)
Charge
Blessing

THE SERVICE FOR PASSION/PALM SUNDAY

GATHERING

If possible, the congregation gathers at a designated place outside the usual worship space, so that all may enter the church in procession.

Palm branches, or branches of other trees or shrubs, are distributed before the service.

CALL TO WORSHIP

The following is sung or said:

Blessed is he who comes in the name of the Lord.

Hosanna in the highest!   *Ps. 118:26*

Or

Rejoice greatly, O daughter of Zion!

Shout aloud, O daughter of Jerusalem!

Lo, your king comes to you;

triumphant and victorious is he,

humble and riding on a donkey,

on a colt, the foal of a donkey.   *Zech. 9:9*

PRAYER

The Lord be with you.

And also with you.

Let us pray.

We praise you, O God,
for the great acts of love by which you redeemed the world
through Jesus Christ our Lord.
Today he entered the holy city of Jerusalem in triumph
and was proclaimed Messiah and king

by those who spread garments and branches along his way.
Let these branches be signs of his victory,
and grant that we who carry them
may follow him in the way of suffering and the cross,
that, dying and rising with him,
we may enter into your kingdom;
through Jesus Christ, who lives and reigns
with you and the Holy Spirit, now and forever.[80]

Amen.

Or

Merciful God,
as we enter Holy Week
and gather at your house of prayer,
turn our hearts again to Jerusalem,
to the life, death, and resurrection of Jesus Christ,
that united with Christ and all the faithful
we may one day enter in triumph
the city not made by human hands,
the new Jerusalem, eternal in the heavens,
where with you and the Holy Spirit,
Christ lives in glory forever.[81]

Amen.

PROCLAMATION OF THE ENTRANCE INTO JERUSALEM

Year A: Matthew 21:1–11   (1993, 1996, 1999)
Year B: Mark 11:1–10
      or John 12:12–16   (1994, 1997, 2000)
Year C: Luke 19:28–40   (1992, 1995, 1998)

PROCESSION INTO THE CHURCH

The procession into the church begins. The hymn "All Glory, Laud, and Honor" or Psalm 118:19–29 is sung.

The procession may be concluded with the singing or saying of the following:

Blessed is he who comes in the name of the Lord.

Hosanna in the highest! *Ps. 118:26*

PRAYER OF THE DAY

The prayer of the day is said, unless a prayer for illumination is to follow:

Everlasting God,
in your tender love for the human race
you sent your Son to take our nature,
and to suffer death upon the cross.
In your mercy enable us to share in his obedience to your will
and in the glorious victory of his resurrection;
through Jesus Christ our Lord,
who lives and reigns with you and the Holy Spirit,
one God, forever and ever.[82]

Amen.

Or

God of all,
you gave your only-begotten Son
to take the form of a servant,
and to be obedient even to death on a cross.
Give us the same mind that was in Christ Jesus,
that sharing in his humility,
we may come to be with him in his glory;
who lives and reigns with you and the Holy Spirit,
one God, now and forever.[83]

Amen.

LITURGY OF THE WORD

PRAYER FOR ILLUMINATION

If the prayer of the day was not said, a prayer for illumination, such as the following, may be said:

Eternal God,
whose word silences the shouts of the mighty,
quiet within us every voice but your own.
Speak to us through the suffering and death of Jesus Christ,
that by the power of your Holy Spirit
we may receive grace to show Christ's love
in lives given to your service.[84]

Amen.

SCRIPTURE LESSONS

First Lesson: Isaiah 50:4–9a
Psalm: Psalm 31:9–16; 118:19–29
Second Lesson: Philippians 2:5–11
Gospel Lesson:
   Year A: Matthew 26:14–27:66   (1993, 1996, 1999)
         or Matthew 27:11–54
   Year B: Mark 14:1–15:47   (1994, 1997, 2000)
         or Mark 15:1–39 (47)
   Year C: Luke 22:14–23:56   (1992, 1995, 1998)
         or Luke 23:1–49

SILENT REFLECTION and/or SERMON

Silent reflection or a brief sermon may follow.

A hymn of the passion is sung.

CREED or AFFIRMATION OF FAITH (optional)

The people may sing or say a creed of the church or an affirmation drawn from scripture.

PRAYERS OF INTERCESSION
[*Or* SOLEMN REPROACHES OF THE CROSS]

Prayers for worldwide and local concerns are offered.

Or, the Solemn Reproaches of the Cross may be said, if there is no Good Friday service (see Service for Good Friday, pp. 178–181).

OFFERING

Silence or appropriate music may accompany the gathering of the people's offerings.

As the offerings are brought forward, a psalm or hymn may be sung.

THE PEACE

The minister says:

The peace of Christ be with you.

Peace be with you.

The people may exchange with one another, by words and touch, signs of reconciliation.

THE EUCHARIST

If the Eucharist is to be celebrated, the table is prepared with bread and wine. The bread and wine may be brought to the table or uncovered if already in place.

If the Eucharist is not to be celebrated, the service proceeds on page 151.

INVITATION TO THE LORD'S TABLE

The minister invites the people to the Sacrament using these or other words from scripture.

Jesus said:
I am the bread of life.
Whoever comes to me will never be hungry,
and whoever believes in me will never be thirsty.   *John 6:35*

GREAT PRAYER OF THANKSGIVING

The Lord be with you.

And also with you.

Lift up your hearts.

We lift them to the Lord.

Let us give thanks to the Lord our God.

It is right to give our thanks and praise.

It is truly right and our greatest joy to praise you,
O Lord our God, creator and ruler of the universe.
In your wisdom you made all things
and sustain them by your power.
You made us in your image,
setting us in your world to love and serve you
and to live in peace with your whole creation.
From generation to generation you have guided us,
sending prophets to turn us from wayward paths
into the way of righteousness.
Out of your great love for the world
you sent your only Son among us to redeem us
and to be the way to eternal life.

Therefore, we praise you,
joining our voices with the choirs of heaven,
and with the faithful of every time and place,
who forever sing to the glory of your mighty name:

**Holy, holy, holy Lord, God of power and might,
heaven and earth are full of your glory.**
Hosanna in the highest.

Blessed is he who comes in the name of the Lord.
Hosanna in the highest.

You are holy, O God of majesty,
and blessed is Jesus Christ, your Son, our Lord.
As one of us, he knew our joys and sorrows,
and our struggles with temptation.
He was like us in every way except sin.
In him we see what you created us to be.

Though he was sinless,
he suffered willingly for our sin;
though he was innocent,
he accepted death for the guilty.

On the cross he offered himself, a perfect sacrifice,
for the sin of the whole world.
By his suffering and death,
he freed us from sin and death.
By his rising from the grave,
he led us to the joy of new life.

*The words of institution may be said here or in relation to the breaking
of the bread.*

[We give you thanks that on the night before he died,
Jesus took bread.
After giving thanks to you, he broke it,
and gave it to his disciples, saying,
"Take, eat.
This is my body, given for you.
Do this in remembrance of me."

In the same way he took the cup, saying,
"This cup is the new covenant sealed in my blood,
shed for you for the forgiveness of sins.
Do this in remembrance of me."]

In remembrance of your acts of love in Jesus Christ,
we take from your creation this bread and this wine
and celebrate his dying and rising,
as we await the day of his coming.
With thanksgiving we offer our very selves to you
to be a living and holy sacrifice,
dedicated to your service.

So we proclaim the mystery of faith.

**Dying you destroyed our death,
rising you restored our life.
Lord Jesus, come in glory.**

Gracious God,
pour out your Holy Spirit
upon us and upon these your gifts of bread and wine.
In broken bread and shared cup,
make us the body of Christ
and confirm your covenant with us.

By your Spirit bind us to the living Christ,
that we may be bound in faith to all who share this feast,
united in service throughout the world.
Give us strength to serve you faithfully
until the promised day of resurrection,
when with all the redeemed,
we feast with you in your kingdom.

Through Christ, with Christ, in Christ,
in the unity of the Holy Spirit,
all glory and honor are yours, God of all ages,
now and forever.[85]

Amen.

THE LORD'S PRAYER

The Lord's Prayer is sung or said.

Or

Our Father in heaven,
hallowed be your name,
your kingdom come,
your will be done,
on earth as in heaven.
Give us today our daily bread.
Forgive us our sins
as we forgive those who sin
   against us.
Save us from the time of trial
and deliver us from evil.
For the kingdom, the power,
   and the glory are yours,
now and forever. Amen.

Our Father, who art in heaven,
hallowed be thy name,
thy kingdom come,
thy will be done,
on earth as it is in heaven.
   Give us this day our daily bread;
and forgive us our debts,
   as we forgive our debtors;
and lead us not into temptation,
   but deliver us from evil.
   For thine is the kingdom,
   and the power, and the glory,
forever. Amen.

BREAKING OF THE BREAD

Or

If the words of institution were included in the great prayer, the minister holds the bread in full view of the people, saying:

If the words of institution were not included in the great prayer, the minister breaks the bread in full view of the people, saying:

Because there is one loaf,
we, many as we are, are one body;
for it is one loaf of which we all
partake.

The minister breaks the bread in full view of the congregation.

When we break the bread,
is it not a sharing in the body of
Christ?

The minister lifts the cup.

When we give thanks over the
cup,
is it not a sharing in the blood of
Christ?

(1 Cor. 10:16–17)

The Lord Jesus, on the night of
his arrest, took bread,
and after giving thanks to God,
he broke it and said,
"This is my body, given for you.
Do this in remembrance of me."

The minister lifts the cup, saying:

In the same way, he took the cup
after supper, saying,
"This cup is the new covenant
sealed in my blood.
Whenever you drink it,
do it in remembrance of me."

Every time you eat this bread and
drink this cup,
you proclaim the death of the
Lord,
until he comes.

(1 Cor. 11:23–26; Luke 22:19–20)

Holding out both the bread and the cup to the people, the minister says:

The gifts of God
for the people of God.

The following, or another version of "Jesus, Lamb of God," may be sung or said.

Jesus, Lamb of God:

have mercy on us.

Jesus, bearer of our sins:

have mercy on us.

Jesus, redeemer of the world:

give us peace.

COMMUNION OF THE PEOPLE

As the bread and wine are given, the following words may be said:

The body of Christ given for you.

Amen.

The blood of Christ shed for you.

Amen.

PRAYER AFTER COMMUNION

*After all are served, the following prayer may be offered by the
minister or by all:*

God our help and strength,
you have satisfied our hunger with this eucharistic food.
Strengthen our faith,
that through the death and resurrection of your Son,
we may be led to salvation,
for he is Lord now and forever.[86]

Amen.

DISMISSAL

A psalm, hymn of praise, or spiritual may be sung.

The people are dismissed with these or other words of scripture:

The peace of God,
which passes all understanding,
keep your hearts and minds
in the knowledge and love of God,
and of God's Son, Jesus Christ our Lord.   *Phil. 4:7*
The blessing of God almighty,
the Father, the Son, and the Holy Spirit,
remain with you always.

Amen.

Go in peace to love and serve the Lord.

Thanks be to God.

If the Eucharist is not celebrated, the service continues here from page 145.

Let us give thanks to the Lord our God.

It is right to give our thanks and praise.

Great God,
we thank you for Jesus, who was punished for our sins,
and suffered shameful death to rescue us.
We praise you for the trust we have in him,
for mercy undeserved,
and for love you pour out on us and on all.
Give us gratitude, O God,
and a great desire to serve you,
by taking our cross,
and following in the way of Jesus Christ the Savior.[87]

Amen.

Sending

A psalm, hymn of praise, or spiritual may be sung.

The people are dismissed with these or other words of scripture:

The peace of God,
which passes all understanding,
keep your hearts and minds
in the knowledge and love of God,
and of God's Son, Jesus Christ our Lord.   *Phil. 4:7*
The blessing of God almighty,
the Father, the Son, and the Holy Spirit,
remain with you always.

Amen.

Go in peace to love and serve the Lord.

Thanks be to God.

OUTLINE OF
TENEBRAE

Psalms 69, 70, and 74
Scripture Lesson
   Lamentations 1:1–5
   Lamentations 1:6–9
   Lamentations 1:10–14
Psalm 63 and Psalm 90 or 143
Canticle of Hezekiah
Psalm 150
Canticle of Zechariah
Psalm 51

TENEBRAE

This service of prayer and meditation is provided for optional use on Wednesday evening of Holy Week. It should not replace the services provided for Maundy Thursday or Good Friday.

Fifteen candles in a triangular holder are lighted before the service begins. The room is dimly lit.

Those leading the worship enter in silence and proceed to their places. The people remain seated.

PSALMS

The service begins with the singing or reciting of the refrain for Psalm 69:

Refrain: **Zeal for your house has consumed me;**
the scorn of those who scorn you has fallen upon me.

Ps. 69:9

PSALM 69 (or 69:1–23) is sung or said.

Following the psalm, two candles are extinguished.

PSALM 70 is sung or said.

Refrain: **Let those be put to shame**
who delight in my misfortune. *Based on Ps. 70:2*

Following the psalm, two candles are extinguished.

PSALM 74 is sung or said.

Refrain: **Arise, O God, and plead your cause.** *Ps. 74:22*

Following the psalm, two candles are extinguished.

Then may be sung or said:

Deliver me, my God, from the hand of the wicked,

from the clutches of the unjust and cruel. *Ps. 71:4*

SCRIPTURE LESSON

A reading from the Lamentations of Jeremiah the Prophet.

Lamentations 1:1–5 is read.

The reader ends the lesson, saying:

Jerusalem, Jerusalem, return to the Lord your God!

Then may be sung or said:

On the Mount of Olives Jesus prayed:

**My Father, if it be possible, let this cup pass from me.
The spirit indeed is willing, but the flesh is weak.**

Matt. 26:39, 41

Watch and pray, that you may not enter into temptation.

Mark 14:38

The spirit indeed is willing, but the flesh is weak.

Lamentations 1:6–9 is read.

The reader ends the lesson, saying:

Jerusalem, Jerusalem, return to the Lord your God!

Then may be sung or said:

My soul is very sorrowful, even to death;

remain here, and watch with me.   *Mark 14:34*
**Now you shall see the crowd who will surround me;
you will flee, and I will go to be offered up for you.**

Behold, the hour is at hand,
and the Son of Man is betrayed into the hands of sinners.

Matt. 26:45

You will flee, and I will go to be offered up for you.

Lamentations 1:10–14 is read.

The reader ends the lesson, saying:

Jerusalem, Jerusalem, return to the Lord your God!

Then may be sung or said:

Lo, we have seen him without beauty or majesty,

nothing in his appearance that we should desire him.

He bore our sins and grieved for us,
he was wounded for our transgressions,
and by his scourging we are healed.

Surely he has borne our griefs and carried our sorrows:

And by his scourging we are healed.   *Based on Isa. 53:2, 4, 5*

PSALMS

PSALM 63 (or 63:1–8) is sung or said.

Refrain: **God did not spare God's own Son,**
              but delivered him up for us all.   *Rom. 18:32*

Following the psalm, two candles are extinguished.

PSALM 90 (or 90:1–12) is sung or said.

Refrain: **Like a lamb led to slaughter,**
              he opened not his mouth.   *Isa. 53:7*

Two candles are extinguished.

PSALM 143 is sung or said.

Refrain: **They shall mourn for him as one mourns for an**
              only child;   *Zech. 12:10*
              for the Lord, who is without sin, is slain.

Following the psalm, two candles are extinguished.

CANTICLE OF HEZEKIAH

The Canticle of Hezekiah (Isaiah 38:10–20) is sung or said.

Refrain: **From the gates of hell, O Lord,
deliver my soul.**

In my despair I said,
"In the noonday of my life I must depart;
my unspent years are summoned to the portals of death."

**And I said,
"No more shall I see the Lord in the land of the living,
never more look on my kind among dwellers on earth.**

My house is pulled down and I am uncovered,
as when a shepherd strikes his tent.

**My life is rolled up like a bolt of cloth,
the threads cut off from the loom.**

Between sunrise and sunset my life is brought to an end;
I cower and hope for the dawn.

**Like a lion he has crushed all my bones;
like a swallow or thrush I utter plaintive cries;
I mourn like a dove.**

My weary eyes look up to you;
Lord, be my refuge in my affliction."

**But what can I say? for he has spoken;
it is he who has done this.**

Slow and halting are my steps all my days,
because of the bitterness of my spirit.

**O Lord, I recounted all these things to you
and you rescued me;
when entreated, you restored my life.**

I know now that my bitterness was for my good,
for you held me back from the pit of destruction,
you cast all my sins behind you.

**The grave does not thank you nor death give you praise;
nor do those at the brink of the grave hang on your promises.**

It is the living, O Lord,
the living who give you thanks as I do this day;
and parents speak of your faithfulness to their children.

You, Lord, are my Savior;
I will praise you with stringed instruments
all the days of my life, in the house of the Lord.

Following the canticle, two candles are extinguished.

PSALM   *Psalm 150 is sung or said.*

Refrain: **O Death, I will be your death;**
          O Grave, I will be your destruction.

Following the psalm, two candles are extinguished.

Then may be sung or said:

My flesh will rest in hope;
you will not let your Holy One see corruption.

Acts 2:26, 27; Ps. 16:9, 10

All may stand.

CANTICLE OF ZECHARIAH

The Canticle of Zechariah (Luke 1:68–79) is sung or said.

During the singing, the candles at the holy table, and all other lights in the church (except the remaining lighted candle on the triangular holder) are extinguished.

Refrain: **Now the women sitting at the tomb made lamentation,**
          weeping for the Lord.

Blessed are you, Lord, the God of Israel,
you have come to your people and set them free.
You have raised up for us a mighty Savior,
born of the house of your servant David.
Through your holy prophets, you promised of old
to save us from our enemies,
from the hands of all who hate us,
to show mercy to our forebears,
and to remember your holy covenant.
This was the oath you swore to our father Abraham:

to set us free from the hands of our enemies,
free to worship you without fear,
holy and righteous before you,
all the days of our life.

And you, child, shall be called the prophet of the Most High,
for you will go before the Lord to prepare the way,
to give God's people knowledge of salvation
by the forgiveness of their sins.
In the tender compassion of our God
the dawn from on high shall break upon us,
to shine on those who dwell in darkness and the shadow of death,
and to guide our feet into the way of peace.

As the refrain is repeated at the end of the canticle, the lighted candle
is taken from the stand and hidden beneath or behind the holy table,
or in some other convenient place.

All kneel, or bow down, for the singing of the following:

Christ for us became obedient unto death,
even death on a cross.
Therefore God highly exalted him
and gave him the name that is above every name.   *Phil. 2:8, 9*

A brief silence is observed.

PSALM   *Psalm 51 is then spoken quietly.*

After the psalm is spoken, the leader says:

Almighty God,
behold this your family,
for whom our Lord Jesus Christ was willing to be betrayed
and given into the hands of sinners,
and to suffer death upon the cross.

Nothing further is said, but a loud noise is made.

The lighted candle is brought from its hiding place and replaced on
the stand.

By its light all depart in silence.

AN OUTLINE OF THE SERVICE FOR MAUNDY THURSDAY

GATHERING

Call to Worship and Greeting
Prayer of the Day
Hymn of Praise, Psalm, or Spiritual
Confession of Sin and Pardon
Act of Praise
The Peace

LITURGY OF THE WORD

Prayer for Illumination
First Lesson
Psalm
Second Lesson
Gospel Lesson
Sermon
Creed or Affirmation of Faith (optional)
Footwashing
Prayers of Intercession
Offering

THE EUCHARIST

Invitation to the Table
Great Prayer of Thanksgiving,
    concluding with the Lord's Prayer
Breaking of the Bread
Communion of the People

Or

The Stripping of the Church   Hymn, Spiritual, or Psalm (optional)
                              Charge

All depart in silence. The service continues on Good Friday.

THE SERVICE FOR MAUNDY THURSDAY

GATHERING

CALL TO WORSHIP

Jesus said:
I give you a new commandment,
that you love one another.
Just as I have loved you,
you also should love one another.   *John 13:34*

GREETING

This is the day
that Christ the Lamb of God
gave himself into the hands of those who would slay him.

This is the day
that Christ gathered with his disciples in the upper room.

This is the day
that Christ took a towel
and washed the disciples' feet,
giving us an example that we should do to others
as he has done to us.

This is the day
that Christ our God gave us this holy feast,
that we who eat this bread
and drink this cup
may here proclaim his holy sacrifice
and be partakers of his resurrection
and at the last day may reign with him in heaven.

PRAYER OF THE DAY

Let us pray.

Holy God, source of all love,
on the night of his betrayal
Jesus gave his disciples a new commandment,

to love one another as he loved them.
Write this commandment in our hearts;
give us the will to serve others
as he was the servant of all,
who gave his life and died for us,
yet is alive and reigns with you and the Holy Spirit,
one God, now and forever.[88]

Amen.

Or

O God, your love lived in Jesus Christ,
who washed disciples' feet on the night of his betrayal.
Wash from us the stain of sin,
so that, in hours of danger,
we may not fail,
but follow your Son through every trial,
and praise him to the world as Lord and Christ,
to whom be glory now and forever.[89]

Amen.

A psalm, hymn, or spiritual may be sung.

CONFESSION OF SIN

The proof of God's amazing love is this:
while we were sinners
Christ died for us.   *Rom. 5:8*
Because we have faith in him,
we dare to approach God with confidence.   *Heb. 4:16*

Let us admit our sin before God.

Eternal God, whose covenant with us is never broken:
we confess that we have failed to fulfill your will for us.
We betray our neighbors and desert our friends,
and run in fear when we should be loyal.
Though you have bound yourself to us,
we will not bind ourselves to you.
God, have mercy on us, weak and willful people.
Lead us once again to your table,

and unite us to Christ,
who is the bread of life
and the vine from which we grow in grace.
To Christ be praise forever.[90]

Or

Merciful God,
we have not loved you with all our heart and mind
and strength and soul.

Silence

Lord, have mercy

Lord, have mercy.

We have not loved our neighbors
as you have taught us.

Silence

Christ, have mercy

Christ, have mercy.

We are indifferent to the saving grace
of your word and life.

Silence

Lord, have mercy

Lord, have mercy.

Forgive and heal us by your steadfast love
made known to us in the passion, death,
and resurrection of Jesus Christ our Lord.[91]

Amen.

The people may sing or say:

Lord, have mercy.
Christ, have mercy.
Lord, have mercy.

DECLARATION OF PARDON

The mercy of the Lord
is from everlasting to everlasting.
I declare to you, in the name of Jesus Christ,
we are forgiven.

May the God of mercy,
who forgives us all our sins,
strengthen us in all goodness,
and by the power of the Holy Spirit
keep us in eternal life.

Amen.

A joyful response is sung or said.

THE PEACE

Since God has forgiven us in Christ,
let us forgive one another.

The peace of the Lord Jesus Christ
be with you all.   *John 20:19, 21, 26*

Peace be with you.

*The people may exchange with one another, by words and touch,
signs of reconciliation.*

LITURGY OF THE WORD

*Before the reading of the scripture lessons, a PRAYER FOR ILLUMI-
NATION may be said by the reader.*

FIRST LESSON: Exodus 12:1–14

PSALM: Psalm 116:12–19

SECOND LESSON: 1 Corinthians 11:23–26

GOSPEL LESSON: John 13:1–17, 31b–35

SERMON

When the Bible has been read, its message is proclaimed in a sermon or other exposition of God's word.

CREED or AFFIRMATION OF FAITH (optional)

The people may sing or say a creed of the church or an affirmation drawn from scripture.

FOOTWASHING

The people may be invited to wash one another's feet, pouring water over the feet and drying them.

During the washing, "Where Charity and Love Prevail" (Ubi Caritas) or another appropriate psalm, hymn, or refrain may be sung. Or the washing may be done in silence.

PRAYERS OF INTERCESSION

Prayers are offered for worldwide and local concerns.

OFFERING

Silence or appropriate music may accompany the gathering of the people's offerings.

As the gifts are brought forward, a doxology, spiritual, or hymn of praise is sung.

THE EUCHARIST

The minister(s) and elders prepare the table with bread and wine during the gathering of the gifts.

The bread and wine may be brought to the table, or uncovered if already in place.

INVITATION TO THE LORD'S TABLE

The minister invites the people to the Sacrament, using the following or other words from scripture:

The Lord Jesus,
on the night of his arrest,
took bread,
and after giving thanks to God,
he broke it and said,
"This is my body, given for you.
Do this in remembrance of me."

In the same way,
he took the cup after supper, saying,
"This cup is the new covenant sealed in my blood.
Whenever you drink it,
do it in remembrance of me."

Every time you eat this bread and drink this cup,
you proclaim the death of the Lord, until he comes.

Based on 1 Cor. 11:23–26 and Luke 22:19–20

GREAT PRAYER OF THANKSGIVING

The minister leads the people in the great prayer:

The Lord be with you.

And also with you.

Lift up your hearts.

We lift them to the Lord.

Let us give thanks to the Lord our God.

It is right to give our thanks and praise.

It is truly right and our greatest joy
to give you praise,
O Lord our God, creator and ruler of the universe.

You bring forth bread from the earth,
and create the fruit of the vine.
You made us in your image,
and freed us from the bonds of slavery.
You claimed us as your people,
and made covenant to be our God.
You fed us manna in the wilderness,

and brought us to a land flowing with milk and honey.
When we forgot you, and our faith was weak,
you spoke through prophets,
calling us to turn again to your ways.

Therefore, we praise you,
joining our voices with choirs of angels,
and with all the faithful of every time and place,
who forever sing to the glory of your name:

The following may be sung or said:

Holy, holy, holy Lord, God of power and might,
heaven and earth are full of your glory.
   Hosanna in the highest.

Blessed is he who comes in the name of the Lord.
   Hosanna in the highest.

You are holy, O God of majesty,
and blessed is Jesus Christ, your Son, our Lord,
whom you sent to deliver us
from the bondage of death and slavery to sin.
In humility he descends from your heights,
to kneel in obedience to love's commands.
He who is boundless takes on the bondage of our sin.
He who is free takes our place in death's prison.

In the deserts of our wanderings, he sustains us,
giving us his body as manna for our weariness,
his blood as drink for our parched souls.
In his death, he ransomed us from death's dominion;
in his resurrection, he opened the way to eternal life.

In remembrance of your acts of grace in Jesus Christ,
we take from your creation this bread and this wine
and celebrate his dying and rising,
as we await the day of his coming.
With thanksgiving we offer our very selves to you
to be a living and holy sacrifice,
dedicated to your service.

So we proclaim the mystery of faith.

One of the following may be sung or said:

Or

Dying you destroyed our death,	**Christ has died,**
rising you restored our life.	**Christ is risen,**
Lord Jesus, come in glory.	**Christ will come again.**

Gracious God,
pour out your Holy Spirit
upon us and upon these your gifts of bread and wine,
that the bread we break and the cup we bless
may be the communion of the body and blood of Christ.

By your Spirit make us one with Christ,
that we may be one with all who share this feast,
united in ministry throughout the world.
Then bring us at the last,
with the people of God of every nation and race,
and from every time and place,
to sit at table in that heavenly banquet
where we will celebrate the victory of Christ.

Through Christ, with Christ, in Christ,
in the unity of the Holy Spirit,
all glory and honor are yours, almighty God,
now and forever.[92]

Amen.

LORD'S PRAYER

As our Savior Christ has taught us,
we now pray:

The Lord's Prayer is sung or said.

Our Father in heaven,	Our Father, who art in heaven,
hallowed be your name,	hallowed be thy name,
your kingdom come,	thy kingdom come,
your will be done,	thy will be done,
on earth as in heaven.	on earth as it is in heaven.
Give us today our daily bread.	Give us this day our daily bread;
Forgive us our sins	and forgive us our debts,
as we forgive those who sin	as we forgive our debtors;
against us.	and lead us not into temptation,
Save us from the time of trial	but deliver us from evil.
and deliver us from evil.	For thine is the kingdom,
For the kingdom, the power,	and the power, and the glory,
and the glory are yours,	forever. Amen.
now and forever. Amen.	

BREAKING OF THE BREAD

Because there is one bread,
we who are many, are one body;
for we all partake of the one bread.

*Here the presiding minister takes the loaf of bread and breaks it in full
view of the congregation, saying:*

The bread that we break,
is it not a sharing in the body of Christ?

The minister lifts the cup.

The cup of blessing that we bless,
is it not a sharing in the blood of Christ?   *1 Cor. 10:16, 17*

*Holding out both the bread and the cup to the people, the minister
says:*

The gifts of God
for the people of God.

The following, or another version of "Jesus, Lamb of God," may be sung or said.

Jesus, Lamb of God:

have mercy on us.

Jesus, bearer of our sins;

have mercy on us.

Jesus, redeemer of the world:

give us peace.

COMMUNION OF THE PEOPLE

During the serving of the Sacrament, psalms, hymns, or spiritual songs may be sung or silence kept.

As the bread and wine are given, the following words may be said:

The body of Christ given for you.

Amen.

The blood of Christ shed for you.

Amen.

PRAYER AFTER COMMUNION

After all are served, the following prayer may be offered by the minister, or by all:

God of grace,
your Son Jesus Christ
left us this holy meal of bread and wine
in which we share his body and blood.
May we who have celebrated this sign of his great love
show in our lives the fruits of his redemption;
through Jesus Christ our Lord,
who lives and reigns with you and the Holy Spirit,
one God, now and forever.[93]

Amen.

STRIPPING OF THE CHURCH

The candles are extinguished, and all linens, paraments, and banners are removed from the worship space. During their removal, Psalm 22 may be read, or the congregation bows in silence.

There is no benediction.

If the church is not stripped, a psalm, hymn, or spiritual is sung.

The people are dismissed with the following charge:

Go in peace.
As Christ has loved you,
love one another.   *John 13:34*

All depart in silence.

The service continues on Good Friday. If no Good Friday service is scheduled, then the service continues with the Easter Vigil, or on Easter.

AN OUTLINE OF THE SERVICE FOR GOOD FRIDAY

GATHERING

Call to Worship
Prayer of the Day
Hymn of Praise, Psalm, or Spiritual

LITURGY OF THE WORD

Prayer for Illumination
Old Testament Lesson
Psalm
Epistle Lesson
Gospel Lesson
Silent Reflection/Sermon
Hymn of the Passion
The Solemn Intercession
The Lord's Prayer
Solemn Reproaches of the Cross
[Psalm, Hymn, or Spiritual]

All depart in silence. The service continues with the Easter Vigil.

SERVICE FOR GOOD FRIDAY

GATHERING

All enter in silence.

CALL TO WORSHIP

Blessed be the name of the Lord our God,

who redeems us from sin and death.

For us and for our salvation,
Christ became obedient unto death,
even death on a cross.   *Based on Phil. 2:8*

Blessed be the name of the Lord.

> *Or*

Surely he has borne our griefs

And carried our sorrows;

Yet we esteemed him stricken,

Smitten by God, and afflicted.   *Isa. 53:4*

> *Or*

Christ bore our sins in his body on the tree,
that we might die to sin
and live for righteousness.

PRAYER OF THE DAY

Let us pray.

Merciful God,
you gave your Son to suffer the shame of the cross.
Save us from hardness of heart,
that, seeing him who died for us,
we may repent, confess our sin,

and receive your overflowing love,
in Jesus Christ our Lord.[94]

Amen.

Or

Almighty God,
we ask you to look with mercy on your family
for whom our Lord Jesus Christ was willing to be betrayed
and to be given over to the hands of sinners
and to suffer death on the cross;
who now lives and reigns with you and the Holy Spirit,
one God, forever and ever.[95]

Amen.

A psalm, hymn, or spiritual may be sung.

LITURGY OF THE WORD

A prayer for illumination is said.

READINGS FROM SCRIPTURE

First Lesson:	Isaiah 52:13–53:12
Psalm:	Psalm 22
Second Lesson:	Hebrews 10:16–25
	or Hebrews 4:14–16; 5:7–9
Anthem (optional)	
Gospel Lesson:	John 18:1–19:42

There may be silent reflection on the readings. A brief sermon may follow.

A hymn on the passion is sung.

THE SOLEMN INTERCESSION

Bidding prayers for the whole family of God and the afflictions of the world are said.

Dear people of God,
God sent Jesus into the world,
not to condemn the world,
but that the world through him might be saved,
that all who believe in him
might be delivered from the power of sin and death
and become heirs with him of eternal life.

In the biddings that follow, the petitions may be adapted as appropriate.

The people may be directed to stand, or to bow down.

The silence should be of significant length.

Let us pray for the one holy catholic
and apostolic Church of Christ throughout the world:

for its unity in witness and service,
for all church leaders and ministers
and the people whom they serve,
for all the people of this presbytery,
for all Christians in this community,
for those about to be baptized (particularly _____),

that God will confirm the church in faith,
increase it in love,
and preserve it in peace.

Silence

Eternal God,
by your Spirit the whole body of your faithful people
is governed and sanctified.
Receive our prayers
which we offer before you
for all members of your holy church,

that in our vocation and ministry
we may truly and devoutly serve you;
through our Lord and Savior Jesus Christ.

Amen.

Let us pray for all nations and peoples of the earth,
and for those in authority among them:

for _____, the President of the United States,
and the Congress and Supreme Court,
for the members and representatives of the United Nations,
for all who serve the common good,

that by God's help
they may seek justice and truth,
and live in peace and concord.

Silence

Almighty God,
kindle, we pray, in every heart
the true love of peace,
and guide with your wisdom
those who take counsel for the nations of the earth,
that justice and peace may increase,
until the earth is filled
with the knowledge of your love;
through Jesus Christ our Lord.

Amen.

Let us pray for all who suffer
and are afflicted in body or in mind:

for the hungry and homeless,
the destitute and the oppressed,
and all who suffer persecution, doubt, and despair,
for the sorrowful and bereaved,
for prisoners and captives
and those in mortal danger,

that God will comfort and relieve them,
and grant them the knowledge of God's love,
and stir up in us the will and patience
to minister to their needs.

Silence

Gracious God,
the comfort of all who sorrow,

the strength of all who suffer,
hear the cry of those in misery and need.
In their afflictions show them your mercy,
and give us, we pray, the strength to serve them,
for the sake of him who suffered for us,
your Son, Jesus Christ our Lord.

Amen.

Let us pray for all
who have not received the gospel of Christ:

for all who have not heard the words of salvation,
for all who have lost their faith,
for all whose sin has made them indifferent to Christ,
for all who actively oppose Christ by word or deed,
for all who are enemies of the cross of Christ,
and persecutors of his disciples,
for all who in the name of Christ have persecuted others,

that God will open their hearts to the truth
and lead them to faith and obedience.

Silence

Merciful God,
creator of the peoples of the earth and lover of souls,
have compassion on all who do not know you
as you are revealed in your Son Jesus Christ.
Let your gospel be preached with grace and power
to those who have not heard it.
Turn the hearts of those who resist it,
and bring home to your fold those who have gone astray;
that there may be one flock under one shepherd,
Jesus Christ our Lord.

Amen.

Let us commit ourselves to God,
and pray for the grace of a holy life,
that with all who have departed this life
and have died in the peace of Christ,
and those whose faith is known to God alone,

we may be accounted worthy
to enter into the fullness of the joy of our Lord,
and receive the crown of life in the day of resurrection.

Silence

O God of unchangeable power and eternal light,
look favorably on your whole church,
that wonderful and sacred mystery.
By the effectual working of your providence,
carry out in tranquillity the plan of salvation.
Let the whole world see and know
that things which were cast down are being raised up,
and things which had grown old are being made new,
and that all things are being brought to their perfection
by him through whom all things were made,
your Son Jesus Christ our Lord;
who lives and reigns with you,
in the unity of the Holy Spirit,
one God, forever and ever.[96]

Amen.

Finally, let us pray for all those things for which our Lord
would have us ask.

Or

Our Father in heaven,	**Our Father, who art in heaven,**
hallowed be your name,	**hallowed be thy name,**
your kingdom come,	**thy kingdom come,**
your will be done,	**thy will be done,**
on earth as in heaven.	**on earth as it is in heaven.**
Give us today our daily bread.	**Give us this day our daily bread;**
Forgive us our sins	**and forgive us our debts,**
as we forgive those who sin	**as we forgive our debtors;**
against us.	**and lead us not into temptation,**
Save us from the time of trial	**but deliver us from evil.**
and deliver us from evil.	**For thine is the kingdom,**
For the kingdom, the power,	**and the power, and the glory,**
and the glory are yours,	**forever. Amen.**
now and forever. Amen.	

A wooden, rough-hewn cross may be carried in procession into the church and placed in front of the people.

During the procession, the following may be said or sung:

Behold the cross
on which was hung the salvation of the whole world.

Come, let us worship.

Behold the cross
on which was hung the salvation of the whole world.

Come, let us worship.

Behold the cross
on which was hung the salvation of the whole world.

Come, let us worship.

SOLEMN REPROACHES OF THE CROSS

The following Reproaches are sung or spoken:

O my people, O my church,
What have I done to you,
or in what have I offended you?
Testify against me.
I led you forth from the land of Egypt
and delivered you by the waters of baptism,
but you have prepared a cross for your Savior.

Lord, have mercy.

Or

**Holy God, holy and mighty,
Holy immortal One, have mercy upon us.**

I led you through the desert forty years,
and fed you with manna:
I brought you through tribulation and penitence,
and gave you my body, the bread of heaven,
but you have prepared a cross for your Savior.

Lord, have mercy.

Or

Holy God, holy and mighty,
Holy immortal One, have mercy upon us.

What more could I have done for you
that I have not done?
I planted you, my chosen and fairest vineyard,
I made you the branches of my vine;
but when I was thirsty, you gave me vinegar to drink
and pierced with a spear the side of your Savior,
and you have prepared a cross for your Savior.

Lord, have mercy.

Or

Holy God, holy and mighty,
Holy immortal One, have mercy upon us.

I went before you in a pillar of cloud,
and you have led me to the judgment hall of Pilate.
I scourged your enemies and brought you to a land of freedom,
but you have scourged, mocked, and beaten me.
I gave you the water of salvation from the rock,
but you have given me gall and left me to thirst,
and you have prepared a cross for your Savior.

Lord, have mercy.

Or

Holy God, holy and mighty,
Holy immortal One, have mercy upon us.

I gave you a royal scepter,
and bestowed the keys to the kingdom,
but you have given me a crown of thorns.
I raised you on high with great power,
but you have prepared a cross for your Savior.

Lord, have mercy.

Or

Holy God, holy and mighty,
Holy immortal One, have mercy upon us.

My peace I gave, which the world cannot give,
and washed your feet as a sign of my love,
but you draw the sword to strike in my name
and seek high places in my kingdom.
I offered you my body and blood,
but you scatter and deny and abandon me,
and you have prepared a cross for your Savior.

Lord, have mercy.

Or

Holy God, holy and mighty,
Holy immortal One, have mercy upon us.

I sent the Spirit of truth to guide you,
and you close your hearts to the Counselor.
I pray that all may be one in the Father and me,
but you continue to quarrel and divide.
I call you to go and bring forth fruit,
but you cast lots for my clothing,
and you have prepared a cross for your Savior.

Lord, have mercy.

Or

Holy God, holy and mighty,
Holy immortal One, have mercy upon us.

I grafted you into the tree of my chosen Israel,
and you turned on them with persecution and mass murder.
I made you joint heirs with them of my covenants
but you made them scapegoats for your own guilt,
and you have prepared a cross for your Savior.

Lord, have mercy.

Or

Holy God, holy and mighty,
Holy immortal One, have mercy upon us.

I came to you as the least of your brothers and sisters;
I was hungry and you gave me no food,
I was thirsty and you gave me no drink,
I was a stranger and you did not welcome me,
naked and you did not clothe me,
sick and in prison and you did not visit me,
and you have prepared a cross for your Savior.[97]

Lord, have mercy.

Or

Holy God, holy and mighty,
Holy immortal One, have mercy upon us.

A psalm, hymn, or spiritual may be sung.

All depart in silence. The service continues with the Easter Vigil, or on Easter Day.

AN OUTLINE OF
THE GREAT VIGIL OF EASTER

LITURGY OF LIGHT

Greeting and Introduction
Opening Prayer
Lighting of the Paschal Candle
Procession into the Church
Easter Proclamation (the Exsultet)

LITURGY OF THE WORD

Greeting
Old Testament Readings
  Between readings:
    Psalms, silence, and prayer
Act of Praise
Prayer of the Day
Epistle Reading
Psalm 114
Gospel Reading
[Sermon]
Psalm, hymn, or anthem

LITURGY OF THE WATER

Or

Baptism	*Reaffirmation of Baptismal Vows*
Presentation	Introduction
Renunciation and Affirmation (including the Apostles' Creed)	Renunciation and Affirmation (including the Apostles' Creed)
Thanksgiving Over the Water	Thanksgiving for the Water
The Act of Baptizing	The Act of Reaffirmation
The Blessing	The Blessing
Welcome	

THE EUCHARIST

Invitation to the Lord's Table
Great Prayer of Thanksgiving,
    followed by the Lord's Prayer
Breaking of the Bread
Communion of the People
Prayer after Communion
Psalm, hymn, or spiritual song
Charge and Blessing

THE GREAT VIGIL OF EASTER
First Service of Easter

The vigil begins in darkness, after nightfall.

If possible, the lighting of the new fire takes place outside the church building; otherwise at the entrance to the church.

All gather in silence at the place where the new fire will be lighted.

A small candle is given to each worshiper.

GREETING

A liturgical leader begins with these or similar words:

Grace and peace from Jesus Christ our Lord.

And also with you.

Sisters and brothers in Christ,
on this most holy night
when our Savior Jesus Christ passed from death to life,
we gather with the church throughout the world
in vigil and prayer.
This is the Passover of Jesus Christ:
Through light and the word,
through water and the bread and wine,
we recall Christ's death and resurrection,
we share Christ's triumph over sin and death,
and with invincible hope
we await Christ's coming again.

Hear the word of God:
In the beginning was the Word,
and the Word was with God,
and the Word was God.
In him was life,
and the life was the light of all people.
The light shines in the darkness,
and the darkness has not overcome it.   *John 1:1, 4–5*

The new fire is lighted.

OPENING PRAYER

Let us pray:

Pause briefly.

Eternal God, in Jesus Christ
you have given the light of life to all the world.
Sanctify this new fire,
and inflame us with a desire to shine forth
with the brightness of Christ's rising,
until we feast at the banquet of eternal light;
through Jesus Christ, the Sun of Righteousness.[98]

Amen.

LIGHTING OF THE PASCHAL CANDLE

The paschal candle is lighted from the new fire, and these words are spoken:

The light of Christ rises in glory,
overcoming the darkness of sin and death.

The candle is lifted so that all may see it.

PROCESSION INTO THE CHURCH

The procession into the darkened church begins, led by the bearer of the paschal candle.

A leader and the people sing or say responsively:

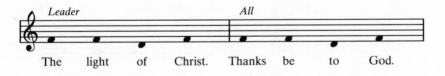

All light their candles from the paschal candle.

At the church door, the leader and people sing or say a second time:

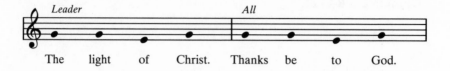

Leader: The light of Christ.
All: Thanks be to God.

The procession continues into the church. When all have reached their places, the leader and people sing or say a third time:

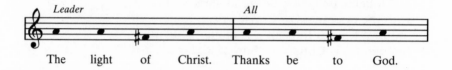

Leader: The light of Christ.
All: Thanks be to God.

At the conclusion of the procession, the paschal candle is placed in its stand, providing a central focus for the congregation.

EASTER PROCLAMATION

The ancient Easter proclamation, the Exsultet, is sung by the choir or a cantor (soloist).

Refrain for Setting I

The refrain is first sung by the choir or a cantor (soloist), then repeated by all. All sing where indicated in the text below. The complete musical setting is on pp. 376ff.

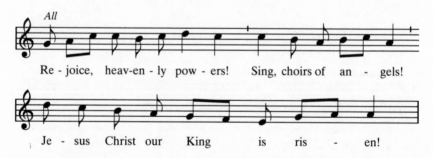

Re - joice, heav-en - ly pow - ers! Sing, choirs of an - gels! Je - sus Christ our King is ris - en!

Refrain for Setting II

The refrain is first sung by the choir or a cantor (soloist), then repeated by all. All sing where indicated in the text below. The complete musical setting is on pp. 382ff.

John Weaver, 1988

Re - joice, heav-en-ly powers! Sing, choirs of an - gels!
Je - sus Christ our King is ris - en!

Rejoice, heavenly powers! Sing, choirs of angels!
Exult, all creation around God's throne!
Jesus Christ our King is risen!
Sound the trumpet of salvation!

Rejoice, heavenly powers!
Sing, choirs of angels!
Jesus Christ our King is risen!

Rejoice, O earth, in shining splendor,
radiant in the brightness of your King!
Christ has conquered! Glory fills you!
Darkness vanishes forever!

Rejoice, heavenly powers!
Sing, choirs of angels!
Jesus Christ our King is risen!

Rejoice, O Mother Church! Exult in glory!
The risen Savior shines upon you!
Let this place resound with joy,
echoing the mighty song of all God's people!

Rejoice, heavenly powers!
Sing, choirs of angels!
Jesus Christ our King is risen!

Responses for Setting I

The Lord be with you. And al - so with you.

Lift up your hearts. We lift them up to the Lord.

Let us give thanks to the Lord our God.

It is right to give our thanks and praise.

Responses for Setting II

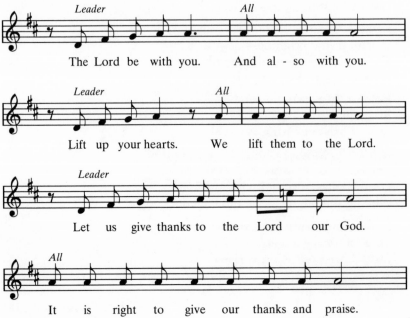

The Lord be with you. And al - so with you.

Lift up your hearts. We lift them to the Lord.

Let us give thanks to the Lord our God.

It is right to give our thanks and praise.

It is truly right that with full hearts and minds
and voices we should praise you,
the unseen God, the all-powerful creator,
and your only Son, our Lord Jesus Christ.
For Christ has ransomed us with his blood,
and paid for us the debt of Adam's sin.

Rejoice, heavenly powers!
Sing, choirs of angels!
Jesus Christ our King is risen!

This is our passover feast,
when Christ, the true Lamb, is slain,
whose blood consecrates the homes of all believers.
This is the night when first you saved our forebears:
you freed the people of Israel from their slavery
and led them dry-shod through the sea.
This is the night when Christians everywhere,
washed clean from sin and freed from all defilement,
are restored to grace and grow together in holiness.
This is the night when Jesus Christ broke the chains of death,
and rose triumphant from the grave.

Rejoice, heavenly powers!
Sing, choirs of angels!
Jesus Christ our King is risen!

Optional ending:

Lord God, how wonderful your care for us!
How boundless your merciful love!
To ransom a slave you gave away your Son.

Most blessed of all nights,
chosen by God to see Christ rising from the dead!

The power of this holy night
dispels all evil, washes guilt away,
restores lost innocence, brings mourners joy;
it casts out hatred, brings us peace,
and humbles earthly pride.
Night truly blessed, when heaven is wedded to earth,
and we are reconciled with God!
Therefore, gracious God, in the joy of this night,

receive our evening sacrifice of praise,
your Church's solemn offering.
May this Easter candle always dispel the darkness of this night!

May the Morning Star which never sets
find this flame still burning:
Christ, that Morning Star,
who came back from the dead,
and shed his peaceful light on all creation,
your Son who lives and reigns forever and ever. Amen.

Rejoice, heavenly powers!
Sing, choirs of angels!
Jesus Christ our King is risen![99]

After the singing of the Proclamation of Easter, the candles of the worshipers are extinguished.

LITURGY OF THE WORD

The paschal candle is moved to the place where the scriptures will be read.

GREETING

In these or similar words the leader says:

Friends in Christ,
let us listen attentively to the word of God,
recalling God's saving deeds throughout history
and how, in the fullness of time,
God's Word became flesh and dwelt among us:
Jesus Christ, our Redeemer!

OLD TESTAMENT READINGS

Nine readings from the Old Testament are provided. At least three are to be read. The reading from Exodus 14 is always included.

Each reading is followed by:
a. a brief period of silence
b. the singing of a psalm [or hymn, or anthem]
c. a prayer

First Reading: **Story of Creation**

Genesis 1:1–2:4a

Silence

Psalm 33:1–11 *(sung)*

Let us pray:

Almighty and eternal God,
you created all things in wonderful beauty and order.
Help us now to perceive
how still more wonderful is the new creation,
by which in the fullness of time
you redeemed your people
through the sacrifice of our Passover, Jesus Christ,
who lives and reigns forever and ever.[100]

Amen.

Second Reading: **The Flood**

Genesis 7:1–5, 11–18; 8:6–18; 9:8–13

Silence

Psalm 46 *(sung)*

Let us pray:

Faithful God,
you placed the rainbow in the skies
as the sign of your covenant with all living things.
May we who are saved through water and the Spirit,
worthily offer to you our sacrifice of thanksgiving.
We ask this in the name of Jesus Christ our Lord.[101]

Amen.

Third Reading: **Abraham's Sacrifice of Isaac**

Genesis 22:1–18

Silence

Psalm 16 *(sung)*

Let us pray:

Gracious God of all believers,
through Abraham's obedience
you made known your faithful love
to countless numbers;
by the grace of Christ's sacrifice,
fulfill in your church and in all creation
your promise of a new covenant.[102]

Amen.

Fourth Reading: **Israel's Deliverance at the Red Sea**

Exodus 14:10–31; 15:20–21

Silence

Exodus 15:1b–6, 11–13, 17–18: Song of Miriam and Moses *(sung)*

Let us pray:

God of steadfast love,
your wonderful deeds of old shine forth even to our own day.
Through the waters of the sea
you once delivered your chosen people from slavery,
a sign for us of the salvation of all nations
through the grace of baptism.
Grant that all of the peoples of the earth
may be numbered among the offspring of Abraham,
and rejoice in the inheritance of Israel;
through Jesus Christ our Lord.[103]

Amen.

Fifth Reading: **Salvation Offered Freely to All**

Isaiah 55:1–11

Silence

Isaiah 12:2–6 *(sung)*

Let us pray:

Eternal God,
by the power of your Word you created all things,
and by your Spirit you renew the earth.
Give now the water of life to all who thirst for you,
and nourish with the spiritual food of bread and wine
all who hunger for you,
that our lives may bear the abundant fruit of your heavenly reign;
through Jesus Christ, the firstborn from the dead,
who, with you and the Holy Spirit,
lives and reigns forever.[104]

Amen.

Sixth Reading: **The Wisdom of God**

Proverbs 8:1–8, 19–21; 9:4–6

Silence

Psalm 19 *(sung)*

Let us pray:

Fountain of wisdom,
by your word you set the universe in space,
and with your hands you molded us in your image.
Everywhere we see signs of your loving care.
Guide us always into your ways,
that in your wisdom we may find life abundant,
and live forever in the splendor of your glory;
through Jesus Christ, the way, the truth, and the life.[105]

Amen.

Seventh Reading: **A New Heart and a New Spirit**

Ezekiel 36:24–28

Silence

Psalms 42 and 43 *(sung)*

Let us pray:

God of holiness and light,
in the mystery of dying and rising with Christ
you have established a new covenant of reconciliation.
Cleanse our hearts
and give a new spirit to all your people,
that your saving grace may be professed
and proclaimed to the whole world;
through Jesus Christ our Lord.[106]

Amen.

Eighth Reading: **The Valley of the Dry Bones**

Ezekiel 37:1–14

Silence

Psalm 143 *(sung)*

Let us pray:

Living God,
by the Passover of your Son
you have brought us out of sin into righteousness,
and out of death into life.
Grant to those who are sealed by your Holy Spirit
the will and power to proclaim you to all the world;
through Jesus Christ our Lord.[107]

Amen.

Ninth Reading: **The Gathering of God's People**

Zephaniah 3:14–20

Silence

Psalm 98 *(sung)*

Let us pray:

God of unchangeable power and eternal light,
look with favor on your whole church,
that wonderful and sacred mystery.
Bring to completion your saving work,
so that the whole world may see and know
that things which were cast down are being raised up,
and things which had grown old are being made new,
and that all things are being brought to their perfection
by him through whom all things were made,
your Son Jesus Christ our Lord.[108]

Amen.

ACT OF PRAISE

> *"Glory to God in the highest," "We Praise You, O God," or some other hymn is sung. Bells may be rung.*

PRAYER OF THE DAY

Let us pray.

Eternal Giver of life and light,
this holy night shines with the radiance of the risen Christ.
Renew your church with the Spirit given to us in baptism,
that we may worship you in sincerity and truth,
and shine as a light in the world;
through Jesus Christ our Lord,
who is alive and reigns with you and the Holy Spirit,
one God, now and forever.[109]

Amen.

EPISTLE READING

Romans 6:3–11

Psalm 114 *(sung)*

GOSPEL READING

Year A: Matthew 28:1–10   (1993, 1996, 1999)
Year B: Mark 16:1–8   (1994, 1997, 2000)
Year C: Luke 24:1–12   (1992, 1995, 1998)

A brief sermon may follow.

The paschal candle is moved in procession to the baptismal font. During the procession, a psalm, hymn, or anthem is sung.

LITURGY OF WATER

BAPTISM

Baptism may follow, using the baptismal liturgy in Holy Baptism and Services for Renewal of Baptism *(Supplemental Liturgical Resource 2), pp. 25–39. Use of the prayer over the water on pp. 35, 36 of* Holy Baptism *is suggested.*

REAFFIRMATION OF BAPTISMAL VOWS

In the event there are no candidates for baptism, the following order for the Reaffirmation of Baptismal Vows is used.

Hear these words from Holy Scripture:

One or more of the following scriptures is said:

Know therefore that the Lord your God is God,
the faithful God who keeps covenant and steadfast love
with those who love God
and keep God's commandments. *Deut. 7:9*

And/or

Once you were darkness,
but now in the Lord you are light.
Live as children of light,
and try to learn what is pleasing to the Lord. *Eph. 5:8, 10*

And/or

You are a chosen race, a royal priesthood,
a holy nation, God's own people,
in order that you may proclaim the mighty acts of him
who called you out of darkness
into his marvelous light.
Once you were not a people,
but now you are God's people;
once you had not received mercy,
but now you have received mercy.   *1 Peter 2:9, 10*

And

Sisters and brothers in Christ,
our baptism is the sign and seal
of our cleansing from sin,
and of our being grafted into Christ.
Through the birth, life, death, and rising of Christ,
the power of sin was broken
and God's kingdom entered our world.

Through our baptism we were made citizens of God's kingdom,
and freed from the bondage of sin.
Let us celebrate that freedom and redemption
through the renewal of the promises made at our baptism.

I ask you, therefore, once again
to reject sin,
to profess your faith in Christ Jesus,
and to confess the faith of the church,
the faith in which we were baptized.

Do you renounce the forces of evil,
which defy God's righteousness and love?

I renounce them.

Do you renounce the evil powers of this world
which corrupt and destroy the creatures of God?

I renounce them.

Do you renounce the ways of sin
that draw you away from the love of God?

I renounce them.

Do you turn to Jesus Christ
and accept him as your Lord and Savior?

I do.

Do you intend to be Christ's faithful disciple,
obeying his word, and showing his love,
to your life's end?

I do.

With the whole church,
let us confess our faith.

The congregation affirms the faith in the words of the Apostles' Creed:

Do you believe in God the Father?

**I believe in God, the Father almighty,
  creator of heaven and earth.**

Do you believe in Jesus Christ, the Son of God?

**I believe in Jesus Christ, God's only Son, our Lord,
  who was conceived by the Holy Spirit,
  born of the virgin Mary,
  suffered under Pontius Pilate,
  was crucified, died, and was buried;
  he descended to the dead.
  On the third day he rose again;
  he ascended into heaven,
  he is seated on the right hand of the Father,
  and he will come to judge the living and the dead.**

Do you believe in God the Holy Spirit?

I believe in the Holy Spirit,
   the holy catholic church,
   the communion of saints,
   the forgiveness of sins,
   the resurrection of the body,
   and the life everlasting. Amen.

Water is poured into the font at this time.

The minister leads the people in prayer, saying:

The Lord be with you.

And also with you.

Let us give thanks to the Lord our God.

It is right to give our thanks and praise.

Holy and gracious God,
ruler over all creation,
in you alone we find life;
by your power we are upheld.

Glory to you forever and ever.

We praise you,
for in the beginning,
your Spirit swept across the watery chaos,
and order and life were called forth.
By the gift of water,
you nourish and sustain all living things.

Glory to you forever and ever.

In the water of the flood, you destroyed evil,
but gave righteousness a new beginning,
by saving Noah and his family,
who found favor in your sight.

Glory to you forever and ever.

By the pillar of cloud and fire,
you led Israel through the water of the sea,
out of slavery into freedom.
Across the water of the Jordan,
you brought your chosen ones into the land of your promise.

Glory to you forever and ever.

In the water of the Jordan,
Jesus was baptized by John
and anointed with the Spirit.
By the baptism of his death,
he set us free from bondage to sin and death.
By his resurrection,
he opened the way to eternal life.

Glory to you forever and ever.

We praise you for the countless ways
you have revealed yourself in ages past,
and for the signs of your grace you have given us.

Glory to you forever and ever.

We thank you for the gift of baptism.
In the waters of baptism
we are buried with Christ in his death;
from the water
we are raised to share in his resurrection;
through the water
we are reborn by the power of the Holy Spirit.

Glory to you forever and ever.

We praise you for claiming us through our baptism
and for upholding us by your grace.
We remember your promises given to us in our baptism.
By your Holy Spirit renew us,
that we may be empowered to do your will,
and continue forever in the risen life of Christ,
to whom, with you and the Holy Spirit,
be all glory and honor,
now and forever.[110]

Amen.

Or

During the singing of a hymn, the minister walks through the congregation sprinkling water from the font, with an evergreen bough, saying:	*The minister may place his or her hand in the water of the font, lift up some water, let it fall back into the font, and then make the sign of the cross over the people while saying:*

Remember your baptism
and be thankful.

Remember your baptism
and be thankful.

In the name of the Father
and of the Son
and of the Holy Spirit.

Amen.

A hymn is sung.

The minister says these or similar words:

The peace of our Lord Jesus Christ be with you.

And also with you.

LITURGY OF THE EUCHARIST

The paschal candle is moved in procession to the holy table.

During the procession, a psalm, hymn, or anthem is sung.

INVITATION TO THE LORD'S TABLE

Text no. 180 in The Service for the Lord's Day *(Supplemental Liturgical Resource 1) is suggested.*

GREAT PRAYER OF THANKSGIVING

Use the great prayer provided for Easter, pp. 204–207 of this resource, or Great Prayer E (text no. 187) in The Service for the Lord's Day *(Supplemental Liturgical Resource 1).*

BREAKING OF THE BREAD

Use text no. 209 or 210 in The Service for the Lord's Day *(Supplemental Liturgical Resource 1), depending upon whether or not the words of institution are included in the great prayer.*

COMMUNION OF THE PEOPLE

PRAYER AFTER COMMUNION

Gracious God,
you have made us one
with all your people in heaven and on earth.
We have recalled your mighty acts in holy history.
We have seen your power
in sending light to conquer darkness,
water to give us life;
and the bread of heaven to nourish us in love.
Send us with your salvation and joy to all the world,
in the name of Jesus Christ our Lord.[111]

Amen.

A psalm, hymn, or spiritual is sung.

CHARGE AND BLESSING

The minister gives God's blessing to the congregation using a scriptural benediction:

Go in peace to love and serve the Lord
in the power of his resurrection. Alleluia!

The grace of the Lord Jesus Christ,
the love of God,
and the communion of the Holy Spirit
be with you all.   *2 Cor. 13:13*

Amen.

Christ is risen!

Christ is risen!

Christ is risen!

Christ is risen!

Christ is risen!

**Christ is risen indeed!
Alleluia, alleluia!**

EASTER SUNDAY THROUGH SIXTH SUNDAY OF EASTER

PRAYER OF ADORATION

Glory to you, O God,
who on this day won victory over death,
raising Jesus from the grave
and giving us eternal life.

Glory to you, O Christ,
who for us and for our salvation overcame death
and opened the gate to everlasting life.

Glory to you, O Holy Spirit,
who lead us into the truth.

Glory to you, O blessed Trinity,
now and forever.[112]

Amen.

PRAYER OF CONFESSION

Mighty God,
by your power Christ is raised from death
to rule this world in love.
We confess that we have not believed in him,
but fall into doubt and fear.
Gladness has no home in our hearts,
and gratitude is slight.
Forgive our dread of dying,
our hopelessness,
and set us free for joy in the victory of Jesus Christ,
who was dead but lives,
and will put down every power to hurt or destroy,
when your promised kingdom comes.[113]

GREAT PRAYER OF THANKSGIVING

It is suggested that text no. 180 in The Service for the Lord's Day
*be used as the invitation to the table, when the following prayer is
used.*

The Lord be with you.

And also with you.

Lift up your hearts.

We lift them to the Lord.

Let us give thanks to the Lord our God.

It is right to give our thanks and praise.

It is truly right and our greatest joy
to give you thanks and praise,
eternal God, creator and ruler of the universe.
At your word the earth was made
and spun on its course among the planets.
Your hand formed us from the dust of the earth
and set us among all your creatures
to love and to serve you.

When we were unfaithful to you
you kept faith with us;
your love remained steadfast.
When we were enslaved in Egypt,
you broke the bonds of slavery,
led us through the sea to freedom,
and made covenant to be our God.

By a pillar of fire you led us through the desert
to a land flowing with milk and honey,
and set before us the way of life.
You spoke of love and justice in the prophets,
and in the Word made flesh,
you lived among us manifesting your glory.
He died that we might live,
and is risen to raise us to new life.

Therefore, we praise you,
singing with angels and archangels,
and with all the faithful of every time and place,
to the glory of your mighty name:

Holy, holy, holy Lord, God of power and might,
heaven and earth are full of your glory.
   Hosanna in the highest.

Blessed is he who comes in the name of the Lord.
  Hosanna in the highest.

You are holy, O God of majesty,
and blessed is Jesus Christ, your Son, our Lord,
whom you sent to save us.
He came with healing in his touch,
and was wounded for our sins.
He came with mercy in his voice,
and was mocked as one despised.
He came with peace in his heart,
and met violence and death.

By your power he broke free from the prison of the tomb;
and at his command the gates of hell were opened.
The one who was dead now lives,
The one whose name is above all names,
before whom every knee shall bow,
is raised to rule over all creation.
In ascending on high,
he promised to be with us always.

> *The words of institution may be said here, or in relation to the
> breaking of the bread.*

[On the night before he died,
Jesus took bread.
After giving thanks to you, he broke it,
and gave it to his disciples, saying,
"Take, eat.
This is my body, given for you.
Do this in remembrance of me."

In the same way he took the cup, saying,
"This cup is the new covenant sealed in my blood,
shed for you for the forgiveness of sins.
Do this in remembrance of me."]

In remembrance of your mighty acts in Jesus Christ,
we take from your creation this bread and this wine
and celebrate his dying and rising,
as we await the day of his coming.
With thanksgiving we offer our very selves to you

to be a living and holy sacrifice,
dedicated to your service.

So we proclaim the mystery of faith:

Christ has died,
Christ is risen,
Christ will come again.

Gracious God,
pour out your Holy Spirit
upon us and upon these your gifts of bread and wine,
that in breaking this bread and sharing this cup,
our eyes may be opened to recognize Christ present.

By your Spirit make our hearts burn within us,
that we may welcome him as host at this table.
Fed by his gracious hand,
make us one with all who share this feast.
Keep us faithful in your service,
until Christ comes in final victory
and we feast with him at the banquet of heaven.
Through Christ, with Christ, in Christ,
in the unity of the Holy Spirit,
all glory and honor are yours, almighty God,
now and forever.[114]

Amen.

PRAYER OF THANKS

For use when the Eucharist is not celebrated.

Let us give thanks to the Lord our God.

It is right to give our thanks and praise.

Eternal and ever-living God,
we praise you that your glory has dawned on us,
and brought us into this Day of Resurrection.
We rejoice that the grave could not hold your Son,
and that he has conquered death,
risen to rule over all powers of this earth.
We praise you that he summons us into new life,

to follow him with joy and gladness.
By your Spirit,
lift us from doubt and despair,
and set our feet in Christ's holy way,
that our lives may be signs of his life,
and all we have may show forth his love.[115]

Amen.

Or

Let us give thanks to the Lord our God.

It is right to give our thanks and praise.

Eternal and ever blessed God,
Lord of heaven and earth:
we praise your glorious majesty.
Your wisdom is seen in all your works;
your grace and truth are revealed in Jesus Christ, your Son;
your power and presence are given to us through your Holy Spirit;
wherefore we adore your holy home, O blessed Trinity,
forever and ever.[116]

Amen.

Or

Let us give thanks to the Lord our God.

It is right to give our thanks and praise.

We give you thanks, great God,
for the hope we have in Jesus,
who died but is risen, and rules over all.
We praise you for his presence with us.
Because he lives, we look for eternal life,
knowing that nothing past, present, or yet to come
can separate us from your great love
made known in Jesus Christ our Lord.[117]

Amen.

EASTER SUNDAY

Call to Worship

Alleluia! The Lord is risen!

The Lord is risen indeed! Alleluia!   *Based on Luke 24:34*

Or

Do not be afraid;
I know you are looking for Jesus who was crucified.
He is not here;
for he has been raised, as he said.   *Matt. 28:5b–6*

Alleluia!

Or

Christ our Passover has been sacrificed for us;
therefore let us keep the feast.   *1 Cor. 5:7, 8*

Prayer of the Day

Lord of life and power,
through the mighty resurrection of your Son
you overcame the old order of sin and death
to make all things new in him:
May we, being dead to sin
and alive to you in Jesus Christ,
reign with him in glory,
who with you and the Holy Spirit is alive,
one God, now and forever.[118]

Amen.

Or

O God,
you gave your only Son
to suffer death on the cross for our redemption,

and by his glorious resurrection
you delivered us from the power of death.
Make us die every day to sin,
so that we may live with him forever
in the joy of the resurrection;
through Jesus Christ our Lord,
who lives and reigns with you and the Holy Spirit,
one God, now and forever.[119]

Amen.

Or

Mighty God,
you raised up Jesus from death to life.
Give us such trust in your power
that we may be glad through all our days,
looking to that perfect day
when we celebrate your victory with Christ the Lord,
to whom be praise and glory.[120]

Amen.

SECOND SUNDAY OF EASTER

CALL TO WORSHIP AND
PRAYER OF THE DAY

Call to Worship

Blessed are those who have not seen
and yet have come to believe.   *John 20:29*

Or

O give thanks to the Lord,
for the Lord is good;

God's steadfast love endures forever.   *Ps. 118:1*

Prayer of the Day

Almighty and eternal God,
the strength of those who believe
and the hope of those who doubt,
may we, who have not seen, have faith
and receive the fullness of Christ's blessing,
who is alive and reigns with you and the Holy Spirit,
one God, now and forever.[121]

Amen.

Or

God of mercy,
we no longer look for Jesus among the dead,
for he is alive and has become the Lord of life.
From the waters of death you raise us with him
and renew your gift of life within us.
Increase in our minds and hearts
the risen life we share with Christ,
and help us to grow as your people
toward the fullness of eternal life with you;
through Jesus Christ our Lord.[122]

Amen.

THIRD SUNDAY OF EASTER

CALL TO WORSHIP AND
PRAYER OF THE DAY

Call to Worship

Call on the name of the Lord in praise;
Make known God's deeds among the nations!

**Sing to God with joyful songs;
tell of God's wonderful deeds!**   *Ps. 105:1–5*

Or

Christ being raised from the dead will die no more;
death has no more dominion over him.   *Rom. 6:9*

Prayer of the Day

O God,
whose Son made himself known to his disciples
in the breaking of bread:
Open the eyes of our faith,
that we may see him in his redeeming work;
who is alive and reigns with you and the Holy Spirit,
one God, now and forever.[123]

Amen.

FOURTH SUNDAY OF EASTER

CALL TO WORSHIP AND
PRAYER OF THE DAY

Call to Worship

I am the good shepherd, says the Lord:
I know my own
and my own know me.   *John 10:14*

Prayer of the Day

God of all power,
you called from death our Lord Jesus,
the great shepherd of the sheep.
Send us as shepherds to rescue the lost,
to heal the injured,
and to feed one another
with knowledge and understanding;
through your Son, Jesus Christ our Lord,
who lives and reigns with you and the Holy Spirit,
one God, now and forever.[124]

Amen.

Or

Almighty God,
you sent Jesus, our good shepherd,
to gather us together:

May we not wander from his flock,
but follow wherever he leads us,
listening for his voice and staying near him,
until we are safely in your fold,
to live with you forever;
through Jesus Christ our Lord.[125]

Amen.

FIFTH SUNDAY OF EASTER

Call to Worship

A

I am the way, and the truth, and the life, says the Lord.
No one comes to the Father except through me.   *John 14:23*

Or

B

I am the vine, you are the branches, says the Lord.
Those who abide in me and I in them
bear much fruit.   *John 15:5*

Or

C

I give you a new commandment,
that you love one another.
Just as I have loved you,
you also should love one another.   *John 13:34*

Prayer of the Day

Almighty God,
your Son Jesus Christ is the way, the truth, and the life.
Give us grace to love one another
and walk in the way of his commandments,

who lives and reigns with you and the Holy Spirit,
one God, now and forever.[126]

Amen.

Or

O God,
form the minds of your faithful people into a single will.
Make us love what you command
and desire what you promise,
that, amid all the changes of this world,
our hearts may be fixed where true joy is found;
through Jesus Christ our Lord,
who lives and reigns with you and the Holy Spirit,
one God, now and forever.[127]

Amen.

SIXTH SUNDAY OF EASTER

CALL TO WORSHIP AND
PRAYER OF THE DAY

Call to Worship

A
If you love me, says the Lord,
you will keep my commandments.   *John 14:15*

Or

B
You did not choose me, but I chose you.
And I appointed you to go and bear fruit,
fruit that will last.   *John 15:16*

Or

C
Those who love me will keep my word,
and my Father will love them,
and we will come to them
and make our home with them.   *John 14:23*

Prayer of the Day

O God,
you have prepared for those who love you
riches beyond imagination.
Pour into our hearts such love toward you,
that we, loving you above all things,
may obtain your promises,
which exceed all that we can desire;
through Jesus Christ our Lord,
who is alive and reigns with you and the Holy Spirit,
one God, forever and ever.[128]

Amen.

ASCENSION OF THE LORD
AND SEVENTH SUNDAY OF EASTER

CALL TO WORSHIP AND
PRAYER OF THE DAY

Call to Worship

Since we have a great high priest
who has passed through the heavens,
Jesus the Son of God,
let us hold fast to our confession.

**Let us approach the throne of grace with boldness,
so that we may receive mercy
and find grace to help
in time of need.**   *Heb. 4:14, 16*

Or

Go and make disciples of all nations, says the Lord;
I am with you always,
to the end of time.   *Matt. 28:19a, 20b*

Alleluia!

Or

Why do you stand looking up toward heaven?
This Jesus will come in the same way as you saw him go into heaven.
                                                        Acts 1:11

Alleluia!

Prayer of the Day

Almighty God,
your Son Jesus Christ ascended to the throne of heaven
that he might rule over all things as Lord.
Keep the church in the unity of the Spirit
and in the bond of his peace,
and bring the whole of creation
to worship at his feet,

who is alive and reigns with you and the Holy Spirit,
one God, now and forever.[129]

Amen.

PRAYER OF CONFESSION

**Almighty God,
you have raised Jesus from the grave
and crowned him Lord of all.
We confess that we have not bowed before him,
or acknowledged his rule in our lives.
We have gone along with the way of the world,
and failed to give him glory.
Forgive us,
and raise us from sin,
that we may be your faithful people,
obeying the commands of our Lord Jesus Christ,
who rules the world
and is head of the church, his body.[130]**

GREAT PRAYER OF THANKSGIVING

Use great prayer for Easter (pp. 204–207).

PRAYER OF THANKS

For use when the Eucharist is not celebrated.

Let us give thanks to the Lord our God.

It is right to give our thanks and praise.

Great and mighty God,
we praise you that Christ has ascended
to rule at your right hand.
We rejoice before the throne of his power and peace,
for he has put down tyrannies that would destroy us,
and unmasked idols claiming our allegiance.
We thank you that he alone is Lord of our lives.
By your Spirit,
give us freedom to love with his love,

and to embrace the world with his compassion.
Accept the offering of our lives,
that we may obey your commands to serve
in the name and for the sake of Jesus Christ, our Lord.[131]

Amen.

Or

Let us give thanks to the Lord our God.

It is right to give our thanks and praise.

Mighty God,
by your power you raised Jesus Christ to rule over us.
We praise you that he puts down tyrannies
that threaten to destroy us,
and unmasks powers that claim our allegiance.
We thank you that he alone commands our lives,
and gives us freedom to love the world.
Glory to you for the gift of his life!
Glory to you for his saving death!
Glory to you for Jesus Christ,
who lives and reigns as our risen Lord.[132]

Amen.

SEVENTH SUNDAY OF EASTER

CALL TO WORSHIP AND
PRAYER OF THE DAY

Call to Worship

Jesus prayed:
As you have sent me into the world,
so I have sent them into the world.   *John 17:18*

Or

Jesus prayed:
I pray that they may be one, as we are one,
so that the world may know that you have sent me.
                              Based on John 17:20–23

Prayer of the Day

Almighty God
you have exalted your only Son Jesus Christ
with great triumph to your kingdom in heaven.
Mercifully give us faith to know
that, as he promised,
he abides with us on earth to the end of time;
who is alive and reigns with you and the Holy Spirit,
one God, now and forever.[133]

Amen.

DAY OF PENTECOST

CALL TO WORSHIP AND
PRAYER OF THE DAY

Call to Worship

The word of the Lord to the prophet:
I will pour out my Spirit on all flesh;
your sons and your daughters shall prophesy,
your old shall dream dreams
and your young shall see visions.   *Joel 1:1a, 2:28–29*

    Or

You will receive power
when the Holy Spirit has come upon you,
and you shall be my witnesses
to the ends of the earth.   *Acts 1:8*

    Or

The love of God has been poured into our hearts
through the Holy Spirit that has been given to us.   *Rom. 5:5*

Prayer of the Day

Almighty and everliving God,
who fulfilled the promises of Easter
by sending us your Holy Spirit
and opening to every race and nation
the way of life eternal,
keep us in the unity of your Spirit,
that every tongue may tell of your glory;
through Jesus Christ our Lord,
who lives and reigns with you and the Holy Spirit,
one God, now and forever.[134]

Amen.

Or

God eternal,
as you sent upon the disciples
the promised gift of the Holy Spirit,
look upon your church
and open our hearts to the power of the Holy Spirit.
Kindle in us the fire of your love,
and strengthen our lives for service in your kingdom;
through your Son, Jesus Christ our Lord,
who lives and reigns with you in the unity of the Holy Spirit,
one God, now and forever.[135]

Amen.

Or

God our creator, earth has many languages,
but your gospel proclaims your love
to all nations in one heavenly speech.
Make us messengers of the good news
that, through the power of your Spirit,
everyone everywhere may unite in one song of praise;
through your Son, Jesus Christ our Lord,
who lives and reigns with you in the unity of the Holy Spirit,
one God, now and forever.[136]

Amen.

LITANY FOR PENTECOST

Holy Spirit, Creator,
in the beginning you moved over the waters.
From your breath all creation drew life.
Without you, life turns to dust.

Come, Holy Spirit!

Holy Spirit, Counselor,
by your inspiration, the prophets spoke and acted in faith.
You clothed them in power to be bearers of your Word.

Come, Holy Spirit!

Holy Spirit, Power,
you came as fire to Jesus' disciples;
you gave them voice before the rulers of this world.

Come, Holy Spirit!

Holy Spirit, Sanctifier,
you created us children of God;
you make us the living temple of your presence;
you intercede within us with sighs too deep for words.

Come, Holy Spirit!

Holy Spirit, Giver of life,
you guide and make holy the church you create;
you give gifts—
    the spirit of wisdom and understanding,
    the spirit of counsel and fortitude,
    the spirit of knowledge and piety
    the spirit of the fear of the Lord,
that the whole creation may become what you want it to be.

Come, Holy Spirit!

    After a brief silence, the leader concludes the litany:

True and only Light,
from whom comes every good gift,
send your Spirit into our lives
with the power of a mighty wind.
Open the horizons of our minds
by the flame of your wisdom.
Loosen our tongues to show your praise,
for only in your Spirit
can we voice your words of peace
and acclaim Jesus as Lord.[137]

Amen.

PRAYER OF CONFESSION

**Almighty God,
who sent the promised power of the Holy Spirit**

to fill disciples with willing faith:
**We confess that we resist the force of your Spirit among us;
that we are slow to serve you,
and reluctant to spread the good news of your love.
God, have mercy on us.
Forgive our divisions,
and by your Spirit draw us together.
Inflame us with a desire to do your will
and be your faithful people;
for the sake of your Son, our Lord, Jesus Christ.**[138]

LITANY OF INTERCESSION FOR PENTECOST

Christ has gathered the church in unity through the Spirit.
With sure hope, let us pray.

Maker of all things,
in the beginning, you created heaven and earth.
In the fullness of time, you restored all things in Christ.
Renew our world, in this day, with your grace and mercy.

Lord, hear our prayer.

Life of the world,
you breathed life into the flesh you created.
By your Spirit breathe new life into the children of earth.
Turn hatred into love,
sorrow into joy,
and war into peace.

Lord, hear our prayer.

Lover of concord,
you desire the unity of all Christians.
Set aflame the whole church with the fire of your Spirit.
Unite us to stand in the world as a sign of your love.

Lord, hear our prayer.

God of compassion,
through your Spirit you supply every human need.
Heal the sick,
comfort the distressed,

befriend the friendless,
and help the helpless.

Lord, hear our prayer.

Source of peace,
your Spirit restores our anxious spirits.
In our labor, give us rest;
in our temptation, give us strength;
in our sadness, give us consolation.

Lord, hear our prayer.

Other brief petitions may here be offered.

Faithful God,
your Spirit empowered the first disciples to be witnesses to
    your truth.
Empower us and all who believe,
to speak your word and do your will,
that the world may know its true and only light,
Jesus Christ our Lord.[139]

Amen.

GREAT PRAYER OF THANKSGIVING

The Lord be with you.

And also with you.

Lift up your hearts.

We lift them to the Lord.

Let us give thanks to the Lord our God.

It is right to give our thanks and praise.

It is right to give you thanks and praise,
Eternal God, Ruler of the Universe.
By the majesty of your hand,
you shaped this world and all that is in it.
By the breath of your Holy Spirit,
you brought us to life from the earth,

and set us on the earth to praise and serve you.
When we wandered from your ways
and were lost in sin's wilderness,
your truth burned in the hearts of prophets.
Through them you proclaimed your justice,
calling your people to return
to the path of righteousness.
In the fullness of time
you sent your Son to be our deliverer.
In every age your Holy Spirit has led us in your ways.

Therefore, we praise you,
singing with the choirs of angels,
and with all the faithful of every time and place,
to the glory of your mighty name:

**Holy, holy, holy Lord, God of power and might,
heaven and earth are full of your glory.
Hosanna in the highest.**

**Blessed is he who comes in the name of the Lord.
Hosanna in the highest.**

You are holy, O God of majesty,
and blessed is Jesus Christ, your Son, our Lord.
At his baptism by John,
your Spirit came with gentle wings,
settling on him your blessing.
In the wilderness of temptation,
your Spirit stood by with power.
In his life and ministry,
your Spirit led him to serve the poor,
proclaim freedom from sin's bondage,
open eyes with faith's sight,
and befriend the friendless and outcast.
In all he did and said,
he announced the coming of your saving might.

By his death on the cross and rising from the tomb,
he broke the power of death,
and led the way to eternal life.
Ascending to rule from on high,
Christ prays for us and promises the coming of peace and power.

The words of institution may be said here, or in relation to the breaking of the bread.

[On the night before he died,
Jesus took bread.
After giving thanks to you, he broke it,
and gave it to his disciples, saying,
"Take, eat.
This is my body, given for you.
Do this in remembrance of me."

In the same way he took the cup, saying,
"This cup is the new covenant sealed in my blood,
shed for you for the forgiveness of sins.
Do this in remembrance of me."]

Remembering your mighty acts in Jesus Christ,
we take this bread and this wine
and celebrate this holy sacrament.
With thanksgiving we offer our very selves to you,
to be a living and holy sacrifice
dedicated to your service.

So we proclaim the mystery of faith:

Christ has died,
Christ is risen,
Christ will come again.

Gracious God,
give us your Holy Spirit,
that we may know Christ present here,
our host at this table,
feeding us with the bread of his life,
and covenanting with us in the blood of his sacrifice.
Pour out the fire of your Spirit
that we may be forged into one church,
many and different people welcomed into the unity of Christ's
    embrace.
Enflame your church with spiritual zeal
to serve you as joyful disciples,
until Christ comes in final victory
and we feast with him in eternity.

Through Christ, with Christ, in Christ,
in the unity of the Holy Spirit,
all glory and honor, praise and adoration are yours,
now and forever.[140]

Amen.

Prayer of Thanks

For use when the Eucharist is not celebrated.

Let us give thanks to the Lord our God.

It is right to give our thanks and praise.

God of all might and power,
we praise you that
you forged your church in the fire of the Spirit,
and breathed life into your people
that we might be the Body of Christ.
We rejoice that our Lord came to rescue us from sin
and to deliver us beyond the grave
to a rebirth and newness of life.
By your Spirit,
baptize us again with your flame of faith,
fill us with the breath of zeal,
inspire us with the witness of martyrs and saints,
and send us forth into your world
to live Christ's life in power and compassion.
Take us, O God,
and shape us according to your will,
in the service of Jesus Christ, our Lord and Savior.[141]

Amen.

ORDINARY TIME
BETWEEN DAY OF PENTECOST
AND FIRST SUNDAY OF ADVENT

TRINITY SUNDAY

Call to Worship

Holy, holy, holy is the Lord of hosts;

the whole earth is full of God's glory. *Isa. 6:3*

Or

I am the alpha and the omega says the Lord God,
who is and who was and who is to come, the almighty. *Rev. 1:8*

Or

The Lord is a great God who says:
I am the Alpha and Omega,
the first and the last,
the beginning and the end. *Rev. 22:13*

Prayer of the Day

Father, we praise you;
through your Word and Holy Spirit you created all things.
You reveal your salvation in all the world
by sending to us Jesus Christ, the Word made flesh.
Through your Holy Spirit
you give us a share in your life and love.
Fill us with the vision of your glory,
that we may always serve and praise you,
Father, Son, and Holy Spirit,
one God, forever and ever.[142]

Amen.

Or

Almighty and ever-living God,
you have given us grace,

by the confession of a true faith,
to acknowledge the glory of the eternal Trinity
and, in the power of your divine majesty,
to worship the Unity.
Keep us steadfast in this faith and worship,
and bring us at last to see you in your eternal glory,
one God, now and forever.[143]

Amen.

PRAYER OF CONFESSION

Holy God,
we confess that we have failed to love you
with all our heart, soul, and mind.
We have ignored your commandments
and have strayed from your ways.

In your mercy,

Hear our prayer.

Lord Jesus Christ,
we confess that we have not loved our neighbors as ourselves.
We fail to reach out to people in need,
and have not told your story to all the world.

In your mercy,

Hear our prayer.

Holy Spirit,
we confess that we are slow to follow your leading.
We prefer to do things our own way,
and ignore your presence in our lives.

In your mercy,

Hear our prayer.

Blessed Trinity,
Father, Son and Holy Spirit,
have mercy upon us.
Forgive our sin, and raise us to new life

that we may serve you
and honor your holy name.[144]

Amen.

GREAT PRAYER OF THANKSGIVING

The Lord be with you.

And also with you.

Lift up your hearts.

We lift them to the Lord.

Let us give thanks to the Lord our God.

It is right to give our thanks and praise.

It is right to give you thanks and praise,
eternal and triune God,
whom we worship as Father, Son and Holy Spirit.
With Jesus Christ you spoke the word
that brought the world into being.
With the Holy Spirit
you brought order out of chaos
and breathed life into your creatures.
As our parent,
you persisted in love in spite of our disobedience,
correcting us with gracious reproof,
and welcoming us again into your loving embrace.

Therefore, we praise you,
singing with all the inhabitants of heaven,
and with the faithful of every time and place,
to the glory of your mighty name:

Holy, holy, holy Lord, God of power and might,
heaven and earth are full of your glory.
   Hosanna in the highest.

Blessed is he who comes in the name of the Lord.
   Hosanna in the highest.

You are holy, O God of majesty,
and blessed is Jesus Christ, your Son, our Lord.
He cared for all your children,
forgiving their failures,
healing their hurts,
and nurturing their faith,
giving himself in utter sacrifice for those he loved.
He inspired ordinary folk to Spirit-filled living
and displayed in his life, death and rising again
the power of your Spirit.

> *The words of institution may be said here, or in relation to the breaking of the bread.*

[On the night before he died,
Jesus took bread.
After giving thanks to you, he broke it,
and gave it to his disciples, saying,
"Take, eat.
This is my body, given for you.
Do this in remembrance of me."

In the same way he took the cup, saying,
"This cup is the new covenant sealed in my blood,
shed for you for the forgiveness of sins.
Do this in remembrance of me."]

Remembering your mighty acts in Jesus Christ,
we take this bread and this wine
and celebrate this holy sacrament.
With thanksgiving we offer our very selves to you,
to be a living and holy sacrifice
dedicated to your service.

So we proclaim the mystery of faith:

Christ has died,
Christ is risen,
Christ will come again.

Gracious God, by your Holy Spirit,
may this bread of the earth and fruit of the vine
be for us communion in the body and blood of Christ.

Nurture us at this table,
that we may grow to the stature of Jesus Christ.
Make us one with Christ,
that we may be one with all your children who share this feast,
united in ministry throughout the world,
until Christ comes in final victory
and we feast with him in eternity.

Through Christ, with Christ, in Christ,
in the unity of the Holy Spirit,
all glory and honor, praise and adoration are yours,
now and forever.[145]

Amen.

PRAYER OF THANKS

For use when the Eucharist is not celebrated.

Let us give thanks to the Lord our God.
It is right to give our thanks and praise.

Gracious Father,
giver of all good things:
For our home on earth
and for your unfailing mercy,

we give you thanks.

Christ, our redeemer:
For your sacrifice on the cross
and rising from death that we might live,

we give you thanks and praise.

Holy Spirit, giver of life:
For your abiding presence in our lives
and for comforting and guiding us,

we give you thanks, praise, and glory.

O triune God:
To you be glory and praise
now and forever.[146]

Amen.

OTHER SUNDAYS BETWEEN TRINITY SUNDAY AND CHRIST THE KING

CALL TO WORSHIP AND PRAYER OF THE DAY

NINTH SUNDAY IN ORDINARY TIME

Sunday between May 29 and June 4 inclusive
(If after Trinity Sunday)

Call to Worship

I am the vine, you are the branches.
Those who abide in me and I in them bear much fruit.
Apart from me you can do nothing.   *John 15:5*

> *Or*

Your word, O Lord, is truth;
sanctify us in the truth.   *John 17:17*

Prayer of the Day

Lord God of the nations,
you have revealed your will to all people
and promised us your saving help.
May we hear and do what you command,
that the darkness may be overcome
by the power of your light;
through Jesus Christ our Lord,
who lives and reigns with you and the Holy Spirit,
now and forever.[147]

Amen.

> *Or*

Almighty God,
whose chosen servant Abraham obeyed your call,
rejoicing in your promise

that in him the family of earth is blessed,
give us faith like his,
that in us your promises may be fulfilled;
through Jesus Christ our Lord,
who lives and reigns with you and the Holy Spirit,
one God, now and forever.[148]

Amen.

TENTH SUNDAY IN ORDINARY TIME

Sunday between June 5 and 11 inclusive
(If after Trinity Sunday)

Call to Worship

The Spirit of the Lord has anointed me
to bring good news to the poor
and release to the captives.   *Luke 4:18*

> *Or*

The ruler of this world will be driven out.
And I, when I am lifted up from the earth,
will draw all people to myself.   *John 12:31, 32*

Prayer of the Day

O God,
you have assured the human family of eternal life
through Jesus Christ our Savior.
Deliver us from the death of sin
and raise us to new life in him,
who lives and reigns with you and the Holy Spirit,
one God, now and forever.[149]

Amen.

ELEVENTH SUNDAY IN ORDINARY TIME

Sunday between June 12 and 18 inclusive
(If after Trinity Sunday)

Call to Worship

The kingdom of God has come near;
repent, and believe in the good news.   *Mark 1:15*

> Or

In this is love,
not that we loved God
but that God loved us
and sent God's Son into the world
so that we might live through him.   *1 John 4:10*

Prayer of the Day

Almighty God,
without you we are not able to please you.
Mercifully grant that your Holy Spirit
may in all things direct and rule our hearts;
through Jesus Christ our Lord,
who is alive and reigns with you and the Holy Spirit,
one God, now and forever.[150]

Amen.

TWELFTH SUNDAY IN ORDINARY TIME

Sunday between June 19 and 25 inclusive
(If after Trinity Sunday)

Call to Worship

The Spirit of truth will bear witness to me, says the Lord;
and you also are witnesses.   *John 15:26, 27*

> Or

In Christ God was reconciling the world to Godself,
not counting their trespasses against them,
and entrusting the message of reconciliation to us.   *2 Cor. 5:19*

Or

My sheep hear my voice, says the Lord.
I know them, and they follow me. *John 10:27*

Prayer of the Day

Pour out upon us, O God,
the power and wisdom of your Spirit,
that we may walk with Christ the way of the cross,
ready to offer even the gift of our lives
to show forth to the world our hope in your kingdom.
We ask this through our Lord Jesus Christ,
who lives and reigns with you
in the unity of the Holy Spirit,
one God, forever and ever.[151]

Amen.

Or

B
O God our defender,
storms rage about us and cause us to be afraid.
Rescue your people from despair,
deliver your sons and daughters from fear,
and preserve us all from unbelief;
through Jesus Christ our Lord,
who lives and reigns with you and the Holy Spirit,
one God, now and forever.[152]

Amen.

THIRTEENTH SUNDAY IN ORDINARY TIME

Sunday between June 26 and July 2 inclusive

Call to Worship

You are a chosen race, a royal priesthood,
a holy nation, God's own people,
that you may proclaim the mighty acts
of the One who called you
out of darkness into marvelous light. *1 Peter 2:9*

Or

Our Savior, Christ Jesus, abolished death
and brought life and immortality to light
through the gospel.   *2 Tim. 1:10*

Or

Speak Lord, for your servant is listening;   *1 Sam. 3:9*
you have the words of eternal life.   *John 6:68*

Prayer of the Day

O God,
you have prepared for those who love you
joys beyond understanding.
Pour into our hearts such love for you
that, loving you above all things,
we may obtain your promises,
which exceed all that we can desire;
through Jesus Christ our Lord.[153]

Amen.

FOURTEENTH SUNDAY IN ORDINARY TIME

Sunday between July 3 and 9 inclusive

Call to Worship

The Spirit of the Lord has anointed me
to bring good news to the poor
and release to the captives.   *Luke 4:18*

Or

Happy are they who hear the word,
hold it fast in an honest and good heart,
and bear fruit with patient endurance.   *Luke 8:15*

Or

The harvest is plentiful,
but the laborers are few.
Ask the Lord of the harvest
to send out laborers into the harvest.   *Luke 10:25*

Prayer of the Day

Almighty God,
your Son Jesus Christ has taught us
that what we do for the least of your children
we do also for him.
Give us the will to serve others
as he was the servant of all,
who gave up his life and died for us,
but lives and reigns with you and the Holy Spirit,
one God, now and forever.[154]

Amen.

FIFTEENTH SUNDAY IN ORDINARY TIME

Sunday between July 10 and 16 inclusive

Call to Worship

The word is very near to you;
it is in your mouth
and in your heart for you to observe.   *Deut. 30:14*

Or

The words you have spoken are spirit and life, O Lord;
you have the words of eternal life.   *John 6:63, 68*

Prayer of the Day

Almighty God,
you have made us for yourself,
and our hearts are restless
until they find their rest in you.
May we find peace in your service,

and in the world to come, see you face to face;
through Jesus Christ our Lord,
who lives and reigns with you and the Holy Spirit,
one God, now and forever.[155]

Amen.

Or

A
Almighty God,
we thank you for planting in us the seed of your word.
By your Holy Spirit help us to receive it with joy,
live according to it,
and grow in faith and hope and love;
through Jesus Christ our Lord.[156]

Amen.

Or

C
Almighty God,
you have taught us through Christ
that love fulfills the law.
May we love you with all our heart,
all our soul, all our mind, and all our strength,
and may we love our neighbor as ourselves;
through Jesus Christ our Lord,
who lives and reigns with you and the Holy Spirit,
one God, now and forever.[157]

Amen.

SIXTEENTH SUNDAY IN ORDINARY TIME

Sunday between July 17 and 23 inclusive

Call to Worship

My word shall accomplish that which I purpose,
and succeed in the thing for which I sent it.   *Isa. 55:11*

Or

My sheep hear my voice, says the Lord.
I know them and they follow me;
and I give them eternal life. *John 10:27, 28a*

Or

Whatever you do, in word or deed,
do everything in the name of the Lord Jesus. *Col. 3:17*

Prayer of the Day

Almighty God,
in Jesus Christ you opened for us
a new and living way into your presence.
Give us pure hearts and constant wills
to worship you in spirit and in truth;
through Jesus Christ our Lord,
who lives and reigns with you and the Holy Spirit,
one God, now and forever.[158]

Amen.

SEVENTEENTH SUNDAY IN ORDINARY TIME

Sunday between July 24 and 30 inclusive

Call to Worship

Lord, to whom can we go?
You have the words of eternal life. *John 6:68*

Or

When we cry, "Abba! Father!"
it is that very Spirit bearing witness with our spirit
that we are children of God. *Rom. 8:15, 16*

Or

Ask, and it will be given you;
search, and you will find;
knock, and the door will be opened for you. *Luke 11:9*

Prayer of the Day

Gracious God,
you have placed within the hearts of all your children
a longing for your Word and a hunger for your truth.
Grant that, believing in the One whom you have sent,
we may know him to be the true bread of heaven
and food of eternal life,
Jesus Christ our Lord,
to whom with you and the Holy Spirit be glory and honor
forever and ever.[159]

Amen.

EIGHTEENTH SUNDAY IN ORDINARY TIME

Sunday between July 31 and August 6 inclusive

Call to Worship

One does not live by bread alone,
but by every word that comes from the mouth of God. *Matt. 4:4*

Or

If you have been raised with Christ,
seek the things that are above, where Christ is,
seated at the right hand of God. *Col. 3:1*

Prayer of the Day

AB
Gracious God,
your blessed Son came down from heaven
to be the true bread which gives life to the world.
Give us this bread,

that he may live in us and we in him,
Jesus Christ our Lord.[160]

Amen.

Or

C
Almighty God,
judge of us all,
you have placed in our hands the wealth we call our own.
Give us such wisdom by your Spirit
that our possessions may not be a curse in our lives,
but an instrument for blessing;
through Jesus Christ our Lord.[161]

Amen.

NINETEENTH SUNDAY IN ORDINARY TIME

Sunday between August 7 and 13 inclusive

Call to Worship

I wait for the Lord, my soul waits,
and in God's word is my hope. *Ps. 130:5*

Or

I am the living bread that came down from heaven.
Whoever eats of this bread will live forever. *John 6:51*

Or

Watch and be ready,
for you do not know on what day your Lord is coming.

Matt. 24:42, 44

Prayer of the Day

Almighty and everlasting God,
you are always more ready to hear
than we are to pray,

and to give more than we either desire or deserve.
Pour upon us the abundance of your mercy,
forgiving us those things
of which our conscience is afraid,
and giving us those good things
for which we are not worthy to ask,
except through the merit of your Son
Jesus Christ our Lord.[162]

Amen.

Or

B
Grant, O Lord,
that we may see in you the fulfillment of all our need,
and may turn from every false satisfaction
to feed on the true and living bread
which you have given us in Jesus Christ;
who lives and reigns with you and the Holy Spirit,
one God, now and forever.[163]

Amen.

TWENTIETH SUNDAY IN ORDINARY TIME

Sunday between August 14 and 20 inclusive

Call to Worship

The word of God is living and active,
it is able to judge the thoughts and intentions of the heart.   *Heb. 4:12*

Or

B
Those who eat my flesh and drink my blood
abide in me, and I in them, says the Lord.   *John 6:56*

Or

C

Since we are surrounded by so great a cloud of witnesses,
let us also lay aside every weight
and the sin that clings so closely,
and let us run with perseverance the race that is set before us,
looking to Jesus, the pioneer and perfecter of our faith.

Heb. 12:1, 2b

Prayer of the Day

Almighty God,
you have broken the tyranny of sin
and sent into our hearts the Spirit of your Son.
Give us grace to dedicate our freedom to your service,
that all people may know the glorious liberty
of the children of God;
through Jesus Christ our Lord,
who lives and reigns with you and the Holy Spirit,
one God, now and forever.[164]

Amen.

Or

B

Holy God,
we do not deserve crumbs from your table,
for we are sinful and dying.
May we have grace to praise you
for the bread of life you give in Jesus Christ,
the Lord of love, and the Savior of us all.[165]

Amen.

Or

C

Almighty and everliving God,
increase in us your gift of faith,
that, forsaking what lies behind
and reaching out to what is before,

we may run the way of your commandments
and win the crown of everlasting joy;
through Jesus Christ our Lord,
who lives and reigns with you and the Holy Spirit,
one God, forever and ever.[166]

Amen.

TWENTY-FIRST SUNDAY IN ORDINARY TIME

Sunday between August 21 and 27 inclusive

Call to Worship

A
Jesus is the Christ,
the Son of the living God.   *Matt. 16:16*

> *Or*

B
Lord, to whom can we go?
You have the words of eternal life.
We have come to believe and know
that you are the Holy One of God.   *John 6:68*

> *Or*

I am the way, and the truth, and the life, says the Lord.
No one comes to the Father except through me.   *John 14:6*

Prayer of the Day

Almighty God,
we are taught by your word
that all our deeds without love are worth nothing.
Send your Holy Spirit and pour into our hearts
that most excellent gift of love,
the true bond of peace and of all virtue;
through Jesus Christ our Lord,
who lives and reigns with you and the Holy Spirit,
one God, now and forever.[167]

Amen.

Or

A
O God, fount of all wisdom,
in the humble witness of the apostle Peter
you have shown the foundation of our faith.
Give us the light of your Spirit,
that, recognizing in Jesus of Nazareth
the Son of the living God,
we may be living stones
for the building up of your holy church,
through Jesus Christ our Lord,
who lives and reigns with you
in the unity of the Holy Spirit,
one God, forever and ever.[168]

Amen.

TWENTY-SECOND SUNDAY IN ORDINARY TIME

Sunday between August 28 and September 3 inclusive

Call to Worship

A
If any want to become my followers,
let them deny themselves
and take up their cross and follow me.   *Matt. 16:24*

Or

God gave us birth by the word of truth,
so that we would become a kind of first fruits of his creatures.
James 1:18

Or

Take my yoke upon you, and learn from me;
for I am gentle and humble in heart,
and you will find rest for your souls.   *Matt. 11:29*

Prayer of the Day

God of power,
author and giver of all good things,
graft in our hearts the love of your name,
increase in us true religion,
nourish us in all goodness,
and keep us in your great mercy;
through Jesus Christ our Lord.[169]

Amen.

Or

C
O God,
you call the poor and the sinful to take their place
in the festive assembly of the new covenant.
May your church always honor the presence of the Lord
in the humble and the suffering,
and may we learn to recognize each other
as brothers and sisters,
gathered together around your table.
We ask this through our Lord Jesus Christ,
who lives and reigns with you
in the unity of the Holy Spirit,
one God, forever and ever.[170]

Amen.

TWENTY-THIRD SUNDAY IN ORDINARY TIME

Sunday between September 4 and 10 inclusive

Call to Worship

In Christ God was reconciling the world to Godself,
not counting their trespasses against them,
and entrusting the message of reconciliation to us.   *2 Cor. 5:19*

Or

B

Every generous act of giving,
with every perfect gift,
is from above,
coming down from the Father of lights,
with whom there is no variation
or shadow due to change.   *James 1:17*

Or

C

Make your face shine upon your servant
and teach me your statutes.   *Ps. 119:135*

Prayer of the Day

Lord of the ages,
you have called your church
to keep watch in the life of the world
and to discern the signs of the times.
Grant us the wisdom which your Spirit bestows,
that with courage we may proclaim your prophetic word,
and as faithful disciples and witnesses of the cross
may finish the work you have given us to do;
through Jesus Christ our Lord.[171]

Amen.

TWENTY-FOURTH SUNDAY IN ORDINARY TIME

Sunday between September 11 and 17 inclusive

Call to Worship

I give you a new commandment,
that you love one another
as I have loved you.   *John 13:34*

Or

May I never boast of anything
except the cross of our Lord Jesus Christ,
by which the world has been crucified to me,
and I to the world.   *Gal. 6:14*

Or

C

There is joy in the presence of the angels of God
over one sinner who repents.   *Luke 15:10*

Prayer of the Day

Almighty God,
you call your church to witness
that in Christ we are reconciled to you.
Help us so to proclaim the good news of your love,
that all who hear it may turn to you;
through Jesus Christ our Lord,
who lives and reigns with you and the Holy Spirit,
one God, now and forever.[172]

Amen.

TWENTY-FIFTH SUNDAY IN ORDINARY TIME

Sunday between September 18 and 24 inclusive

Call to Worship

It is my prayer that your love may abound more and more,
so that you may approve what is excellent,
and may be pure and blameless for the day of Christ.   *Phil. 1:9, 10*

Or

You know the grace of our Lord Jesus Christ,
that though he was rich,
yet for your sake he became poor,
so that by his poverty you might become rich.   *2 Cor. 8:9*

Prayer of the Day

Almighty God,
you have created the heavens and the earth,
and ourselves in your image.
Teach us to discern your hand in all your works
and to serve you with reverence and thanksgiving;
through Jesus Christ our Lord,
who is alive and reigns with you and the Holy Spirit,
one God, now and forever.[173]

Amen.

  Or

B
God and Father of all,
you have willed that the last should be first,
and you have made a little child the measure of your kingdom.
Give us that wisdom which is from above,
so we may understand that, in your sight,
the greatest of all is the one who serves.
We ask this through our Lord Jesus Christ,
who lives and reigns with you
in the unity of the Holy Spirit,
one God, forever and ever.[174]

Amen.

TWENTY-SIXTH SUNDAY IN ORDINARY TIME

Sunday between September 25 and October 1 inclusive

Call to Worship

O taste and see that the Lord is good;
happy are those who take refuge in the Lord.   *Ps. 34:8*

  Or

Your word, O Lord, is truth;
Sanctify us in the truth.   *John 17:17*

You know the grace of our Lord Jesus Christ,
that though he was rich,
yet for your sake he became poor,
so that by his poverty you might become rich.   *2 Cor. 8:9*

Prayer of the Day

Grant, O merciful God,
that your church,
being gathered by your Holy Spirit into one,
may show forth your power among all peoples,
to the glory of your name;
through Jesus Christ our Lord,
who lives and reigns with you and the Holy Spirit,
one God, now and forever.[175]

Amen.

TWENTY-SEVENTH SUNDAY IN ORDINARY TIME

Sunday between October 2 and 8 inclusive

Call to Worship

I chose you and appointed you, says the Lord,
to go and bear fruit,
fruit that will last.   *John 15:16*

Or

God is love,
and those who abide in love abide in God,
and God abides in them.   *1 John 4:16b*

Or

C
God did not give us a spirit of cowardice,
but rather a spirit of power and of love
and of self-discipline.   *2 Tim. 1:7*

Prayer of the Day

Almighty God,
you have built your church
on the foundation of the apostles and prophets,
Jesus Christ himself being the chief cornerstone.
Join us together in unity of spirit by their teaching,
that we may become a holy temple, acceptable to you;
through Jesus Christ our Lord,
who lives and reigns with you and the Holy Spirit,
one God, now and forever.[176]

Amen.

TWENTY-EIGHTH SUNDAY IN ORDINARY TIME

Sunday between October 9 and 15 inclusive

Call to Worship

May God give you a spirit of wisdom and revelation
so that you may know the hope to which you are called.

Eph. 1:17, 18

Or

I will put my laws in their minds,
and write them on their hearts,
and I will be their God,
and they shall be my people.

Heb. 8:10

Or

Give thanks in all circumstances
for this is the will of God in Christ Jesus for you.　　　*1 Thess. 5:18*

Prayer of the Day

Almighty God,
in our baptism you adopted us for your own.
Quicken, we pray, your Spirit within us,
that we, being renewed both in body and mind,
may worship you in sincerity and truth;
through Jesus Christ our Lord,

who lives and reigns with you and the Holy Spirit,
one God, now and forever.[177]

Amen.

TWENTY-NINTH SUNDAY IN ORDINARY TIME

Sunday between October 16 and 22 inclusive

Call to Worship

Shine like stars in the world,
holding fast to the word of life.   *Phil. 2:15, 16*

  Or

The Son of Man came not to be served
but to serve,
and to give his life a ransom for many.   *Mark 10:45*

  Or

The word of God is living and active.
It is able to judge the thoughts and intentions of the heart.
                Heb. 4:12

Prayer of the Day

Almighty and everlasting God,
in Christ you have revealed your glory among the nations.
Preserve the works of your mercy,
that your church throughout the world
may persevere with steadfast faith
in the confession of your name;
through Jesus Christ our Lord.[178]

Amen.

THIRTIETH SUNDAY IN ORDINARY TIME

Sunday between October 23 and 29 inclusive

Call to Worship

Those who love me will keep my word,
and my Father will love them,

and we will come to them
and make our home with them. *John 14:23*

Or

Our Savior Christ Jesus abolished death,
and brought life and immortality to light through the gospel.
2 Tim. 1:10

Or

In Christ God was reconciling the world to Godself,
not counting their trespasses against them,
and entrusting the message of reconciliation to us. *2 Cor. 5:19*

Prayer of the Day

Almighty and everlasting God,
increase in us the gifts of faith, hope, and love;
and, that we may obtain what you promise,
make us love what you command;
through your Son, Jesus Christ our Lord.[179]

Amen.

THIRTY-FIRST SUNDAY IN ORDINARY TIME

Sunday between October 30 and November 5 inclusive

Call to Worship

A
You have one Father, who is in heaven.
You have one Teacher, the Christ. *Matt. 23:9, 10*

Or

Those who love me will keep my word,
and my Father will love them,
and we will come to them
and make our home with them. *John 14:23*

Prayer of the Day

Lord our God,
in Jesus Christ you have taught us
that love is the fulfilling of the law.
Send your Holy Spirit upon us,
and pour into our hearts
that most excellent gift of love,
that we may love you with our whole being,
and our neighbors as ourselves;
through Jesus Christ our Lord.[180]

Amen.

THIRTY-SECOND SUNDAY IN ORDINARY TIME

Sunday between November 6 and 12 inclusive

Call to Worship

Watch and be ready,
for you do not know on what day your
Lord is coming.   *Matt. 24:42, 44*

Or

Blessed are the poor in spirit,
for theirs is the kingdom of heaven.   *Matt. 5:3*

Or

Jesus Christ, the firstborn of the dead . . .
to him be glory and dominion forever and ever.   *Rev. 1:5, 6*

Prayer of the Day

O God,
whose blessed Son came into the world
that he might destroy the works of evil
and make us children of God and heirs of eternal life:
Grant that, having this hope,
we may purify ourselves as he is pure;
that, when he comes again with power and great glory,

we may be made like him
in his eternal and glorious kingdom;
where he lives and reigns with you and the Holy Spirit,
one God, forever and ever.[181]

Amen.

THIRTY-THIRD SUNDAY IN ORDINARY TIME

Sunday between November 13 and 19 inclusive

Call to Worship

Be alert at all times,
praying that you may stand before the Son of Man.   *Luke 21:36*

> Or

Look up and raise your heads,
because your redemption is drawing near.   *Luke 21:28*

Prayer of the Day

Everliving God,
before the earth was formed
and even after it shall cease to be, you are God.
Break into our short span of life
and show us those things that are eternal,
that we may serve your purpose in all we do,
through Jesus Christ our Lord.[182]

Amen.

> Or

Almighty God,
whose sovereign purpose none can make void:
Give us faith to be steadfast
amid the tumults of this world,
knowing that your kingdom shall come
and your will be done,
to your eternal glory;

through Jesus Christ our Lord,
who lives and reigns with you and the Holy Spirit,
one God, now and forever.[183]

Amen.

ALL SAINTS' DAY—NOVEMBER 1

All Saints' Day may be celebrated on the first Sunday in November.

CALL TO WORSHIP AND
PRAYER OF THE DAY

Call to Worship

A

After this I looked,
and there was a great multitude that no one could count,
from every nation, from all tribes and peoples and languages,
standing before the throne and before the Lamb,
robed in white, with palm branches in their hands.
They cried out in a loud voice, saying:

**Salvation belongs to our God
who is seated on the throne,
and to the Lamb!**   *Rev. 7:9–10*

Or

B

Since we are surrounded by so great a cloud of witnesses,
let us also lay aside every weight,
and the sin that clings so closely,

and let us run with perseverance the race that is set before us.
Heb. 12:1

Or

C

People will come from east and west,
from north and south,

and will eat in the kingdom of heaven.   *Luke 13:29*

Prayer of the Day

Eternal God,
from whose love neither death nor life can separate us:

Grant that we may serve you faithfully here on earth,
and in heaven rejoice with all your saints,
who ceaselessly proclaim your glory;
through Jesus Christ our Lord,
who lives and reigns with you and the Holy Spirit,
one God, forever and ever.[184]

Amen.

PRAYER OF CONFESSION

Eternal God,
in every age you have raised up men and women
to live and die in faith.
Forgive our indifference to your will.
You have commanded us to speak,
but we have been silent.
You have called us to do what is just,
but we have been fearful.
Have mercy on us, your faithless servants.
Keep before us faithful people for us to follow,
so that living with courage and love,
we may inherit the kingdom promised in Jesus Christ,
and reign with him forever.[185]

GREAT PRAYER OF THANKSGIVING

It is recommended that, with this prayer, the invitation to the Lord's Table "Friends, this is the joyful feast. . . ." (text no. 180 in The Service for the Lord's Day, *Supplemental Liturgical Resource 1, be used, and that the words of institution (text no. 209 in the same resource) accompany the breaking of the bread.*

The Lord be with you.

And also with you.

Lift up your hearts.

We lift them to the Lord.

Let us give thanks to the Lord our God.

It is right to give our thanks and praise.

It is truly right and our greatest joy
to give you thanks and praise,
O Lord our God, creator and ruler of the universe.

We praise you for saints and martyrs,
for the faithful in every age,
who have followed your Son
and witnessed to his resurrection.
From every race and tongue,
from every people and nation,
you have gathered them into your kingdom.
You have shown them the path of life
and filled them with the joy of your presence.
How glorious is your heavenly kingdom
where the multitude of your saints rejoice with Christ!

Therefore, we praise you,
joining our voices with choirs of angels,
with prophets, apostles, and martyrs,
and with all the faithful of every time and place,
who forever sing to the glory of your name:

The following may be sung or said:

Holy, holy, holy Lord, God of power and might,
heaven and earth are full of your glory.
  Hosanna in the highest.

Blessed is he who comes in the name of the Lord.
  Hosanna in the highest.

Holy are you, O Lord,
and blessed is your only Son, Jesus Christ,
sent to be our Savior.
Taking our flesh, he dwelt among us
full of grace and truth.
His words are true.
His touch brings healing.
To those who follow him, he gives abundant life.
When evil sought to destroy him,
and he lay in the darkness of death,
you raised him from the grave.
He is our risen Lord forever!

In remembrance of your mighty acts in Jesus Christ,
we take this bread and this wine
and celebrate his death and resurrection,
as we await the day of his coming.

We offer ourselves as a living and holy sacrifice,
dedicated to your service,
that our lives may proclaim the mystery of faith:

Christ has died,
Christ is risen,
Christ will come again.

Gracious God,
pour out your Holy Spirit
upon us and upon these your gifts of bread and wine,
that the bread we break and the cup we bless
may be the communion of the body and blood of Christ.

By your Spirit unite us with Christ,
and with the faithful of every time and place,
that, strengthened by their witness
and supported by their fellowship,
we may run with perseverance the race that is set before us,
and with them receive the unfading crown of glory,
and feast together in your eternal kingdom.

Through Christ, with Christ, in Christ,
in the unity of the Holy Spirit,
all glory and honor, praise and adoration are yours,
now and forever.[186]

Amen.

PRAYER OF THANKS

For use when the Eucharist is not celebrated.

Let us give thanks to the Lord our God.

It is right to give our thanks and praise.

God of the ages,
we praise you for all your servants,
who have done justice, loved mercy,
and walked humbly with their God.

For apostles and martyrs and saints
of every time and place,
who in life and death have witnessed to your truth,

we praise you, O God.

For all your servants who have faithfully served you,
witnessed bravely and died in faith,
who still are shining lights in the world,

we praise you, O God.

For those no more remembered,
who earnestly sought you in darkness,
who held fast their faith in trial,
and served others,

we praise you, O God.

For those we have known and loved,
who by their faithful obedience and steadfast hope
have shown the same mind that was in Christ Jesus,

we praise you, O God.

Keep us grateful for their witness,
and, like them, eager to follow in the way of Christ.
Then at the last, bring us with them
to share in the inheritance of the saints in light;
through Jesus Christ our Savior.[187]

Amen.

CHRIST THE KING

Sunday between November 20 and 26 inclusive

CALL TO WORSHIP AND PRAYER OF THE DAY

Call to Worship

The Lord is a great God who says:
I am the Alpha and Omega,
the first and the last,
the beginning and the end. *Rev. 22:13*

Or

Blessed is the one who comes in the name of the Lord!
Hosanna in the highest! *Mark 11:9, 10b*

Prayer of the Day

God of power and love,
you raised Jesus from death to life,
resplendent in glory to rule over all creation.
Free the world to rejoice in his peace,
to glory in his justice,
and to live in his love.
Unite all humankind in Jesus Christ your Son,
whose kingdom is with you and the Holy Spirit,
one God, forever and ever.[188]

Amen.

Or

Almighty and everlasting God,
whose will is to restore all things
in your well-beloved Son, our Lord and King,
grant that the people of earth,
now divided and enslaved by sin,
may be freed and brought together
under his gentle and loving rule;

who lives and reigns with you and the Holy Spirit,
one God, now and forever.[189]

Amen.

Or

Eternal God,
you set Jesus Christ to rule over all things,
and made us servants in your kingdom.
By your Spirit empower us to love the unloved,
and to minister to all in need.
Then at the last bring us to your eternal realm,
where we may worship and adore you
and be welcomed into your everlasting joy;
through Jesus Christ our Lord,
who lives and reigns with you and the Holy Spirit,
one God, now and forever.[190]

Amen.

GREAT PRAYER OF THANKSGIVING

The Lord be with you.

And also with you.

Lift up your hearts.

We lift them to the Lord.

Let us give thanks to the Lord our God.

It is right to give our thanks and praise.

It is right to give you thanks and praise,
for you fashioned this world in love,
and rule over all the earth with grace and peace.
Nations and monarchs rise and fall,
but your reign is for all time,
and your mercy is without end.

In love you made us to love and serve you.
When we have turned from you
and bent our knees to gods of our own making,

you spoke through prophets
to bring us back to your ways.
You gave us a vision of your holy kingdom
that we might hunger after righteousness
and thirst for justice,
and long for the day when peace will triumph mightily
over the pride and greed of nations.

Therefore, we praise you,
singing with the servants around heaven's throne
and with all the faithful of every time and place,
to the glory of your mighty name:

Holy, holy, holy Lord, God of power and might,
heaven and earth are full of your glory.
   Hosanna in the highest.

Blessed is he who comes in the name of the Lord.
   Hosanna in the highest.

You are holy, O God of majesty,
and blessed is Jesus Christ your Son, our Lord.
Born as king in David's line,
he lived with the lowly
and cared for the least of your children.
His power was revealed in weakness,
his majesty in mercy.
His captors knelt before him in ridicule,
giving him bruises instead of praises,
and piercing thorns for a crown.
His only earthly throne was a cross to die on.
Even there his arms stretched out
to embrace friends and foes in love.
From the grave you raised him to your right hand
where he rules again from heaven,
and commands true loyalty from peoples and nations.

> *The words of institution may be said here, or in relation to the*
> *breaking of the bread.*

[On the night before he died,
Jesus took bread.
After giving thanks to you, he broke it,
and gave it to his disciples, saying,
"Take, eat.
This is my body, given for you.
Do this in remembrance of me."

In the same way he took the cup, saying,
"This cup is the new covenant sealed in my blood,
shed for you for the forgiveness of sins.
Do this in remembrance of me."]

Remembering your sovereign rule in Jesus Christ,
we take this bread and this wine
and celebrate this holy sacrament.
With thanksgiving we offer our very selves to you
to be a living and holy sacrifice
dedicated to your service.

So we proclaim the mystery of faith:

Christ has died,
Christ is risen,
Christ will come again.

Gracious God, give us your Holy Spirit,
that these your gifts to us of bread and wine
may be a communion in the body and blood of Christ,
a foretaste of the banquet in his kingdom.

By your Spirit make us one with Christ,
that we may be one with all who share this feast.
Unite us in ministry to be your emissaries throughout the world,
until Christ comes in final victory
and we feast with him in eternity.

Through Christ, with Christ, in Christ,
in the unity of the Holy Spirit,
all glory and honor, praise and adoration are yours,
now and forever.[191]

Amen.

PRAYER OF THANKS

For use when the Eucharist is not celebrated.

Let us give thanks to the Lord our God.

It is right to give our thanks and praise.

We praise you, great God,
for you are Ruler of the universe,
and have sent your Son to be King of kings.
We rejoice that he has triumphed
   over all the powers of this world,
and governs the nations in justice and righteousness.
We celebrate his victory
in his life, death, resurrection,
   and ascension to honor and might at your side.
By your Spirit,
claim our complete loyalty,
establish Christ's rule
   in every land and in every heart.
Accept our homage
as we offer our lives in the service of Christ's kingdom.[192]

Amen.

COMMENTARY ON THE
LITURGICAL RESOURCES

AN OUTLINE OF
THE SERVICE FOR THE LORD'S DAY

GATHERING
Call to Worship
Prayer of the Day
Hymn of Praise
Confession of Sin
Declaration of Pardon
Act of Praise

LITURGY OF THE WORD
Prayer for Illumination
First Lesson
Psalm
Second Lesson
Hymn, Spiritual, or Anthem
Gospel Lesson
Sermon
Creed or Affirmation of Faith
Prayers of Intercession
The Peace
Offering

*If the Eucharist
is not celebrated:*

THE EUCHARIST

Invitation to the Lord's Table	
Great Prayer of Thanksgiving, concluding with the Lord's Prayer	Prayer of Thanks, concluding with the Lord's Prayer
Breaking of the Bread	
Communion of the People	
Prayer after Communion	

SENDING
Hymn, Spiritual, or Psalm
Charge and Blessing

HOW TO USE THIS RESOURCE

The liturgical texts in the previous section are intended for use with the order of service contained in *The Service for the Lord's Day*, Supplemental Liturgical Resource 1.[1] On the opposite page is an outline of that order of service with slight modifications resulting from testing since *The Service for the Lord's Day* was published.

This resource supplements the texts available in that volume by providing texts for use during the festivals and seasons in the liturgical calendar. You will find the following in this resource (pp. 61–270):

Call to Worship
Prayer of the Day
Prayer of Confession
Great Prayer of Thanksgiving
Prayer of Thanks

Call to Worship

Sentences of scripture are provided for use as a call to worship. There is a text for each Sunday and festival. When a text relates to the lectionary readings for a particular day, it is identified with an A, B, or C, indicating the cycle for which its use is intended. A combination AB, AC, or BC indicates that it is appropriate for use in either of the two cycles identified. If no letter appears, the text is appropriate on that day in any of the three cycles.

Prayer of the Day

A prayer of the day is provided for each Sunday and festival. As with the sentences of scripture, many have a direct relationship with the lectionary readings for the particular day, and are also so indicated with A, B, C, AB, AC, or BC.

The prayer of the day may be used in either of two ways. It may be used as an opening prayer, and would immediately follow the call to worship. This would enable a prayer for illumination to be used (texts 101–111 in *The Service for the Lord's Day*). Or the prayer of the day may be used to conclude the opening rite, which is here called: Gathering. When this is done, a prayer for illumination would not be used before the readings from scripture. The alternatives are as follows:

Or

GATHERING	**GATHERING**
Call to Worship	Call to Worship
Prayer of the Day	
Hymn of Praise	Hymn of Praise
Confession of Sin	Confession of Sin
Declaration of Pardon	Declaration of Pardon
Act of Praise	Act of Praise
	Prayer of the Day

LITURGY OF THE WORD	**LITURGY OF THE WORD**
Prayer for Illumination	
First Lesson	First Lesson
Psalm	Psalm
. . .	. . .

Prayer of Confession

The prayers of confession supplement those in *The Service for the Lord's Day* (texts 74–82) and are provided for each season and festival. They may be used as alternatives to those in *The Service for the Lord's Day*.

Great Prayer of Thanksgiving

While recognizing that the norm of Christian worship is to celebrate the Lord's Supper as often as each Lord's day, for several years Presbyterian churches have been encouraged to celebrate the Lord's Supper at least on those days which are especially appropriate to celebrate the Sacrament. These are:

First Sunday of Advent
Christmas Eve
Christmas Day
Epiphany
Baptism of the Lord
Transfiguration of the Lord
First Sunday in Lent
Passion/Palm Sunday
Maundy Thursday
The Paschal Vigil
Easter Sunday
All other Sundays of the Easter season
Ascension of the Lord
Pentecost
World Communion Sunday
All Saints' Day
Christ the King.[2]

Churches following this pattern ordinarily will also celebrate the Sacrament at least monthly during Ordinary Time. This breaks the pattern of mechanically scheduling an observance according to the secular calendar (e.g., first Sunday of each quarter, or first Sunday of each month). By celebrating the Sacrament on the festivals that focus our attention on the saving acts of God in Jesus Christ, people will the more readily associate the Sacrament with the Gospel story. This especially will be true if the eucharistic prayer recounts the fullness of that story. The Eucharist will the more readily be received as a feast of celebrating the fullness of God's revelation, rather than being simply a memory aid to ponder the death of Jesus.

With this increase in frequency of eucharistic celebration, there is a need for more eucharistic prayers. This resource addresses this need. Fifteen new eucharistic prayers are included in this resource with a separate prayer for each festival and season. These prayers incorporate images and themes of the particular day or season.

Among the eight eucharistic prayers in *The Service for the Lord's Day* are three (texts A, C, and F) that include prefaces for use on the various festivals of the liturgical calendar.[3] The new prayers are offered for use along with those in *The Service for the Lord's Day*. The prayers in *The Service for the Lord's Day* will continue to provide variety during Ordinary Time.

In this resource, the particular text for the invitation to the Lord's Table, or for the breaking of the bread from *The Service for the Lord's Day*, is suggested in some instances. Where no such suggestion is given, the Words of Institution may be said before the prayer (as a warrant), or during the prayer (as one of the mighty acts of God for which we give God praise), or after the prayer (with the breaking of the bread). The Words of Institution are always to be included in a celebration of the Lord's Supper, but are said only once in a service.

Prayer of Thanks

At least one prayer of thanks is provided for each season and festival. This prayer is for use when the Eucharist is not celebrated. It is used in the place in the order where the eucharistic prayer is normally said (see outline of the service on page 274).

Other Texts

A prayer of adoration is provided for Christmas (p. 73) and for Easter (p. 204). This is for use immediately after the call to worship and may be used instead of the prayer of the day when that prayer is used as an opening prayer.

A text for lighting of the Advent candles and a Litany for Advent are provided. A Litany for Pentecost and a Litany of Intercession for Pentecost are also provided. These will be discussed below in relation to Advent and Pentecost.

Music (pages 325–412)

A variety of refrains are provided for the seasons and festivals for singing at various places in the liturgy.

A refrain may appropriately be interjected, sensitively and creatively, at several places in a service. Normally, only one refrain is used in a single service, although it may be repeated at several places in the service, thereby contributing a sense of unity to the service.

Examples include: following the call to worship, before and/or follow-ing the confession of sin, between the reading of the second lesson and the Gospel lesson, preceding the prayers of intercession or be-tween the petitions of the intercession, after the charge and blessing.

Most of the refrains written by John Weaver are responsorial. The refrain is easily grasped by a congregation since it is lined out by a cantor (soloist) or choir. The refrain is always sung first by the cantor or choir, the congregation then repeats it. Because it is lined out for the worshipers, there is no need to reproduce it in a church bulletin. In this way a greater sense of spontaneity is conveyed.

Additional refrains are set to simple tones or melodies that are easy for a congregation to learn and sing. Congregations that have pur-chased this resource are free to reproduce the melody line and text of these refrains (as they appear on pages 405–412) in a church bulletin for a one-time use without seeking permission (see copyright page). Lines from hymns that may be used as refrains are also suggested (pages 373–375).

Two settings for the Exsultet for use in the Paschal Vigil are also included in the music section for use by a cantor or choir and accom-panist. The text and music as they appear on pages 186–190 may be reproduced and placed in a church bulletin to enable the congregation to participate.

Services

It was noted above that the Service for the Lord's Day is the basic order into which texts in this resource are to be incorporated. There-fore, the only complete services in this resource are those which deviate significantly from the structure of the Service for the Lord's Day. Each of these services will be discussed in the commentary that follows.

THE CHRISTMAS CYCLE

Advent

Advent originated as a three-week fast in preparation for baptism at Epiphany, and it evolved into a period of preparation for the coming of Christ as judge, and so assumed a penitential mood, a shorter Lent. In contrast, Advent today is seen as a season of hope and joy, anticipating the fulfillment of the rule of God in Christ's coming in the future. The scripture that is read, the liturgical texts used, the music, the environment, and the ceremonial actions should all convey this sense of expectant, joyful longing for the fulfillment of God's promised reign.

Lighting of the Advent Candles (pages 61–62)

The hanging of an Advent wreath during the season is a common feature of Advent. The Advent wreath is a large wreath with four candles in the wreath itself, and often with another candle in the center. A candle is lighted the first week and an additional one each week thereafter, culminating in the lighting of the center one on Christmas. Ordinarily, the wreath candles are purple (or blue), the color traditional to the season, and the center candle white. In some traditions the candle that is lighted on the Third Sunday of Advent is rose-colored. Some congregations replace the candles with white candles for Christmas Eve.

The origin of the Advent wreath is obscure. It apparently emanated from the Lutheran tradition, but it has been appropriated by almost all other traditions. A review of the origin of the wreath makes it clear that the candles do *not* represent any single event, person, or doctrine. What the candles do signify and communicate is the increasing crescendo of light throughout the season. The dominant natural symbol is *increasing* light during Advent. As Advent draws nearer to Christmas, the congregation experiences the increasing brightness radiated by the wreath. This is the significance of the wreath, and should not be lost by trying to give each candle some special meaning such as hope, joy, shepherds, angels, etc. Let the focus be not on the proper meaning of the candles, but on the light generated by the candles. The tradition of the lighting of candles on the Advent wreath is simply a symbol, powerful though it may be, that helps us experience the cruciality of the coming Christmas season.

People remember the lighting of a growing number of candles throughout the weeks of Advent. The lighting of the Advent wreath often triggers memories and hopes of the season. Music, mood, colors, signs, biblical texts are recalled, and, above all, the symbol of lighting candles on a wreath.

On pages 61–62 is a model for lighting the Advent wreath based on the Common Lectionary's Old Testament readings for the weeks of Advent (Cycle A). No attempt is made to identify each candle with any person, event, or doctrine. Rather, the natural symbol of light is simply accompanied by biblical word-pictures of the coming Savior. By combining the reading of "stories" of the hopes of Advent with the lighting of candles on a wreath insures that the growing light serves to reflect on and flow from the Word.

Instructions for Lighting the Advent Wreath. Invite different persons for each of the four Sundays of Advent, as well as for Christmas Eve, to *light* a candle on the Advent wreath, and/or *read* an appropriate text.

In selecting people, try to include a broad range of persons—a cross-section of the entire congregation (e.g., young child, "senior citizen," college student, teenager, middle-aged parent or single person, and so forth). "Twosomes" or even "threesomes" are encouraged, particularly during the second half of Advent when the reading portion becomes extended and, therefore, can be shared. (Note: Since, this is *not* a nuclear family event, but a *church family* ritual, nuclear family teams are ordinarily discouraged, and combinations of random members of the congregation are encouraged.)

Distribute to each person, well in advance, appropriate instructions for lighting of the wreath. To be sure everyone understands what is expected, rehearse the lighting of the candle(s).

Third Sunday of Advent. A frequently asked question is, "Why do some churches light a pink or rose-colored candle on the Third Sunday of Advent?"

During the fourth century in Gaul, Advent evolved as a period of preparation for the coming of Christ as judge and, therefore, its mood was penitential.

In the Middle Ages, the appointed epistle for the Third Sunday of Advent was Philippians 4:4–6, which begins with the Latin word *Gaudete,* meaning "rejoice": "Rejoice in the Lord always; again I will say, Rejoice. Let your gentleness be known to everyone. The Lord is near." Philippians 4:4–6 also served as the introit for the day (entrance song), which was interspersed by the antiphon of Psalm 84:2: "My soul longs, indeed it faints for the courts of the LORD; my heart and flesh sing for joy to the living God."

Thus, the penitential mood of Advent was momentarily suspended by the joyous character of the Philippians text. Since this anticipated joy of the end time was an exception during a penitential Advent, Paul's injunction to the Philippians, *Gaudete in Domino semper* ("Rejoice in the Lord always") had the effect of interrupting the period of fasting. Therefore, the opening word of the text gave its name to this Third Sunday of Advent, Gaudete Sunday, by which it is still known in some traditions. And, a candle on the Advent wreath was changed to pink or rose as a sign of a brief delight in the midst of fasting in preparation for the Christmas feast. In traditions where the Third Sunday of Advent is observed as Gaudete Sunday, the paraments are also rose.

In the Common Lectionary, we find this Philippians text as the appointed epistle for the Third Sunday of Advent in Year C. On that same day and cycle, you will also hear Zephaniah's psalm of celebration (3:14–20): "Rejoice and exult with all your heart."

In Year B, the Common Lectionary's appointed epistle for the Third Sunday of Advent is 1 Thessalonians 5:16–24, in which, at the close of one of his earliest letters, Paul offers some final admonitions, beginning with the words, "Rejoice always."

In Year A, the Common Lectionary's appointed Old Testament text for the Third Sunday of Advent is Isaiah 35:1–10, in which the opening metaphor concerns the transformation of the land: "The desert will rejoice, and the *rose* will bloom in the wastelands. The desert will sing and shout for joy." Do you believe the messianic rose can bloom in the wilderness?

The decision to use or not to use a pink or rose candle on the Third Sunday of Advent is at the discretion of particular churches. With or without the pink candle, the biblical note of joy on this Third Sunday of Advent does intensify the anticipation, for truly, "The Lord is near" (Phil. 4:5b).

Litany of Advent—O Antiphons (pages 71–72)

The Litany for Advent incorporates a series of texts called the O Antiphons, so called because all seven of them begin with the interjection "O."

The O Antiphons, with their recurring "Come, Lord Jesus," effectively capture the hope of Advent. During the season, the biblical readings selected from Isaiah and other prophets announce the coming of the Messiah. The closer Christmas comes to us, the more the liturgy accentuates its call to the Savior with the cry, *Veni!* ("Come!"). Ultimately, "Come" is humanity's only valid prayer: it sums up all of our needs of God. Ever since the expulsion from paradise, "Come" has been the ceaseless cry of humanity.[4]

While we do not know for sure when or by whom the O Antiphons were conceived, they probably originated in Rome about the ninth century. They enjoyed great popularity during the Middle Ages.

For centuries each O Antiphon has been sung on one of the seven days (December 17–23) preceding the Vigil of Christmas (December 24). Traditionally, they are sung in full both before and after the canticle (Canticle of Mary, the Magnificat: Luke 1:46–55) during Vespers (evening prayer) on the following days:

Dec. 17—"O Wisdom . . ."	*Proverbs 8:22*
Dec. 18—"O Adonai . . ."	*Exodus 20:2*
Dec. 19—"O Root of Jesse . . ."	*Isaiah 11:1, 10*
Dec. 20—"O Key of David . . ."	*Isaiah 22:22*
Dec. 21—"O Radiant Dawn . . ."	*Zechariah 6:12*
Dec. 22—"O Ruler of the Nations . . ."	*Haggai 2:8*
Dec. 23—"O Immanuel . . ."	*Isaiah 7:14*

Each antiphon is addressed to the Son, and begins with an exclamation which is a scriptural title: "O Wisdom!" "O Adonai!" The title is then amplified with other biblical images.[5] The antiphon concludes with a petition to the coming Savior. Each is structured in this way:

Address—invocation to the Messiah with a title inspired by the Old Testament (e.g., "O Wisdom")

Amplification—stating an attribute of the Messiah, and foreshadowing the petition (e.g., "coming forth from the mouth of the Most High, pervading and permeating all creation, you order all things with strength and gentleness")

Appeal/Petition—commencing always with "Come" and referring to the initial invocation (e.g., "come now and teach us the way to salvation")

The litany incorporating the O Antiphons is provided for use on the Sunday that falls on or between December 17 and 23. It may be used at the beginning of the service instead of the prayer of the day, and is especially effective when sung.

In using the litany in the liturgy, a cantor (soloist) sings the O Antiphons, either improvising or using a chant tone, and the congregation sings the refrain "Come, Lord Jesus." In the service, the cantor first sings the refrain. The congregation then repeats it. This familiarizes the congregation with the refrain. The cantor then sings each of the O Antiphons. At the conclusion of each O Antiphon, the cantor with a simple motion of the hand invites the congregation to sing the refrain. Silence follows the singing of the refrain after the last O Antiphon. The concluding petition is then spoken by a worship leader. The litany is most effective when sung without organ accompaniment, with a handbell striking the note at the beginning of each O Antiphon.

The tone for Psalm 146 (number 254) in *The Presbyterian Hymnal*[6] with refrain 26 in this book (pages 360, 405) may effectively be employed for singing the litany. Tone 5 on page 3 of *Psalm Refrains and Tones for the Common Lectionary*, by Hal H. Hopson[7] with refrain 26 in this book (pages 360, 405), is an alternative, as is one of the tones (or combination of tones 1–4) on page 8 of the same resource, with refrain 51 in this book (pages 368, 410). Other tones are available in *The Psalter*.[8]

Congregations may find use of the O Antiphons enriching in other ways as well. Most congregations do not currently conduct evening prayer on the seven days (December 17–23) preceding Christmas Eve, when the O Antiphons traditionally are sung. An alternative to daily use might be to sing all seven of the O Antiphons throughout the service on the Fourth Sunday of Advent. A fine series of settings of the O Antiphons by John Weaver may be found in *Reformed Liturgy*

& *Music*, vol. 23, no. 3 (Fall 1988), pp. 152–166. Or, stanzas of the familiar hymn "O Come, O Come, Emmanuel" (tune: VENI EMMAN-UEL) may be used in the same way.

The text for the hymn "O Come, O Come, Emmanuel" derives from the Latin O Antiphons and originally was sung responsively by two choirs seated opposite each other in the chancel. In the twelfth century, the antiphons were reduced from seven to five, and made into the hymn "O Come, O Come, Emmanuel," with a refrain added (tune: VENI EMMANUEL). It is this hymn with which we are now familiar.[9]

Since the O Antiphons allow worshipers to express their "ceaseless cry," the O Antiphons should be played and sung boldly. O Antiphons are neither mournful nor plaintive in mood, but insistent, outspoken, almost a demanding cry for the Lord to come. Because they are very poetic and symbolic, the O Antiphons increase the feeling of expectancy and longing for the coming of Christ.

Customarily, the largest bell was rung throughout the singing of the O Antiphon and the Canticle of Mary (Magnificat—Luke 1:46–55), which it accompanied. Thus, it would be desirable to ring the largest bell available during the singing of the antiphons during Advent, but particularly on the Fourth Sunday of Advent if all the O Antiphons are sung.

Music and Environment for Advent

Music. The selection of music for Advent may be difficult for many congregations. The scriptures invite us to wait, watch, and prepare. Musical responses reflect these messages and bid Christ come: "Maranatha," "O Come, O Come, Immanuel." The music of the season should move from reflection on Christ's coming at the end of time to preparing for celebrating Christ's first coming. Careful consideration of instrumentation can enhance the mood of Advent. Consider, on occasion, use of a capella singing to create a sense of longing. Consider also instrumentation of hymns intended to convey expectancy. The Advent section in *The Presbyterian Hymnal*, and some responses from *Music from Taizé*, and the responses on pages 329–330, 360 of this resource will assist the congregation in understanding the dual nature of the season.

Neither the readings in the lectionary for Advent nor our understanding of the nature of the season of Advent lend themselves to the use of Christmas carols during Advent. These should be saved for the celebration of the incarnation at Christmas. Concerts of Christmas music are best scheduled during the twelve days of Christmas and not during Advent.

Setting. The counsel regarding music pertains also to decorating the place of worship. Let Advent speak its own message by delaying any Christmas decorations in the space for worship until Christmas Eve. Allow the symbol of light in the Advent wreath to speak without ambiguity. In addition, the Advent message might be accented in designing banners using the signs of the season (e.g., messianic rose, the peaceable kingdom, root or tree of Jesse), or the principal figures in focus during Advent (Isaiah, John the Baptist, and Mary), or the symbolic, eschatological words: *Maranatha,* or *Come, Lord Jesus.*

Liturgical Color. Traditional color for Advent is purple, although use of blue is gaining popularity. Blue is expressive of the hope that is at the heart of Advent, and is less penitential than purple.

Christmas and Epiphany

Christmas-Epiphany engages us in joyful praise of the incarnation, God's coming to us in Jesus Christ. When Advent is observed as a time of preparation and anticipation and is characterized by the plaintive sounds of the Advent hymns, Christmas comes to us as a time for jubilant praise of Christ's coming to dwell with us.

Let the Christmas Eve service be the first occasion for the church to be decorated in the manner that is the local custom for Christmas. Let the decorations be a surprise to the people and contribute to their sense of joy in the coming of the feast of the incarnation of the Lord. Decorations should be simple, well planned, and artistically done. In decorating, care should be taken to insure the integrity of the pulpit, font, and table. Nothing should impede any of the liturgical actions or obstruct any exit.

The meaning of the season is conveyed in a variety of ways. Christmas Eve, Christmas Day, and Epiphany are all occasions for celebrating the Eucharist. A candlelight Communion on Christmas Eve is a common practice. Epiphany and the Sunday following (The Baptism of the Lord) are appropriate times to celebrate Baptism. Many congregations set up a Christmas crèche on Christmas Eve, maintaining it for the twelve days of the season, removing it after the Epiphany service. Banners and bulletins can portray the many symbols of the season.

Gold and white are the traditional colors of the season. Congregations are encouraged to use the finest and most elegant fabrics available for vestments and paraments, to express the joy of the incarnation.

In contrast to the discipline of selecting service music and hymns for Advent, the task of planning for Christmas music is easy. We find ourselves dealing, for the most part, with the favorite and familiar carols that have been sung and played in our secular environs since before Thanksgiving. Our primary dilemma will be having opportunities to sing enough carols in the services on Christmas Eve, Christmas Day, the First and Second Sundays after Christmas, and Epiphany, to satisfy congregations that have not sung carols during Advent. A Festival of Lessons and Carols and caroling activities will help meet this need. In addition to the two or three hymns ordinarily sung on Sunday, selected carol fragments or verses of carols may be incorporated as responses to the offering, during Communion, and after the benediction. This is both effective and pastoral. Various instruments may be used to complement the organ, e.g., trumpets, handbells, tympani, cymbals, recorders, French horn, harp, glockenspiel. On Christmas Eve and Christmas Day, carolers on the front walk or in the narthex might sing to welcome worshipers.

Epiphany music needs to be selected with theological breadth. The congregation is cheated if Epiphany represents only the visit of the three magi. The baptism of Jesus is well reflected in the *Presbyterian Hymnal*. There are also appropriate hymns that focus on light and the Light of the Word. Hymns that center on the miracle at Cana, another traditional focus of Epiphany (now Third Sunday after Epiphany in Cycle C), are not generally available in most hymnals. "Songs of Thankfulness and Praise" (tune: SALZBURG), in *Rejoice in the Lord*, is one of the only hymns from the classical hymn tradition that reflects the miracle at Cana. There are, however, instrumental selections and anthems that can balance this lack of hymns.

Festival of Lessons and Carols (pages 82–84)

The Festival of Lessons and Carols was originally prepared for use in Truro Cathedral in England in the nineteenth century and was adapted for use in King's College Chapel, Cambridge, in 1918. It has found its way into many congregations at Christmas, especially as an evening candlelight service during the twelve days of the season. The congregation may sing the more familiar hymns and carols, and a choir the less familiar. The Service for Lessons and Carols should not replace a Christmas celebration of the Eucharist.

The text and order on pages 82–84 draw upon the tradition at King's College Chapel. The following music is in accord with that tradition:

Processional Hymn: "Once in Royal David's City" (Tune: IRBY)

Hymn: "Of the Father's Love Begotten" (Tune: DIVINUM MYSTERIUM)

First Lesson—Genesis 3:8–15
Carol: "Adam Lay Ybounden" (Text: 15th century; Music: Boris Ord, or Benjamin Britten)

Second Lesson—Genesis 22:15–18
Hymn: "O Come, O Come, Emmanuel" (Tune: VENI EMMANUEL)

Third Lesson—Isaiah 9:2, 6–7
Carol: "Lo, How a Rose E'er Blooming" (Tune: ES IST EIN' ROS')

Fourth Lesson—Micah 5:2–4
Carol: "O Little Town of Bethlehem" (Tune: FOREST GREEN)

Fifth Lesson—Luke 1:26–35, 38
Carol: "There Is No Rose" (Text: 15th century; Music: Benjamin Britten)

Sixth Lesson—Matthew 1:18–21
Carol: "Infant Holy, Infant Lowly" (Tune: W ZLOBIE LEZY) *and/or* "Lullay My Liking" (Text: 15th century; Music: Gustav Holst)

Seventh Lesson—Luke 2:8–20
Carol: "The First Nowell" (Tune: THE FIRST NOWELL)

Eighth Lesson—Matthew 2:1–11
Carol: "In the Bleak Midwinter" (Tune: CRANHAM), *and/or* "On This Day Earth Shall Ring" (Tune: PERSONENT HODIE)

Ninth Lesson—John 1:1–14
Carol: "Silent Night, Holy Night" (Tune: STILLE NACHT)

Concluding Hymn: "O Come, All Ye Faithful" (Tune: ADESTE FIDELES)

Other hymn and carol alternatives after the lessons include:

	HB	WB	PH
First Lesson—Genesis 3:8–15			
As Morning Dawns—Psalm 5 (vs. 2–4)	—	—	161
Come, Thou Long-expected Jesus (vs. 1–2)	151	342	1
Comfort, Comfort You My People (v. 1)	—	347	3
Second Lesson—Genesis 22:15–18			
O Come, O Come, Emmanuel	147	489	39
		490	
Third Lesson—Isaiah 9:2, 6–7			
Break Forth, O Beauteous Heavenly Light	—	314	26
Lo, How a Rose E'er Blooming	162	455	48
Fourth Lesson—Micah 5:2–4			
O Little Town of Bethlehem	171	511	43
Fifth Lesson—Luke 1:26–35, 38			
The Angel Gabriel from Heaven Came	—	—	16
To a Maid Engaged to Joseph	—	—	19
Sixth Lesson—Matthew 1:18–21			
The First Nowell	156	585	56
Gentle Mary Laid Her Child (vs. 1, 3)	167	375	27
Hark! The Herald Angels Sing (v. 2)	163	411	31
Seventh Lesson—Luke 2:8–20			
Angels, from the Realms of Glory	168	298	22
Angels We Have Heard on High	158	299	23
Go, Tell It on the Mountain (African-American)	—	380	29
Hark! The Herald Angels Sing	163	411	31
Holy Night, Blessed Night—Sheng Ye Qing, Sheng Ye Jing (Mandarin)	—	—	33
Midnight Stars Make Bright the Sky (Chinese)	—	—	65
See Amid the Winter's Snow	—	—	51
Sheep Fast Asleep—Hitsuji Wa (Japanese)	—	—	52
Eighth Lesson—Matthew 2:1–11			
As with Gladness Men of Old	174	302	63
Brightest and Best of the Stars of the Morning	175	318	67
On This Day Earth Shall Ring	—	538	46

	HB	WB	PH
From a Distant Home—De Tierra Lejana			
Venimos (Puerto Rico)	—	—	64
We Three Kings of Orient Are	176	—	66

Ninth Lesson—John 1:1–14

	HB	WB	PH
Born in the Night, Mary's Child	—	312	30
Creator of the Stars of Night	—	348	4
Hark! The Herald Angels Sing	163	411	31
O Gladsome Light (vs. 1, 3)	61	494	549
Silent Night, Holy Night	154	567	60

THE EASTER CYCLE

Ash Wednesday (pages 115–126)

Ash Wednesday centers both upon human mortality and on the confession of sin before God. The service provided in this resource maintains this dual focus in the light of God's redeeming love in Jesus Christ.

Entrance

When a procession begins the service, it is to take place in silence in keeping with the austere character of the Ash Wednesday service, thus encouraging thoughtful meditation on the meaning of the day.

Confession of Sin

Psalm 51 is always used in this service as a confession of sin. Since the time between Ash Wednesday and Maundy Thursday is traditionally a time of penitence, the tradition is to not include a declaration of pardon on Ash Wednesday and throughout Lent, until Maundy Thursday.

Ashes

Traditionally, the ashes for this service are prepared by burning the palm branches from the previous year's Palm Sunday. Ordinarily, the palms from the service are returned on the Sunday before Ash

Wednesday (The Transfiguration of the Lord). No empirical historical reason exists for the burning of the previous year's palms for Ash Wednesday. But, it is often suggested that the returned palms signify the enthusiasm from the last year's palm procession that has now wilted to brittle, dry, dead fronds. Burned to ash, they remind us of our dashed dreams of faithful discipleship and, ultimately, our mortality: "You are dust, and to dust you shall return" (Gen. 3:19). In this sense, the burning of the previous year's palms might imply a relationship between one year's Passion/Palm Sunday and the following year's Ash Wednesday. The natural symbols of palms that are part of the conclusion of Lent become part of the subsequent year's introduction to Lent.

The ashes should be ground into a fine powder with a spoon. Working them through a screen will make them even finer. A damp towel (or large paper tissues) should be available for the hands of those who have imposed ashes.

For pastoral reasons, some congregations may choose not to impose ashes. This issue has clear educational implications, and it might take time to prepare a congregation for participation in a service which includes imposition. In an initial year, ashes might merely be present in the service. A second step might be for the congregation to see the ashes poured from one container into another.

Before the thanksgiving over the ashes, the worship leader should observe a brief period of silence. The silence should be more than a pause.

People come in procession to the front of the church to receive the imposition of ashes. The ashes are imposed on the forehead of those who come to receive the imposition. The one imposing the ashes dips his or her thumb in the ashes, and marks the forehead in the form of a cross, while saying the words, "Remember that you are dust, and to dust you will return."

Music

Music for Ash Wednesday will probably be the most somber of the year, except for Good Friday. A musical setting of the biblical text of Psalm 51 may be found in *PH* 196. Appropriate choices of hymns for the service include:

	HB	WB	PH
Forty Days and Forty Nights	—	—	77
God of Compassion, in Mercy Befriend Us	122	261	261
Have Mercy on Us, Living Lord (Psalm 51, paraphrase)	—	—	195
Just as I Am, Without One Plea	272	—	370
Lord Jesus, Think on Me	270	—	301
Lord, Who Throughout These Forty Days	181	470	81

Liturgical Color

The liturgical color for the day is purple, the color traditional to Lent, although some prefer the use of gray. Consider rough textured fabrics, such as monk's cloth or burlap, perhaps using earth tones for Ash Wednesday and the weeks that follow during Lent.

The Service for Passion/Palm Sunday (pages 139–151)

The Service for Passion/Palm Sunday maintains an inherent tension between the joyful entry of the palm procession and the somberness of the passion (the focus of Holy Week). The triumphal entry is celebrated as a gateway to the week by a congregational procession into the sanctuary. Christ's suffering and death for all is then proclaimed through the passion narrative according to Matthew, Mark, or Luke.

The Setting

Liturgical Color. Red is now commonly used on Passion/Palm Sunday. Some traditions begin the service (the entrance rite of prayer, proclamation, and palm processional) with red vestments in celebration of Christ's impending sacrificial death. The color red also manifests the triumphant singing and joyful excitement of this opening part of the service. At the conclusion of the hymn of praise, or immediately prior to the liturgy of the Word, vestments are changed to the traditional purple which continues the penitential color of Lent. Some traditions reverse this color sequence, understanding the purple to represent the majesty of the entering king, and red the blood of Christ shed for our salvation.

Congregations using somber earthen tones of gray or brown throughout Lent may wish to continue such colors on this day, but still might use red during the entrance rite.

Other Visual Signs. As with liturgical colors, each congregation will decide for itself what visual signs are consistent with the day as well as in the particular setting of the liturgy. Remember, it is the first day of Holy Week with shifts in music, mood, texture, and tone from joyfulness to solemnity. The shadow of the cross in the passion narrative falls on the exuberance of the triumphal entry.

Therefore, visual signs of the triumphal entry—crown, palms, and donkey—as well as signs of the passion—whip, flogging post, crown of thorns, seamless robe, dice, nails, ladder—are appropriate.

Music

Since Passion/Palm Sunday moves us from the procession into Jerusalem through the crucifixion, the choices of hymns for this service will need to be selected carefully. Suggestions are given at appropriate places below.

Entrance Rite

Gathering of People. If possible, the congregation gathers at a designated place outside the usual worship space. A brief introduction to the service may be given, noting any unfamiliar elements, musical responses, and so forth. Perhaps, special instruction or practice may be required to insure not only awareness but also smoothness in the conduct of the day's service.

Palm branches, or flowering branches indigenous to the area, may be distributed to all the people so they may carry or wave them as they sing the hymn(s) of praise during the palm processional.

Call to Worship and Proclamation of the Entrance into Jerusalem. Consider enhancing the entrance rite and/or the reading of the Gospel account of Jesus' entrance into Jerusalem by letting the people sing the *Benedictus qui venit* ("Blessed is he who comes . . ."—Psalm 118:26) as it appears in: (a) the entrance rite; (b) each Gospel reading of the Entrance Into Jerusalem (Matthew 21:9; Mark 11:9; Luke 19:38); (c) concluding the entrance rite, *or* as introductory words to the prayer for illumination. Sources of musical settings are noted below under "Response" (page 295).

Procession into the church. A palm procession (used since at least the fourth century) involving touch, sight, and hearing heightens a congregation's appreciation of the story of Jesus' triumphal entry into Jerusalem. Therefore, consider the possibilities of a palm procession. Distance and degree of incline (including steps) must be considered in order to sensitively incorporate people who may have difficulty walking with ease.

If an outdoor procession is not possible, a congregation can gather in the worship space and conduct a palm procession within that space by inviting the people to proceed around the outside aisles to the rear and then down the center aisle(s) to their seats. The action of the procession is a symbolic movement by the congregation from outside to the inside of the worship space.

Since the ninth century, "All Glory, Laud, and Honor" (*HB* 187, *WB* 284, *PH* 88) has been sung on this day. This hymn relates to the scripture just read and expresses a festive spirit. Consider varying the voices singing the stanzas and refrain of the hymn among combinations of alto and soprano voices, and tenor and bass voices. Enhancing the accompaniment with varied instrumentations adds to the festive nature of this processional hymn. An alternative to this hymn is the singing of Psalm 118:19–29. A setting of this psalm is found in *The Presbyterian Hymnal* (no. 232).

During the processional hymn or psalm, choirs, liturgical leaders, dancers, musicians (brass and percussion instrumentalists are particularly suitable), with the whole congregation proceed into the place of worship bearing their palms. Since it may prove cumbersome for some people to hold a hymnbook in one hand and a palm branch in the other, consider printing the text of the hymn in the order for worship or on a separate sheet. It will be necessary to secure permission to reprint the hymn if a hymn is chosen that is under copyright.

Response. Echoing the opening of the service, the responsive words "Blessed is he who comes . . ." from Psalm 118:26 frame the entrance rite, as well as assist transition to the Liturgy of the Word with its distinctly different mood. Three settings are provided in this resource: 11 (page 340), 30 (page 360), 55 (page 369). A response can also be formed from the "Blessed is he who comes . . ." portion of the "Holy, holy, holy Lord," used in celebrations of the Eucharist such as those in *The Worshipbook,*[10] pages 229, 249, 269, or in *The Presbyterian Hymnal,*[11] pages 568, 581.[12]

A prayer of confession is usually omitted from the service, particularly if a palm procession is incorporated in the entrance rite. In keeping with the penitential discipline of the entire season of Lent, as well as the ensuing reading of a passion narrative, a prayer of confession is redundant on this day.

Liturgy of the Word

Gospel Lesson. Various modes of proclaiming the passion narrative could include any one or combination of the following. All will require advance planning and careful practice:

Choral Reading.[13] At the reading of Matthew 27:31; Mark 15:20; or Luke 23:26, it is customary for the congregation to stand and remain standing through the remainder of the reading. An extended period of silence follows the reading of Matthew 27:50; Mark 15:37; and Luke 23:46.

Dramatization. This could include art forms such as mime, readers' theater, dance, music, or visual arts.

A Vocal setting may be sung by the choir or an individual, perhaps including congregational responses.

A Lessons and Hymns format may be used, such as the following:

	HB	WB	PH
CYCLE A			
Matthew 26:14–35			
An Upper Room Did Our Lord Prepare (vs. 1, 2)	—	—	94
Matthew 26:36–75			
Go to Dark Gethsemane (vs. 1, 2)	193	—	96
or			
When We Are Tempted to Deny Your Son (vs. 1, 2)	—	640	86

Matthew 27:1–32

	HB	WB	PH

At the words: "Then they led him away to crucify him" (Matthew 27:31), it is customary for the congregation to stand and remain standing through the remainder of the reading.

	HB	WB	PH
Ah, Holy Jesus	191	280	93
or			
O Sacred Head, Now Wounded	194	524	98

Matthew 27:33–50

An extended period of silence follows the reading of Matthew 27:50, after which one of the following may be sung:

	HB	WB	PH
Alas! and Did My Savior Bleed	199	—	78
or			
Throned Upon the Awful Tree	197	605	99
or			
Why Has God Forsaken Me?	—	—	406

Matthew 27:51–66

	HB	WB	PH
Deep Were His Wounds, and Red	—	—	103
or			
O Love, How Deep, How Broad, How High!	—	518	83
or			
Were You There?	201	—	102
or			
What Wondrous Love Is This	—	—	85

	HB	WB	PH
or			
When I Survey the Wondrous Cross	198	635	100, 101

CYCLE B

Mark 14:1–31
An Upper Room Did Our Lord Prepare (vs. 1, 2) — — 94

Mark 14:32–72
Go to Dark Gethsemane (vs. 1, 2) 193 — 96

or

When We Are Tempted to Deny Your Son
(vs. 1, 2) — 640 86

Mark 15:1–37

At the words, "Then they led him out to crucify him" (Mark 15:20), it is customary for the congregation to stand and remain standing through the remainder of the reading.

An extended period of silence follows the reading of Mark 15:37, after which one of the following may be sung:

O Sacred Head, Now Wounded	194	524	98
Throned Upon the Awful Tree	197	605	99
Why Has God Forsaken Me?	—	—	406

Mark 15:38–47
Deep Were His Wounds, and Red — — 103

or

Were You There? 201 — 102

	HB	WB	PH
or			
When I Survey the Wondrous Cross	198	635	100, 101

CYCLE C

Luke 22:14–38
An Upper Room Did Our Lord Prepare (vs. 1, 2)   — — 94

Luke 22:39–71
Go to Dark Gethsemane (vs. 1, 2)   193 — 96

Luke 23:1–31

*At the words, ". . . they laid the cross on him, and
made him carry it behind Jesus" (Luke 23:26), it is
customary for the congregation to stand and remain
standing through the remainder of the reading.*

Ah, Holy Jesus   191 280 93

Luke 23:32–46

*An extended period of silence follows the reading of
Luke 23:46, after which one of the following may be
sung:*

Alas! and Did My Savior Bleed   199 — 78
He Never Said a Mumbalin' Word   — — 95
Jesus, Remember Me   — — 599

Luke 23:47–56
Deep Were His Wounds, and Red   — — 103

or

Were You There?   201 — 102

or

When I Survey the Wondrous Cross   198   635   100,
                                                      101

Sermon. The proclamation of the lessons for the day may replace the sermon, or a brief sermon may precede, interweave, or follow the readings for the day.

Prayers of Intercession. Consider using a seasonal sung or spoken response following each intercession, such as refrain 53 on page 368.

The Solemn Reproaches of the Cross (see Service for Good Friday, pages 178–181). The Reproaches are probably more effective on Good Friday, but some congregations fittingly may wish to use them on Passion/Palm Sunday, especially if the congregation will not gather again for corporate worship until Easter Day. If a prayer of confession has been included earlier in the service, do not use the Reproaches.

The Eucharist

Music that attends the Sacrament needs to be carefully selected to be in keeping with the reading of the passion narrative. A hymn such as "Bread of Heaven, on Thee We Feed" (*WB* 313, *PH* 501), which reflects on Christ's death and is set in a minor key, is especially appropriate for use during the serving of the people.

Sending

The Service for Passion/Palm Sunday draws people into contrasts of mood—the exuberant entry of the palm procession, the solemn reading of the passion of Christ, and a celebration of the Lord's Supper—"the joyful feast of the people of God." The conclusion of this service, therefore, needs to be carefully planned.

The people depart in silence. Or, a hymn reflective of the week, may first be sung, such as "Ah, Holy Jesus, How Have You Offended" (*HB* 191, *WB* 313, *PH* 501) perhaps a capella accompanied by a simple one note melody. An appropriate refrain from the music section of this resource (pages 329-375) would provide a dramatic close to the service.

Tenebrae (pages 152–158)

This book contains a tenebrae service for use by congregations desiring a service of prayer and meditation to use on Wednesday evening of Holy Week.

The tenebrae, meaning "darkness" or "shadows," dates from medieval times. Tenebrae was originally a series of sung services in monastic communities constituting morning and evening prayer. These services were held each day, morning and evening, from Wednesday night of Holy Week through Saturday. Each of the services featured fifteen candles. After the singing of each psalm in the service, a candle was extinguished. Nine were extinguished in morning prayer, and five in evening prayer. One candle remained burning. This lighted candle was then hidden, leaving the community in darkness. At the end of the service, there was a loud noise, and the lighted candle was returned to its stand in anticipation of the resurrection. The tenebrae in this resource is adapted from this tradition.

Certain cautions need to attend the incorporation of a tenebrae service during Holy Week. A tenebrae service may amount to what is often called an "as if liturgy," a service *as if* Christ had not risen. Such a liturgy also raises the question whether the services during Holy Week are a historical recounting (even reenacting) *or* an evangelical celebration of the cross.

During the past twenty years of ecumenical liturgical reform, the more significant services for Maundy Thursday and for Good Friday have been restored. In this restoration, the tenebrae is eclipsed by the more important liturgies. Although a tenebrae can be very moving, the importance of the services for Maundy Thursday and Good Friday outweighs any values a tenebrae may have. The tenebrae should therefore not replace either the Service for Maundy Thursday or the Service for Good Friday, so that those services may have their fullest expression. The tenebrae, therefore, is provided here for use on the evening before Maundy Thursday as a service of prayer and meditation.

The most prominent feature of the tenebrae is the reading, or singing, from the Lamentations, and the gradual extinguishing of candles and other lights in the church, until only a single candle remains burning. This lone candle symbolizes Jesus Christ. The hiding of this candle symbolizes the apparent victory of evil. The loud noise at the end of the service symbolizes the earthquake at the resurrection (Matt. 28:2). The restoration of the lighted candle is a further symbol of Christ's victory over death.

There is no musical prelude or postlude at this service.

The traditional stand for the fifteen candles, called a "hearse," is a large triangular candle holder with fifteen candles, with the highest candle, at the point of the triangle, the one that is not extinguished.

The psalms may be sung or recited antiphonally, with the refrains sung or recited before and after each psalm. The Lamentations text may be sung.[14] It is recommended that the same style of music be used throughout the service, thereby providing a unity to the liturgy.

During the first set of three psalms, seven candles are extinguished at suitable intervals. During the second set of three psalms, seven more candles are extinguished. All other candles and lights are extinguished during the Canticle of Zechariah (Benedictus—Luke 1:68–79) except for one candle. This candle is hidden, usually behind the Communion table (if the base of the table is enclosed). The people remain seated for the psalms and for the reading from Lamentations.

In the darkened church, people may bow down for the Lord's Prayer, Psalm 51 (which may be recited by the choir), and for the final prayer. Because this portion of the service is in darkness, Psalm 51 and other texts at the end of the service will need to be memorized by those chosen to read. The choir will need to memorize the text from Philippians which is appointed to be sung.

After the psalm is sung, the prayer is said. There is then a loud noise signifying the earthquake. The noise can be made in a variety of ways, e.g., two boards firmly slapped together, a book slammed flat on a table, a group beating vigorously on the backs of the pews. The hidden candle is then returned to its place in the candle holder. Without further word the people depart in silence.

The Service for Maundy Thursday (pages 159–170)

How can we respect the paradoxical nature of the Maundy Thursday service—somber and celebrative?[15]

Since most services will occur in the evening, perhaps lighting the worship space by many candles, or by illuminating the worship space in subdued fashion, can effectively assist. Periods of silent meditation juxtaposed with joyful expression, and vice versa, may also help. We need not fret about trying to create a proper mood, because the acts of confession, the declaration of pardon, the reading and preaching of the Word, the footwashing, the Lord's Supper, and the stripping of the church will draw us all into the paradoxical mood of this first service of the Triduum.

Arrangement of the Worship Space

Services on Maundy Thursday demonstrate a wider variety of celebration than perhaps any other day of the year. Modest to fancy fellowship meals, unadorned church meeting halls to elegantly decorated sanctuaries, reserved to convivial moods, simple to elaborate services are all common to Maundy Thursday. At root, all communities of faith gather on the first night of the Triduum to hear the Word and to break bread together.

Pastoral sensitivity to adapt to local circumstances is a necessity in order to conduct the service for Maundy Thursday "decently and in order" and with dignity, while avoiding a contented mood or uncomfortable setting. Decide how to arrange the worship space in order to establish an environment suitable to the solemn celebration of this day.

Depending upon the flexibility of the worship space and the intended mood and movement of the service, some congregations arrange the space so that the bread and the cup are served to the people seated at tables.

For example, small groups of people may be seated at individual tables located throughout the room, with the Lord's table serving as a "head table" from which the liturgical leaders preside. Congregations are discouraged, however, from setting up only tables of twelve as a means to reliving a historical moment in the life of Christ. Liturgy may be dramatic and historic but it is not a reenacted historical drama.

Another example consists of one, room-sized Lord's table around which all the people gather. This may be achieved by arranging a series of tables, all connected in some fashion, the length of a hall or around the room.

A third example consists of a semicircular or half-wheel arrangement with the Lord's table as the hub and the tables, at which the people sit, as the spokes.

Congregations desiring to serve the bread and the cup to people who come forward to the Lord's table or to stations where the bread and the cup are served, may also arrange their worship space in varying ways to accommodate easy movement of the congregation.

Liturgical Color

Continue the same colors and worship environment employed throughout the season of Lent. Though the traditional color is purple, some churches use somber earth tones of brown or gray. Whichever color is used, consider rough textured fabrics as a suitable means of conveying the mood of the season. Special visual art or use of shades of colors appropriate to the day can be added to enhance the stories and the shifting moods of this service. Keep in mind that the concluding act is the stripping of the church (worship space) when the stark, bare environment reflects the tone of the concluding days and services of the Triduum in preparation for Easter.

The Entrance Rite

Gathering of the People. Music played or sung as the people gather for worship will set the mood of the service. Therefore, first decide the tone to be established, then carefully choose instrumental or choral music to match.

Call to Worship. The sentences of scripture proclaim who God is and what God has done in Christ, mindful of the overarching themes of the day.

Confession and Pardon. Either a prayer or penitential psalm, spoken or sung, is appropriate. Use of a sung Kyrie ("Lord, have mercy") will reinforce the penitential note. Choices include *The Worshipbook*, pages 213 and 235; *The Presbyterian Hymnal*, nos. 565, 572–574; *Music from Taizé*, vol. I, pages 12–14; *Lutheran Book of Worship*, pages 57, 78, 99; and *The Hymnal 1982*, pages S85–S98.

For many Christians, the "penitential season" commences on Ash Wednesday and culminates finally in a great absolution on Maundy Thursday (the custom of reconciling penitents on this day is an ancient practice). Thus, Ash Wednesday to Maundy Thursday is kept as a time of penitence, with the long-awaited absolution on Maundy Thursday concluding the Lenten discipline.

In response to the pardon, a hymn of praise, such as the first stanza of "There's a Wideness in God's Mercy" (tune: IN BABILONE), would be an appropriate response to the joy of forgiveness. For other suggestions see *The Service for the Lord's Day*, Supplemental Liturgical Resource 1 (pages 55–57).

The Peace. The momentous words of forgiveness call for action. We have been forgiven, and we have sung praise. Now we extend forgiveness to neighbors and become a reconciled community. Therefore, the first act of the community following the climax of the penitential season is the exchange of the peace. The community thus symbolizes its reconciliation with God and with neighbors by exchanging signs of peace following the announcement of our forgiveness in Jesus Christ.

Since the peace is exchanged at this point in the service, it should not be repeated later. If the peace is not exchanged at this point in the service, another possible location would be immediately preceding the celebration of the Lord's Supper, again as a sign of a community reconciled to God and with neighbors.

Liturgy of the Word

The Scripture Lessons. Following the completion of the season of penitence with the declaration of pardon, the last three days of Lent truly begin, with an intense meditation upon the mystery of redemption through the cross and resurrection of Christ. Thus, scripture lessons according to the Common Lectionary focus on a range of texts over its three-year cycle, including:

—preparation and celebration of the Passover (Exodus 12:1–14)
—sealing of the Mosaic covenant (Exodus 24:3–8)
—promise of a new covenant and the fulfillment of this promise through Christ's sacrifice (Jeremiah 31:31–34; Hebrews 10:16–25)
—understanding our sharing in the body and blood of Christ (1 Corinthians 10:16–17)
—footwashing by Jesus (John 13:1–15)
—Pauline and Gospel accounts of the institution of the Lord's Supper (1 Corinthians 11:23–26; Mark 14:12–26; Luke 22:7–20)

Creed or Affirmation of Faith. In keeping with the solemnity of the service, most Christian traditions omit a creed on Maundy Thursday. The act of footwashing is itself an act of professing faith. We are doing what Jesus did for the reason he did it—in love and service of our brothers and sisters. However, since the Reformed tradition is a confessional tradition, particular churches may wish to use suitable segments of historic confessions.

Footwashing. If a footwashing is included in the service, it should be conducted in an open area of the worship space, preferably in view of the whole congregation.

Depending on the size of the congregation and the amount of space available, either all who wish to may participate, or representative members of the congregation may be selected. The simple yet powerful act of washing the feet of another person best represents the intention of the "new commandment." Therefore, try to avoid having minigroups of two people wash only each other's feet as mutual footwashing may connote "mutual back-scratching" and, therefore, diminish the radical nature of the unilateral action of footwashing. Some possibilities that may best symbolize servanthood, would include the following: (a) A person washes the feet of another person, whereupon both return to their seats. (b) Upon completion of having one's feet washed, that person then turns to a neighbor and washes his or her feet.

It is usually prudent to prepare the persons whose feet will be washed so they may wear easily removable footwear and socks. The specific people to engage in the footwashing could be arranged beforehand, or an opportunity could be offered to those so moved by the Spirit to step forward at the time of footwashing.

A sufficient number of pitchers of warm water, basins, and towels must be provided for the people washing the feet of another person. Fill the pitchers with hot water before the service so the water may cool to a tepid temperature for the actual washing.

The procedure for the footwashing is as follows:

1. People go to the location of a pitcher, basin, and towels.
2. A pitcher, basin, and towels are passed from one person to another.
3. People whose feet will be washed remove their footwear, while those who will wash the feet of others kneel before them, place the basin under the feet, pour the water over the feet, letting it cascade into the basin, "wash" the feet with the hands, dry the feet with the towel, and assist with putting back on the footwear.

A particularly appropriate hymn for the congregation to sing during the footwashing is "Where Charity and Love Prevail." This hymn is a paraphrase of the ancient Latin hymn *Ubi Caritas* and appears in *The Worshipbook* (no. 641). Particularly effective is an ostinato version that is included in Jacques Berthier, *Music from Taizé*, vol. I (vocal edition, page 28; instrumental edition, page 27).[16] This hymn has long been associated with Maundy Thursday footwashing. The choir may also provide an anthem or responsorial music during the footwashing. Perhaps a combination of hymns, anthems, and silence may enhance the footwashing ritual.

Plan for everyone to participate through acts of washing, being washed, singing, or observing. Also, recognize that footwashing will require movement by at least some people. Plan accordingly for graceful and natural movement.

Prayers of Intercession. Consider using a sung response following each intercession, such as one of the refrains from pages 329–375.

The Eucharist

Words of Institution. If the words of institution were not spoken before the great prayer of thanksgiving, or included in it, then the minister, standing before the people, says them in relationship with the breaking of the bread.

Serving. Possible room arrangements for churches with flexible seating are suggested on page 303. Whatever the room arrangement, plan a mode of distributing the elements so that the bread and the cup, as always, are *served* (i.e., *given*) to the people rather than *taken* by the people.

For example, people can be served at the Lord's table or at one of several stations within the worship space. Or, if people are seated at various tables, the bread and the cup can be passed around or across each table, with each person serving the elements to others at the table. Careful planning is necessary to insure that people understand what is expected of them so that the method of distribution facilitates rather than frustrates the communion of the people.

Stripping of the Church (Worship Space)

The final act of this service is the evocative stripping of the worship space. This is most effectively done in absolute silence, and in an unhurried, orderly fashion. Designate several people to extinguish the candles, strip the Lord's table of all cloths and vessels, and remove all textile hangings, candles and candelabra, flowers, and so forth, carrying all the items out of the room. The stark, bare, unadorned church now reflects Jesus' abandonment during the night in Gethsemane.

The visual aspect of the transformed worship space gives people a dramatic depiction of Christ's desolation. The church remains bare until the Easter Vigil when the process is reversed and the worship space is "dressed" again.

Ordinarily, neither a blessing is given nor a postlude played on this night, as the services for Maundy Thursday, Good Friday, and Holy Saturday (the Easter Vigil) are actually one unified ritual. The opening service of the Triduum continues on Good Friday and concludes with the Easter Vigil at which time a blessing is pronounced.

Some congregations may desire to conclude the service with a psalm, hymn, or spiritual. A setting of Psalm 22 would be appropriate, or a hymn, such as, "I Greet Thee, Who My Sure Redeemer Art" (*HB* 144, *WB* 418, and *PH* 457), which focuses on our redemption in Jesus Christ.

The church remains in semidarkness, and all depart in silence, thus making the transition from the eucharistic celebration to Jesus' crucifixion and death. Symbolically, Christ, stripped of his power and glory, is now in the hands of his captors.

The Service for Good Friday (pages 171–181)

The Good Friday service is intentionally in concert with the broad ecumenical tradition, and is representative of many ecumenical aspects. It therefore reflects a commonality with many strands of Christian tradition.

It is important to retain the paradoxical nature of the day in form, mood, and texts. Good Friday is a day for many contemplative moments, so let the power of silence speak for itself.

No paraments on the table or pulpit, no flowers, candles, or decorative materials are appropriate on Good Friday, except, perhaps, representations of the way of the cross. On Good Friday some traditions drape the cross with red (or black) where it remains until during the paschal vigil.

While the nature of music on Good Friday is somber, hymns which include reflections on resurrection need not be avoided, such as:

	HB	WB	PH
In the Cross of Christ I Glory	195	437	84
O Love, How Deep, How Broad, How High	—	518	83

Liturgy of the Word

Gospel Lesson. We read the passion narrative according to John on Good Friday, because at the heart of John's passion narrative is the good news of the cross—the victory of the cross. Thus, John's emphasis on crucifixion and glory corresponds to the tension and ambiguity of the day.

Various modes of proclaiming the passion narrative could include any one or combination of the following, all of which necessitate not only advance planning but careful practice:

Choral Reading[17]

At the words, "So they took Jesus; and carrying the cross by himself, he went out to what is called The Place of the Skull, which in Hebrew is called Golgotha" (John 19:16b, 17), it is customary for the congregation to stand and remain standing through the remainder of the reading. An extended period of silence follows the reading of John 19:30 ". . . and gave up his spirit."

Dramatization. This could include art forms such as mime, readers' theater, dance, music, or visual arts.

A Vocal setting may be sung by the choir or an individual, perhaps including congregational responses.

A Lessons and Hymns format may be used, such as the following:

	HB	WB	PH
John 18:1–27			
When We Are Tempted to Deny Your Son	—	640	86
John 18:28—19:16a			
Ah! Holy Jesus	191	280	93
John 19:16b–30			

At the words: "So they took Jesus; and carrying the cross by himself, he went out to what is called The Place of the Skull, which in Hebrew is called Golgotha" (John 19:16b, 17), it is customary for the congregation to stand and remain standing through the remainder of the reading.

An extended period of silence follows the reading of John 19:30 ". . . and gave up his spirit," after which one of the following may be sung:

Deep Were His Wounds, and Red	—	—	103
or			
He Never Said a Mumbalin' Word	—	—	95

or

	HB	WB	PH
Were You There? (vs. 1, 2 in *HB*, vs. 1, 2, 3 in *PH*)	201	—	102

or

	HB	WB	PH
Throned Upon the Awful Tree	197	605	99

John 19:31–42

	HB	WB	PH
Were You There (v. 3 in *HB*, v. 4 in *PH*)	201	—	102

or

	HB	WB	PH
When I Survey the Wondrous Cross	198	635	101

Sermon. The proclamation of the lessons for the day may replace the sermon, or a brief sermon may precede, interweave, or succeed the readings for the day. Those who plan the liturgy may consider letting the gospel speak through the power of silence, or through an appropriate liturgical dance or offering of music, which may help deepen reflection on the cross for all worshipers.

The Solemn Intercession. A fitting response to the hearing of the passion of Christ is intercession in the form of bidding prayers for the whole family of God and the afflictions of the world. This is an important element of the Good Friday tradition. Such bidding prayers are signs of our joining in Christ's priestly ministry of fully extending his arms in order to embrace all God's people (i.e., his posture on the cross).[18]

Consider using a sung scriptural response following each bidding prayer, such as "He was wounded for our transgressions and bruised for our iniquities" (Isa. 53:5), no. 14 (page 343) and no. 42 (page 364).

Solemn Reproaches of the Cross. The "Solemn Reproaches" are an ancient text of Western Christendom associated with Good Friday. They need to be read slowly and clearly.[19]

The Solemn Reproaches take the place of confession in this service, so no prayer of confession and declaration of pardon are included in the service. If, however, a prayer of confession with a declaration of pardon are included earlier in the service, or if the Reproaches were used on Passion/Palm Sunday, the Solemn Reproaches are not used.

Consider enhancing the people's response to the Solemn Reproaches by letting the people sing the Kyrie ("Lord, have mercy") or Trisagion ("Holy God . . .").

A congregational sung response of the Kyrie can be adapted from the following: *WB,* page 213 and no. 235, or *PH,* nos. 565, 572–574.

In some traditions, the people's response during the Reproaches is the Trisagion (Greek, literally "the thrice holy"), the name of a hymn in the ancient rite of the Eastern church:

Holy God, holy and mighty,
Holy and immortal One, have mercy upon us.

The Trisagion may be spoken or sung by the congregation adapted from musical settings for the Trisagion. A setting by John Weaver may be found in "Service Music," *Reformed Liturgy & Music,* vol. 18, no. 1 (Winter 1984), pp. 38, 39, 41. Other settings may be found in *The Hymnal 1982,* nos. S99–S102.

Instead of printing the entire text of the Solemn Reproaches in the order for worship, simple rubrics will suffice. Here is an example:

Each reproach ends with the leader saying:

. . . you have prepared a cross for your Savior.

and all the people respond by singing:

Lord, have mercy.

Dismissal

The Service for Good Friday draws people into the story of the passion of Christ. It is composed of contrasting actions and moods of the solemn reading of the passion of Christ and, yet, hopeful look toward the resurrection. What is an appropriate way in which to be dismissed to continue serving?

Following the Solemn Reproaches, some congregations find it meaningful to depart in silence, while others find it useful to sing a hymn of the good news of the cross, extolling the victory of the cross of Christ. For example, a hymn appropriate to the day and the week, such as "Ah, Holy Jesus, How Have You Offended" (*HB* 191; *WB* 280; *PH* 93), might be sung either a capella or softly accompanied by only a simple one note melody. An effective alternative is to sing a response such as "Jesus, Remember Me" (*PH* 599), sung repetitiously with a flute accompaniment. Or, the last portion of the first stanza of "I Sing as I Arise Today" (*WB* 429, tune: DEIRDRE) might be sung. This is a prayer attributed to St. Patrick (c. 389–c. 461):

Christ within me, Christ beside me,
Christ before me, Christ to guide me,
Christ in rising, Christ in sleeping,
Christ in working, Christ in speaking.

It would provide a transition from Good Friday to Holy Saturday.

Following the singing, it is most dramatic and meaningful when all depart in silence. The service continues with the Easter Vigil, or on Easter Day.

The Great Vigil of Easter (pages 182–203)
First Service of Easter

The Structure of the Great Vigil of Easter

The Great Vigil of Easter is the brightest jewel of Christian liturgy traced to early Christian times. It proclaims the universal significance of God's saving acts in history through four related services held on the same occasion, and consists of:

Liturgy of Light. The service begins in the darkness of night. In kindling new fire and lighting the paschal candle, we are reminded that Christ came as a light shining in darkness (John 1:5). Through the use of fire, candles, words, movement, and music, the worshiping community becomes the pilgrim people of God following the "pillar of fire" given to us in Jesus Christ, the light of the world. The paschal candle is used throughout the service as a symbol for Jesus Christ. This candle is carried, leading every procession during the vigil. Christ, the light of the world, thus provides the unifying thread to the service.

Liturgy of the Word. The second part of the vigil consists of a series of readings from the Old and New Testaments. These lessons provide a panoramic view of what God has done for humanity. Beginning with creation, we are reminded of our delivery from bondage in the exodus, of God's calling us to faithfulness through the cry of the prophets, of God dwelling among us in Jesus Christ, and of Christ's rising in victory from the tomb. The readings thus retell our "holy history" as God's children, summarizing the faith into which we are baptized.

Liturgy of Water. In the earliest years of the Christian church, baptisms commonly took place at the vigil. So this vigil includes baptism and/or the renewal of baptismal vows. As with the natural symbol of light, water plays a critical role in the vigil. The image of water giving life—nurturing crops, sustaining life and cleansing our bodies—cannot be missed in this part of the vigil. Nor is the ability of water to inflict death in drowning overlooked. Water brings both life and death. So also there is death and life in baptism, for in baptism we die to sin and are raised to life. Baptism unites believers to Christ's death and resurrection.

Liturgy of the Eucharist. The vigil climaxes in a joyous celebration of the feast of the people of God. The risen Lord invites all to participate in the new life he brings by sharing the feast which he has prepared. We thus look forward to the great Messianic feast of the kingdom of God when the redeemed from every time and place "will come from east and west, and from north and south, and sit at table in the kingdom of God" (Luke 13:29). The vigil thus celebrates what God has done, is doing, and will do.

Background of the Great Vigil

The Great Vigil of Easter is an exciting liturgical recovery. Churches of many traditions have rediscovered the vigil and experienced its potential for renewal of the faith. It is an occasion for worship and fellowship; an annual remembering of all that is fundamental in the history of the faith; an event rich with the mystery and power of the gospel.

The Tradition of the Great Vigil. In the early centuries of the church, Holy Week was observed by a rigorous fast followed by a celebration of the mystery of Easter Eve and Easter Day in one unified liturgy. The Great Vigil contained everything: lighting the new fire and the paschal candle; reading and telling of the mighty acts of God; baptizing persons into the body of Christ; renewing baptismal vows for the entire community of faith; retelling the story of our Lord's dying and rising; and celebrating the Eucharist as a foretaste of the Messianic banquet in the kingdom of God.

Originally the Great Vigil continued through the night climaxing with the celebration of the resurrection as dawn approached. Like the dawning sun ending night, so Christ arose in the splendor of his glory, conquering forever the night of sin.

Clearly, the Great Vigil was the high point of the church's annual liturgical calendar. It was the greatest moment during the year in the life of the church. It was a great occasion when the church baptized the converts to the faith. The vast majority of baptisms were at this service.

The Great Vigil has both historic and symbolic roots in the Jewish Passover. So, many of the images in the vigil are drawn from the Old Testament. In the four liturgies of the vigil we experience our passage from slavery to freedom, from sin to salvation, from death to life.

In medieval times, the proclamation of the gospel was virtually lost from the vigil, smothered by practices which distorted its original purpose. Consequently, the sixteenth-century Reformers saw little worth retaining in the vigil. For this reason the vigil has not generally been observed in the Protestant tradition—not until quite recently in the light of reforms of the vigil.

The liturgy in this resource is based on ancient texts and contemporary editions of the vigil used in many churches, including Roman Catholic, Episcopal, Lutheran, Orthodox, and Methodist. Many Presbyterian congregations throughout the United States, as well as other Reformed churches throughout the world, have begun to observe paschal vigils. Often they are creative and innovative celebrations while based on the tradition of the ancient texts.

Introducing and Planning the Great Vigil

Since the vigil is the most glorious liturgical celebration of the entire year, it requires careful preparation. It takes many weeks or months of planning and education to prepare a congregation for such an occasion.

Congregations planning their first vigil should consider establishing an educational program to introduce the concept to the church several months before Easter. Possibilities include Sunday morning classes using material in this book, or a program centered around a family night supper.

Special attention needs to be given to the details involved in all of the settings for the various components of the vigil. Lighting, processions, the details surrounding the baptisms, the serving of Communion, the lighting of the new fire, and the readings, all need to be carefully planned and rehearsed.

Music should be selected with great care, with particular attention given to the musical settings, hymns and instrumental music used. Brass fanfares and accompaniment to the hymns in the last portion of the vigil adds greatly to the service. The choir's main role will be to assist the congregation in its singing, and during Communion may sing appropriate music.

A paschal candle needs to be purchased or made. This candle is of central importance in the vigil. The paschal candle is a large candle at least two inches in diameter, and at least two feet tall. It is placed in a stand at least three feet high. Traditionally the paschal candle has a cross inscribed upon it with the numerals of the current year and the Greek letters alpha and omega. A new candle is used each year. Paschal candles may be purchased from church supply houses, or may be made by someone in the congregation.[20]

Movement adds a great deal to the vigil, particularly if the church facilities enable the congregation to move to different places during the vigil. As the community moves from place to place around the church property and buildings, there is a symbolic sense of identification with God's pilgrim people. The community also has a sense of physical participation in the vigil.

Since each vigil takes on its own life, those who plan the vigil will need to make some decisions about movement, lessons, music, timing, and placement that might not be addressed in this or any liturgical resource. The vigil is an ancient part of Christian liturgical tradition, but one should not be overly concerned about the *right* way to celebrate the vigil. The vigil should reflect the spirit and essence of the particular community of faith.

It is appropriate for the Great Vigil to commence about 10:30 P.M., and end after midnight. The most dramatic time would of course be for the vigil to begin in the middle of the night so that the vigil would end at dawn. However, the vigil can be observed anytime after dark on Holy Saturday and before sunrise on Easter Sunday.

The Liturgy of Light

The community gathers in silence at an appointed place for the new fire. As worshipers gather, each person is given a candle, which may be purchased at religious supply stores.

Lighting of the Paschal Candle. The new fire should be a simple open fire that can be set up somewhere on the church property. A large metal container on legs about three feet high may be used to contain the fire. The paschal candle is lit from the flames of the fire. It is best to light the paschal candle with a taper or stick from the new fire since it is difficult to light the paschal candle from a blazing, open fire.

If an outside fire is not possible for practical considerations, such as inclement weather, a simple fire in a brazier inside the church building, at the main entrance, can be most effective. It is important that the fire be lighted in as dark a setting as possible. The symbols of light and darkness are far more powerful when the contrast is greatest.

After the lighting of the fire and the paschal candle, the procession into the church begins. The fire is carefully extinguished after the paschal candle and the candles of the people are lighted. A cover may be placed over the container for the fire to smother the flames.

The lighting of worshipers' candles can be accomplished by having the people come to the paschal candle and light their candles from the paschal candle. If the congregation is large, those nearest the paschal candle may light their candles and then pass the light to those nearby until all of the candles are lit. Or the candles of the worshipers may be lighted after the congregation has been seated in the church.

If the lighting of the paschal candle takes place inside the church building, a procession is still included, although it may consist only of the worship leaders and choir. The paschal candle is carried at the head of the procession, as with all processions throughout the vigil.

Customarily, the procession moves in silence, with the silence punctuated at three places when the worship leader sings: "The light of Christ." The congregation responds, singing: "Thanks be to God."

Worship leaders are encouraged to memorize the texts in the Liturgy of Light, since much of the service is conducted in darkness or limited light.

The Easter Proclamation. The Exsultet is the Easter proclamation sung in conjunction with thanksgiving for the paschal candle. It is sometimes known as Laus Cerei ("praise of the candle"). It takes its more familiar Latin name, "Exsultet jam Angelica turba," from its opening words: "Rejoice, heavenly powers! Sing, choirs of angels! Exult, all creation around God's throne! Jesus Christ, our king, is risen!" The text comes from the third or fourth century and is intended to imitate the style of the psalms. It is often attributed to St. Ambrose, bishop of Milan (340–397).

Two settings of the Exsultet are provided. The traditional setting (pages 185–190, 376–381) is sung without accompaniment, by a choir (or cantor) with the congregation singing the recurring refrain as indicated in the text. Organ accompaniment is provided for the contemporary setting (pages 186–190, 382–404). In using either setting, the congregation needs to be provided the text of the Exsultet with the melody line of the appropriate refrain, and responses as displayed on pages 186–188. If it is not possible for the full text of the Exsultet to be sung, it may be read with the congregation singing the refrain at the appointed places. If it is read it should be carefully rehearsed to ensure that its message is effectively conveyed. A hymn inspired by the Exsultet may be found in the *Lutheran Book of Worship*, no. 146. An alternative to the tune in the *Lutheran Book of Worship* is the familiar tune MIT FREUDEN ZART.

The worshipers hold their lighted candles throughout the singing of the Exsultet. After the Exsultet the worshipers' candles are extinguished.

Liturgy of the Word

Traditionally, this part of the service includes the reading of as many as twelve lessons from the Old Testament.[21] Some Eastern liturgies have included as many as seventeen lessons. Nine readings are here provided from the Old Testament, together with an epistle lesson and a reading from one of the Synoptic Gospels. If the situation does not permit all nine Old Testament lessons to be read, a sufficient number should be read to convey a sense of the broad sweep of salvation history. There should always be at least three lessons from the Old Testament, one of which will always be Exodus 14:10–31; 15:20–21. The reading of each lesson is followed by a brief silence. The appointed psalm or canticle (or a suitable hymn) may then be sung. A brief prayer, such as the one provided, follows.

The lessons should be read with care and sensitivity. The planners of the vigil should be as creative as possible in considering a variety of methods to present the lesson. Drama, choral readings, slide and film presentations, liturgical dance, and choral music are some of the possibilities one can consider.

Following are some suggested settings for singing the psalms and canticles that follow the readings.

The *Presbyterian Hymnal* includes settings for some of the psalms:

	PH		PH
Psalm 33	185	Psalm 42	190
Psalm 46	191	Psalm 143	250
Psalm 16	165	Psalm 98	218

Psalms and Canticles for Singing (scheduled for release by Westminster/John Knox Press in late 1992) includes musical settings for all of the psalms and canticles that follow the readings.

Following are some suggestions for congregations that may choose to substitute hymns for some of the psalms:

	HB	WB	PH
Following Genesis 1:1–2:2			
Father Eternal, Ruler of Creation	486	362	—
God of the Sparrow	—	—	272
God, You Spin the Whirling Planets	—	—	285
Many and Great, O God, Are Thy Things	—	—	271
Creating God, Your Fingers Trace	—	—	134
Following Genesis 7:1–5, 11–18; 8:6–18; 9:8–13			
Our God, Our Help in Ages Past	111	549	210
A Mighty Fortress Is Our God	91	274	260
Following Genesis 22:1–18			
God of Our Life	108	395	275
O God of Bethel, By Whose Hand	342	496	269
Following Exodus 14:10–31; 15:20–21			
Call Jehovah Your Salvation	123	322	—
Come, You Faithful, Raise the Strain			
(esp. v. 1)	205	345	114, 5
Following Isaiah 55:1–11			
God Is My Strong Salvation	347	388	179
Following Proverbs 8:1–8, 19–21; 9:4–6			
Immortal, Invisible, God Only Wise	85	433	263
Be Thou My Vision	303	304	339
Following Ezekiel 36:24–28			
Breathe on Me, Breath of God	235	—	316
O Spirit of the Living God	—	528	—
Spirit of God, Descend Upon My Heart	236	275	326
Following Ezekiel 37:1–14			
Breathe on Me, Breath of God	235	—	316
Come Holy Ghost, Our Souls Inspire	237	335	125
Come Holy Spirit, God and Lord	161	336	—

	HB	WB	PH
Following Zephaniah 3:14–20			
Father, We Thank You That You Planted	—	366	—
Joy to the Lord	161	444	40
The Church's One Foundation	437	582	442
Following Romans 6:3–11			
The Church of Christ in Every Age	—	—	421

The "Glory to God in the highest. . . ." is commonly sung after the last Old Testament lesson is read. Some traditions accompany the singing with the ringing of the church bells. In some traditions the "Glory to God in the highest . . ." is not sung until after the singing of Psalm 114 following the reading of Romans 6:3–11, where it occurs immediately before the reading of the resurrection narrative from the Gospel.

A brief sermon may follow the Gospel lesson. Instead of a sermon, in some congregations a portion of the paschal homily of St. John Chrysostom is read.[22]

The Liturgy of Water

At this place in the liturgy baptisms take place. The prayer over the water on pages 35–36 of *Holy Baptism and Services for the Renewal of Baptism* (Supplemental Liturgical Resource 2) is encouraged because of its fuller inclusion of biblical images and of water in the history of salvation. An alternative service of baptism is one ecumenically prepared by the Consultation on Common Texts, in which Reformed, Anglican, Catholic, Lutheran, and other traditions participated.[23]

When there are no candidates for baptism, the Liturgy of Water essentially becomes the renewal of baptismal vows. Worship leaders may move among the people liberally sprinkling the worshipers with water while repeating "Remember your baptism and be thankful" as a symbol of forgiveness and reconciliation we have in Christ. An evergreen bough may be used in sprinkling the people. The bough is dipped into a large basin of water that is carried by the person doing the sprinkling. If an evergreen bough is not available, the water can be lifted out of the font with cupped hands and either returned to the font or splashed over the worshipers.

The sprinkling of the people as a renewal of baptismal vows is most dramatic when it immediately follows a baptism.

Appropriate hymns for use in procession to the font include:

	HB	WB	PH
Glorious Things of Thee Are Spoken	434	379	446
The Church's One Foundation	437	582	442

Appropriate hymns for use during baptism or the renewal of baptismal vows include:

	HB	WB	PH
Baptized in Water	—	—	492
Dearest Jesus, We Are Here	—	310	493
Come Down, O Love Divine	—	334	313
Descend, O Spirit, Purging Flame	—	353	—
Father, We Thank You that You Planted	—	366	—
Jesus, Friend So Kind and Gentle	451	—	—
Lord Jesus Christ, Our Lord Most Dear	452	461	496
O God, This Child from You Did Come	—	501	—
Out of Deep, Unordered Water	—	—	494
Pardoned Through Redeeming Grace	—	550	—
We Know that Christ Is Raised	—	—	495
With Grateful Hearts Our Faith Professing	—	—	497
Wonder of Wonders, Here Revealed (after baptism)	—	—	499

The Eucharist

The passing from darkness to light, from death to resurrection, is now fully consummated. The red (or black) drape of Good Friday is removed. The Easter flowers are displayed. The sanctuary is decorated with white and gold, the traditional colors of Easter.

This part of the vigil lends itself to a grand procession into the sanctuary, if the baptism or renewal of baptismal vows took place in a space other than the sanctuary. Colorful banners, preferably without words, can add to the beauty of the procession. The entire worshiping community follows the paschal candle and banners.

Hymn suggestions for use during the celebration of the Eucharist include:

	HB	WB	PH
Come Risen Lord	—	340	503
Deck Yourself, My Soul, with Gladness	—	351	501

	HB	WB	PH
I Sing as I Arise Today	—	428	—
O Sons and Daughters, Let Us Sing	206	527	116

Hymn suggestions for use before the charge and benediction or during a recessional include:

	HB	WB	PH
Alleluia, Alleluia! Give Thanks	—	—	106
The Day of Resurrection	208	584	118

In traditions where fasts have been maintained during Lent, the fast is broken after the vigil with a breakfast of bread, cheese, milk, honey, and fruit. Such a meal might take place in a fellowship hall.

Easter Sunday Through Pentecost

Congregations are encouraged to celebrate the resurrection throughout the Great Fifty Days of Easter. During these days we remember Christ's rising from the tomb, his post-resurrection appearances, his ascension, and the outpouring of the Holy Spirit at Pentecost. This should be the most festive period of the year.

Some congregations, moving toward weekly Communion, are beginning to celebrate the Eucharist on each Sunday throughout this season, even when they celebrate it less frequently during the rest of the year. Congregations are thus introduced to weekly Communion. It is an easy step toward the ultimate commitment of celebrating the Eucharist each Lord's Day. Weekly Communion during the Easter season further helps congregations to understand that this Sacrament is a resurrection feast. The Lord's Supper derives as much from the postresurrection meals as it does from the Last Supper. Music that attends the Sacrament should therefore not be funereal in tone. Adequate preparation and instruction of the congregation should precede weekly Communion during Easter, even though it is just for the season.

The environment for worship should be in sharp contrast with the austerity of the preceding season of Lent. The traditional Easter colors of white and gold, in the finest and most elegant fabrics, can express the joy of the season. Of course, other festive colors may also be used. Since the Great Fifty Days is as much the Season of Pentecost as it is the Season of Easter, red might be added (beginning on the

Second Sunday of Easter) to the white and gold used at the Vigil and Easter Sunday. This would remain until red becomes dominant on Pentecost Sunday. Symbols common to the liturgical season may be incorporated on banners and on church bulletins.

The paschal candle is particularly important throughout the season. First lighted at the Easter Vigil, it is lighted for each Sunday following through Pentecost Sunday. During the Great Fifty Days it will remain in its stand beside the Communion table. After Pentecost it is placed beside the baptismal font for the rest of the year.

The paschal candle is lighted for every baptism throughout the year, signifying the relationship of our baptism with the death and resurrection of Jesus Christ (see *Holy Baptism and Services for the Renewal of Baptism*, Supplemental Liturgical Resource 2, pages 60–61[24]). It is also lighted at each funeral (where it is placed in its stand at the head of the coffin) and memorial service (see *The Funeral: A Service of Witness to the Resurrection*, Supplemental Liturgical Resource 4, page 80[25]).

Music which proclaims Christ's victory over death and our joyful response befits the season. It is a time to sing lots of hymns with Alleluias. Use of trumpets to punctuate portions of the liturgy, especially the call to worship, will remind us of the significance of the season. The seasonal refrains, pages 329–375, can add further seasonal focus.

Ascension Day. Ascension Day was a festival retained by the sixteenth-century Reformers. As was noted in the Introduction, the doctrine of the ascension of Christ has had an important place in Reformed theology. Congregations are encouraged to restore a service on Ascension Day. To introduce it, a congregation might precede it with a congregational meal. A celebration of the Eucharist is most fitting. The environment should help convey a sense of the transcendent, of Christ enthroned in glory as ruler of all. The Pantocrator iconography of Eastern Orthodoxy might be used in a creative way, such as in visual projections. What is done on Ascension Day needs to carry through the following Sunday, lest the Ascension be seen as an isolated event and not integral to the season that leads to the celebration of Pentecost.

Pentecost Sunday. Pentecost Sunday draws the Great Fifty Days of Easter to a glorious climax. Additional texts are provided for Pentecost Sunday.

The Litany for Pentecost (pages 221–222) may be used as an alternative to the Prayer of the Day and may be sung in a manner similar to that suggested for the Litany of Advent (pages 71–72). Or it may be used as an alternative to a prayer of confession. As with the Litany for Advent, the litany is particularly effective when sung (see page 284 for instructions on singing a litany). Unlike the Advent litany, it is preferable for a choir to sing the text of this litany, and the singing should be accompanied with the organ. One of the tones (or combination of tones 1–4) on page 34 of *Psalm Refrains and Tones for the Common Lectionary*[26] may be used with refrain 32 in this book (page 361). Tones in *Psalms and Canticles for Singing*[27] are other alternatives.

A Litany of Intercession for Pentecost is also provided (pages 223–224).

Red is the traditional color for the day, symbolizing the fire of the Spirit that rested upon the faithful disciples of Christ, and gives life to the church in every age. The use of gold (as throughout the rest of the Great Fifty Days), is common, along with the red on Pentecost Sunday. The colors may be used in a variety of ways, including vestments, paraments, and banners. Some congregations have been very creative in the use of textiles on Pentecost. For example, one congregation used red, orange, and gold streamers of "fire" throughout the worship space. To symbolize the "wind of the Spirit," another congregation used a collection of wind chimes and placed them in the worship space where the chimes would be in the path of the currents of air where they would give a gentle, joyful sound throughout the service. The use of a readers' theater presentation of Acts 2:1–21 or Ezekiel 37:1–14 (Cycle B) is another possibility. Many congregations read the Acts lesson in a variety of languages known to members in the congregation. In planning this service let it be evident that Pentecost is a major festival. A sense of triumphant joy should characterize the liturgy.

The powerful images of rushing wind and tongues of flame lend themselves to use of a variety of instrumentation which might otherwise be resisted in a worship setting. Percussion effects, especially using cymbals, both rolled and crashed, tympani, and contemporary music in almost any instrumentation will convey some sense of this extraordinary event and perhaps even the powerful symbolism of being commissioned for ministry through the gift of the Holy Spirit.

MUSIC

REFRAINS

The musical refrains that follow may be used in the liturgy in a variety of ways, and are useful in emphasizing the particular day or season in the liturgical calendar. For suggestions see pages 278–279. The numbers in the index below refer to the number of the refrain.

Permission is granted by the publisher to reproduce the melody line and text of psalm refrains numbers 26–62 without charge in church bulletins for congregational participation. See pages 405–412 for forms that may be reproduced.

Advent	1, 2, 26, 27, 51, 63
Christmas	3, 4, 35, 36, 64
Epiphany	5, 28, 52
Baptism of the Lord	6, 37
Transfiguration of the Lord	7, 38, 65
Ash Wednesday	8, 9, 29, 39, 54, 66
Lent	9, 10, 39, 41, 53, 54, 68
Passion/Palm Sunday	11, 12, 30, 42, 55, 69, 70
Maundy Thursday	13, 31
Good Friday	12, 14, 42, 43, 70
Easter	15, 16, 23, 44, 46, 48, 56, 60, 71
Ascension of the Lord	17, 50
Pentecost	18, 32, 57
Trinity Sunday	13, 19, 31, 40, 58

Ordinary Time	20, 21, 22, 23, 24, 33,
	34, 46, 47, 49, 56, 61,
	62, 74, 75, 76
All Saints' Day	25, 45, 59
Christ the King	17, 72, 73

Music for the Easter Proclamation (the Exsultet) for the Paschal Vigil is provided in two settings. The traditional setting appears on pages 376–381. A contemporary setting appears on pages 382–404.

ADVENT

1

Based on 1 Cor. 16:22; Rev. 22:20

John Weaver, 1989

Ma - ra - na - tha! Come, Lord Je - sus.

2

Isa. 40:3

John Weaver, 1989

Music © 1989 John Weaver.

CHRISTMAS

Isa. 9:6

John Weaver, 1989

CHRISTMAS

Luke 2:14

John Weaver, 1989

Glo-ry to God in the high-est.

Glo-ry to God in the high-est. Peace to all peo-ple on

earth. Peace to all peo-ple on earth.

Music © 1989 John Weaver.

5

Isa. 60:1

John Weaver, 1989

Moderato

A - rise, shine, for your light is come. A - rise, shine, for your light is come.

Handbells

p

Organ

Man.

fine

Music © 1989 John Weaver.

NOTE: The accompaniment may be either handbells or keyboard (piano or organ) or both, or neither.
The melody is a canon with voices entering one measure apart. The accompaniment should continue repeating
the formula until the last voice finishes. As many different parts as wished may be used, possibly singing the
canon twice, or it may be sung in unison, perhaps with the cantor singing it first and the congregation responding.

BAPTISM OF THE LORD

Based on Mark 1:11

John Weaver, 1989

6

Be - hold, the be-lov-ed of the Lord, Be - hold, the be-lov-ed of the Lord, on whom God's fa - vor rests, On whom God's fa - vor rests.

7

TRANSFIGURATION OF THE LORD

Based on Mark 9:28

John Weaver, 1989

Be - hold, the be - lov - ed of the Lord. Be - hold, the be - lov - ed of the Lord; lis - ten to him, lis - ten to him, lis - ten to him, lis - ten to him. Be -

Music © 1989 John Weaver.

hold, the be-lov-ed of the Lord.   Be - hold, the be-lov-ed of the Lord.

Ped.

ASH WEDNESDAY

8
Gen. 3:19

John Weaver, 1989

9

Ps. 51:10

John Weaver, 1989

Music © 1989 John Weaver.

10

Ps. 143:10

John Weaver, 1989

Teach me to do your will, Teach me to do your will, for you are my God, for you are my God.

Music © 1989 John Weaver.

(for use during gathering rite)

11

Mark 11:9

John Weaver, 1989

PASSION/PALM SUNDAY
(for use after the gathering rite)

12

Isa. 53:7

John Weaver, 1989

Music © 1989 John Weaver.

MAUNDY THURSDAY

13
Based on John 15:12

John Weaver, 1989

Music © 1989 John Weaver.

14

Isa. 53:5

John Weaver, 1989

♩ = 69

Leader

He was wound-ed for our trans-gres-sions.

mp

Man.

All

He was wound - ed for our trans-gres - sions

Ped.

Music © 1989 John Weaver.

Leader

and   bruised   for our in - iq - ui-ties,

Man.

All

and   bruised   for our in - iq - ui-ties.

rit.

Ped.

15

Based on Luke 24:34

John Weaver, 1989

Music © 1989 John Weaver.

16

1 Cor. 15:54

John Weaver, 1989

Allegro   *Leader*

Death is swal-lowed up in   vic - to-ry.

f II

Ped.

All   *Leader*

Death is swal-lowed up in   vic - to-ry.   Al-le - lu   -

I

II

All   *rit.*

ia!   Al - le - lu   -   ia!

rit.

I

17

Phil. 2:10–11

John Weaver, 1989

PENTECOST

John Weaver, 1989

Allegro

Leader

Come, Ho - ly Spir - it.

All

Come, Ho - ly Spir - it, en - flame us with your

Leader

love, en - flame us with your love.

All

rit.

Music © 1989 John Weaver.

TRINITY SUNDAY

John Weaver, 1978

Glo-ry to the Fa-ther, and to the Son, and to the Ho-ly Spir-it: as it was in the be-gin-ning, is now, and will be for-ev-er. A-men! A - men! A - men!

* May be sung as a canon.

Music © 1978 John Weaver.

ORDINARY TIME

20

Based on Eph. 2:6

John Weaver, 1989

You have raised us to new life in Christ. You have

raised   us   to   new   life   in

Christ.

rit.

Ped. 16' + II

21

Eph. 4:4–5

John Weaver, 1989

ORDINARY TIME

Ps. 51:15

John Weaver, 1989

O Lord, o - pen my lips. O Lord, o - pen my lips, and my mouth shall pro-claim your praise, and my mouth shall pro-claim your praise.

Music © 1989 John Weaver.

ORDINARY TIME

Ps. 118:24

John Weaver, 1989

This is the day   which

God has made;   Let us re-joice and be   glad in it.

Music © 1989 John Weaver.

This is the day   which God has made;   Let us re-joice and be

glad   in it.   This is the day   which

This is   the   day

which God has made;   Let us re-joice   and be glad in

God has made;   Let us re-joice   and be   glad in it.

it.

rit.

full Ped.

ORDINARY TIME

24
Amos 5:24

John Weaver, 1989

Let jus-tice roll down like wa - ters, and righ-teous-ness like an ev - er-flow-ing stream. Let jus-tice roll down like wa - ters, and righ-teous-ness like an ev - er-flow - ing stream.

25

Heb. 12:1

John Weaver, 1989

Sur - round - ed by a cloud of wit - ness-es, sur - round - ed by a cloud of wit - ness-es, we

run the race be - fore us,

All

we run the race be - fore

us.

rit.

Words and melody line of the refrains that follow (26–62) are also provided in a form that may be reproduced in church bulletins for congregational participation (see pages 405-412).

26–34   Hal H. Hopson

Music © 1992 Westminster/John Knox Press.

26. ADVENT

Maranatha! Come, Lord Jesus.   *Based on 1 Cor. 16:22;*
                                                                    Rev. 22:20

27. ADVENT

Prepare the way of the Lord.   *Isa. 40:3*

28. EPIPHANY

Arise, shine, for your light is come.   *Isa. 60:1*

29. ASH WEDNESDAY

We are dust; to dust we will re-turn.   *Gen. 3:19*

30. PASSION/PALM SUNDAY

Blessed is he who comes in the name of the Lord.   *Mark 11:9*

31. MAUNDY THURSDAY

Love one another as Christ has loved us.   *John 15:12*

32. PENTECOST

Come, Holy Spirit, enflame us with your love.

33. ORDINARY TIME

You have raised us to new life in Christ.   *Based on Eph. 2:6*

34. ORDINARY TIME

There is one Lord, one faith, one baptism.   *Eph. 4:4–5*

35–36   Hal H. Hopson

Music © 1987 The Westminster Press.

35. CHRISTMAS

Unto us a child is born.*
   To us a Son is given.

36. CHRISTMAS

Glory to God in the highest.*
   Peace to all peo-ple on earth.

BAPTISM OF THE LORD

37

Based on Mark 11:1

St. Meinrad V
Samuel Weber, O.S.B.

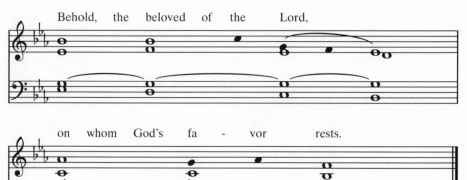

Behold, the beloved of the Lord,

on whom God's fa - vor rests.

TRANSFIGURATION OF THE LORD

38

Based on Mark 9:28

St. Meinrad V
Samuel Weber, O.S.B.

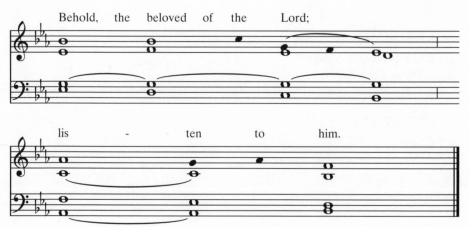

Behold, the beloved of the Lord;

lis - ten to him.

39

Ps. 51:10

St. Meinrad VII
Columba Kelly, O.S.B.
Harm. Samuel Weber, O.S.B.

Create in me a clean heart, O God.

Renew a right spir - it with - in me.

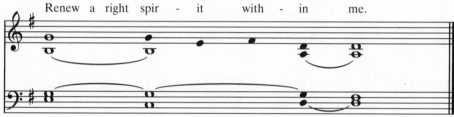

40

Ps. 143:10

St. Meinrad I
Samuel Weber, O.S.B.

Teach me to do your will,

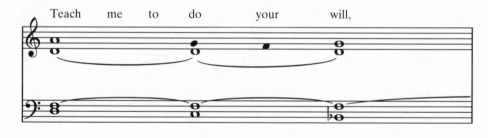

for you are my God.

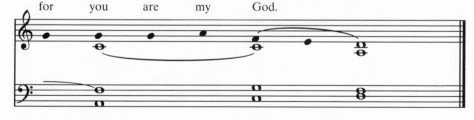

PASSION/PALM SUNDAY

41

Isa. 53:7

St. Meinrad I
Samuel Weber, O.S.B.

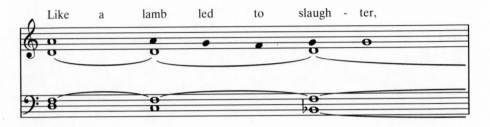

Like a lamb led to slaugh - ter,

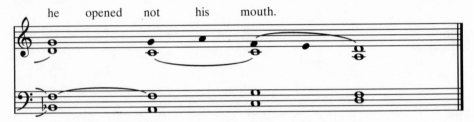

he opened not his mouth.

GOOD FRIDAY

42

Hal H. Hopson

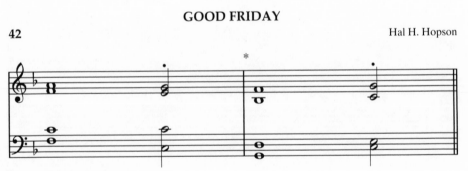

He was wounded for our trans-grèssions,*
and bruised for our in-ïquities.

TRINITY SUNDAY

St. Meinrad VII
Columba Kelly, O.S.B.
Harm. Samuel Weber, O.S.B.

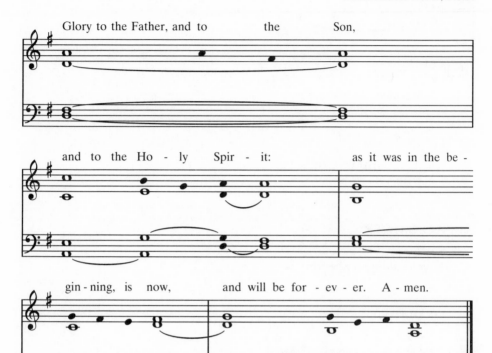

44. EASTER

Alleluia! Christ is risen!*
Christ is ris-en in-deed!

45. ALL SAINTS'

Surrounded by a cloud of witnesses,*
we run the race be-fore us.

46. ORDINARY TIME

This is the day which God has made;*
let us rejoice and be glad in it.

47. ORDINARY TIME

Let justice roll down like waters,*
and righteousness like an ever-flow-ing stream.

48. EASTER

> Death is swallowed up in vic-to-ry.*
> Al-lė-lu-ia!

49. ORDINARY TIME

> O Lord, o-pėn my lips,*
> and my mouth shall pro-claim your praise.

ASCENSION OF THE LORD

50

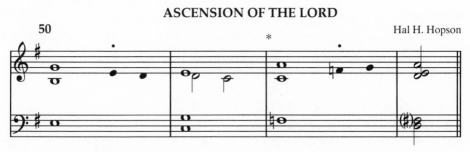

At the name of Jesus every knėe shall bow,*
  and every tongue confess: Jesus Christ is Lord!

ADVENT

51

Hal H. Hopson

Lord, come soon. Lord, come soon.

Music © 1988 Hope Publishing Company.

EPIPHANY

52

Hal H. Hopson

The light shines in the dark-ness. Al-le - lu - ia! Al-le - lu - ia!

Music © 1988 Hope Publishing Company.

LENT

53

Ps. 130:1–2

Hal H. Hopson

Lord, I call to you; O hear my cry.

Music © 1986 Hope Publishing Company.

LENT

54

Ps. 51:10

Hal H. Hopson

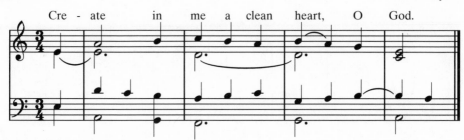

Music © 1988 Hope Publishing Company.

PASSION/PALM SUNDAY

55

Mark 11:9

Hal H. Hopson

Music © 1988 Hope Publishing Company.

EASTER

56

Hal H. Hopson

Music © 1986 Hope Publishing Company.

PENTECOST

57

Psalm 104:30

Hal H. Hopson

Lord, your spir-it re-news the earth. Al-le - lu - ia!

TRINITY SUNDAY

58

Psalm 8:1

Hal H. Hopson

O Lord, our Lord, how glo-ri-ous is your name.

ALL SAINTS'

59

Hal H. Hopson

Join all the saints to praise the Lord. Al - le - lu - ia!

60

Psalm 118:24

Hal H. Hopson

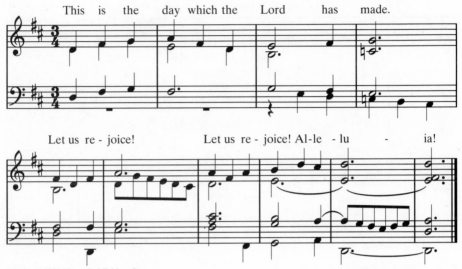

This is the day which the Lord has made.

Let us re - joice! Let us re - joice! Al-le - lu - ia!

Music © 1988 Hope Publishing Company.

ORDINARY TIME

61

Psalm 67:3

Hal H. Hopson

Let the peo - ple praise you, O God; Let

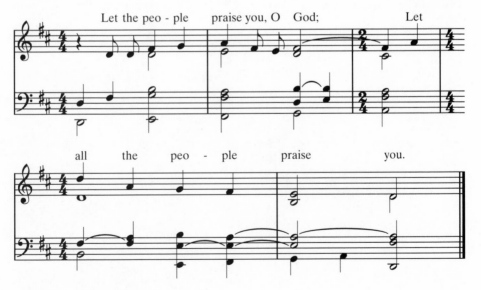

all the peo - ple praise you.

Music © 1986 Hope Publishing Company.

ORDINARY TIME

62

Psalm 135:1

Hal H. Hopson

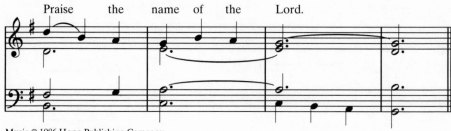

LINES FROM HYMNS USED AS SEASONAL REFRAINS

Portions of hymns can be used as recurring refrains sung throughout a service in the same manner as the refrains on the preceding pages. The following are particularly effective.

		HB	*WB*	*PH*

63. ADVENT

"O come, O come, Emmanuel, and ransom captive
    Israel."
From hymn: "O Come, O Come, Emmanuel"
[Tune: VENI EMMANUEL]   147 489 9

64. CHRISTMAS

"Joy to the world! The Lord is come."
From hymn: "Joy to the World"
[Tune: ANTIOCH]   161 444 40

65. TRANSFIGURATION OF THE LORD

"Still be my vision, O Ruler of all."
From hymn: "Be Thou My Vision"
[Tune: SLANE]   303 304 339

66. ASH WEDNESDAY

"Teach us with thee to mourn our sins and close
    by thee to stay."
From hymn: "Lord, Who Throughout These
    Forty Days"
[Tune: ST. FLAVIAN]   181 470 81

67. LENT

"God be merciful to me, on thy grace I rest my plea."
From hymn: "God, Be Merciful to Me"
[Tune: REDHEAD]   282 — —

68. LENT

"There is a balm in Gilead to heal the sin-sick soul."
From hymn: "There Is a Balm in Gilead"
[Tune: BALM IN GILEAD]   — 600 394

69. PASSION/PALM SUNDAY

"All glory, laud and honor to thee, Redeemer, King!"
From hymn: "All Glory, Laud, and Honor"
[Tune: VALET WILL ICH DIR GEBEN]   187 285   88

70. PASSION/PALM SUNDAY (AND GOOD FRIDAY)

"Were you there when they crucified my Lord?"
From hymn: "Were You There?"
[Tune: WERE YOU THERE]   201   — 102

71. EASTER

"Come, Christians, join to sing, Alleluia! Amen."
From hymn: "Come, Christians, Join to Sing"
[Tune: MADRID]   131 333 150

72. CHRIST THE KING

"Alleluia! Sing to Jesus: his the scepter, his the throne."
From hymn: "Alleluia! Sing to Jesus!"
[Tune: HYFRYDOL]   —   — 144

73. CHRIST THE KING

"Crown him, crown him, crown him, crown him
    Lord of all."
From hymn: "All Hail the Power of Jesus' Name!"
[Tune: MILES' LANE]   132 286   —

74. ORDINARY TIME

"Rejoice, rejoice, rejoice, give thanks and sing!"
From hymn: "Rejoice, Ye Pure in Heart!"
[Tune: MILES' LANE]   407 561 145

75. ORDINARY TIME

"Lord of all, to thee we raise this our hymn of
   grateful praise."
From hymn: "For the Beauty of the Earth"
[Tune: DIX]   2   372   473

76. ORDINARY TIME

"Sing praise to God who reigns above, the God
   of all creation."
From hymn: "Sing Praise to God, Who Reigns
   Above"
[Tune: MIT FREUDEN ZART]   15   568   483

77

THE EASTER PROCLAMATION (THE EXSULTET)
Setting I

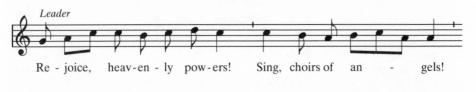

Leader

Re - joice, heav-en - ly pow-ers! Sing, choirs of an - gels!

Ex-ult, all cre-a - tion a-round God's throne! Je-sus Christ our King is ris - en!

All

Sound the trum-pet of sal-va - tion! Re - joice, heav-en - ly pow - ers!

Sing, choirs of an - gels! Je - sus Christ our King is ris - en!

Leader

Re-joice, O earth, in shin-ing splen - dor, ra-diant in the bright-ness of your King!

Christ has con-quered! Glo - ry fills you! Dark-ness van-ish-es for ev - er!

All

Re - joice, heav-en - ly pow - ers! Sing, choirs of an - gels!

Leader

Je-sus Christ our King is ris - en! Re-joice, O Moth-er Church! Ex-ult in glo -

ry! The ris - en Sav - ior shines up - on you!

Let this place re-sound with joy, ech-o-ing the might-y song of all God's peo-ple!

All

Re - joice, heav-en - ly pow - ers! Sing, choirs of an - gels!

Leader

Je - sus Christ our King is ris - en! The Lord be with you.

All   *Leader*

And al - so with you. Lift up your hearts.

All   *Leader*

We lift them up to the Lord. Let us give thanks to the Lord our God.

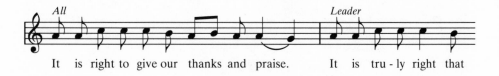

All   *Leader*

It is right to give our thanks and praise. It is tru - ly right that

with full hearts and minds and voic - es

we should praise you, the un-seen God, the all-power - ful Cre - a - tor,

and your on - ly Son, our Lord Je - sus Christ. For Christ has ran-somed us

All

with his blood, and paid for us the debt of Ad-am's sin. Re - joice,

heav-en - ly pow - ers! Sing, choirs of an - gels! Je - sus Christ our King

Leader

is ris - en! This is our pass - o - ver feast, when Christ,

the true Lamb, is slain, whose blood con - se-crates the homes of all be -

liev - ers. This is the night when first you saved our fore - bears:

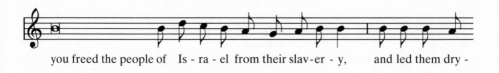

you freed the people of Is - ra - el from their slav-er - y, and led them dry -

shod through the sea. This is the night when the pil-lar of fire de-stroyed the dark-

ness of sin! This is the night when Chris-tians ev - ery-where,

washed clean of sin and freed from all de - file - ment,

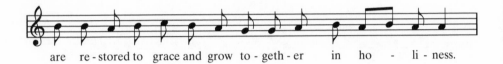

are re - stored to grace and grow to - geth - er in ho - li - ness.

This is the night when Je - sus Christ broke the chains of death

and rose tri - um-phant from the grave. *All* Re - joice, heav-en - ly pow - ers!

Sing, choirs of an - gels! Je - sus Christ our King is ris - en!

OPTIONAL ENDING

Leader

Lord God, how won - der - ful your care for us!

How bound - less your mer - ci - ful love!

To ran-som a slave you gave a - way your Son. Most blessed of

all nights, cho - sen by God to see Christ ris - ing from the dead!

The power of this ho - ly night dis-pels all e - vil, wash-es guilt a-way,

re - stores lost in - no - cence, brings mourn - ers joy;

it casts out ha - tred, brings us peace, and hum-bles earth - ly pride.

Night tru - ly blessed when heav - en is wed - ded to earth

and we are rec - on - ciled with God! There-fore,

gra-cious God, in the joy of this night, re-ceive our eve-ning sac-ri-fice of praise,

your church's sol - emn of - fer-ing. May this Eas - ter can - dle

al-ways dis-pel the dark-ness of this night! May the Morn-ing Star which nev-er sets

find this flame still burn - ing: Christ, that Morn - ing Star,

who came back from the dead and shed his peace-ful light on

all cre - a - tion, your Son who lives and reigns for ev - er and ev - er.

All

A - men. Re - joice, heav - en - ly pow - ers!

Sing, choirs of an - gels! Je - sus Christ our King is ris - en!

78

THE EASTER PROCLAMATION (THE EXSULTET)
Setting II

John Weaver, 1988

Re - joice, heav-en-ly powers! Sing, choirs of an - gels! Je-sus Christ our King is ris - en! Re - joice, heav-en-ly powers! Sing, choirs of an-gels! Je-sus Christ our King is

ris-en! Re - joice, heav-en-ly powers! Sing, choirs of an-gels! Ex-

ult, all cre-a-tion a-round God's throne! Je-sus Christ our King is

ris - en! Sound the trum-pet of sal - va-tion! Re -

joice, heav-en-ly powers! Sing, choirs of an-gels! Je-sus Christ our King is

ris - en! Re - joice, O earth, in shin-ing splen-dor,

ra-diant in the bright-ness of your King! Christ has con-quered!

Glo - ry fills you! Dark-ness van-ish - es for - ev - er! Re -

joice, heav-en-ly powers! Sing, choirs of an - gels! Je-sus Christ our King is

ris - en! Re - joice, O Moth - er Church! Ex -

ult in glo - ry! The ris - en Sav - ior

shines up - on you! Let this place re - sound with joy,

ech - o - ing the might - y song of all God's

peo - ple! Re - joice, heav-en-ly powers! Sing, choirs of an - gels!

Je - sus Christ our King is ris - en!

It is right to give our thanks and praise.

It is tru-ly right that with full hearts and minds and voic-es we should

praise you, the un - seen God, the all pow-er-ful Cre-

a - tor, and your on - ly Son, our Lord Je - sus Christ. For

Christ has ran-somed us with his blood, and paid for us the debt of Ad-am's

sin. Re - joice, heav-en-ly powers! Sing, choirs of an - gels!

Je - sus Christ our King is ris - en!

+reeds,
mixtures

Leader

This is our pass-o-ver

rit.

Sw. 8'4'

Man.

Ped.

feast, when Christ the true Lamb is slain, whose

blood con-se-crates the homes of all be - liev - ers.

This is the night when first you saved our

fore - bears: you freed the peo-ple of Is - rael

from their slav-ery, and led them dry-shod through the sea.

This is the night when Chris-tians ev-ery-where,

washed clean from sin and freed from all de-file-ment, are re-

stored to grace and grow to-geth-er in ho - li-ness.

This is the night when Je - sus Christ broke the chains of

OPTIONAL ENDING:

Lord   God, how won-der-ful your

Sw. 8'4'

care for us! How bound-less your mer-ci - ful love!

To ran - som a slave, you gave a - way your

Son. Most bless - ed of all nights,

cho - sen by God   to   see   Christ

ris - ing from the   dead!

The power of this ho - ly night dis - pels all e - vil,

wash-es guilt a-way, re - stores lost in-no-cence, brings mourn-ers joy; it

casts out ha-tred, brings us peace, and hum - bles

earth - ly pride. Night tru - ly bless - ed, when

heav-en is wed-ded to earth and we are

rec-on-ciled with God. There-fore, gra-cious

God, in the joy of this night, re-ceive our

eve - ning sac - ri - fice of praise, your church's sol - emn

of - fer - ing. *mp* Ac - cept this Eas - ter can - dle.

May it al - ways dis - pel the dark - ness of this

night!   May   the   Morn - ing   Star   which

nev - er   sets   find   this   flame   still   burn - ing:

Re - joice, heav-en-ly powers! Sing, choirs of an - gels!

Je-sus Christ our King is ris - en! Christ, that Morn-ing

Star, who came back from the dead and

Man.

REFRAINS FOR THE CONGREGATION

Free permission is granted by the publisher to reproduce the refrains that follow (on pages 405-412) in church bulletins for congregational participation.

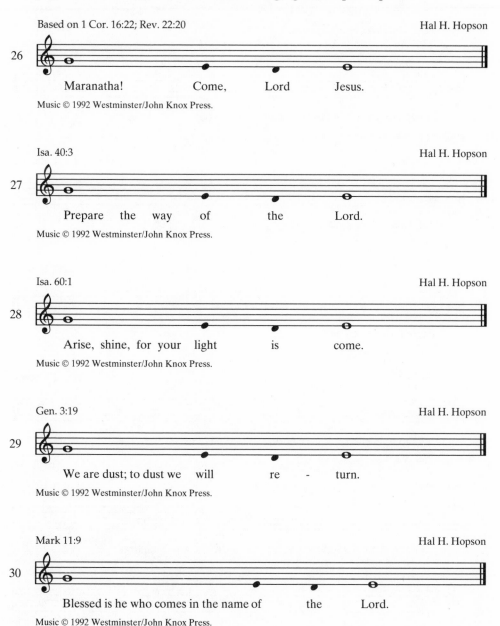

Based on 1 Cor. 16:22; Rev. 22:20

Hal H. Hopson

26

Maranatha!   Come,   Lord   Jesus.

Music © 1992 Westminster/John Knox Press.

Isa. 40:3

Hal H. Hopson

27

Prepare   the   way   of   the   Lord.

Music © 1992 Westminster/John Knox Press.

Isa. 60:1

Hal H. Hopson

28

Arise, shine, for your   light   is   come.

Music © 1992 Westminster/John Knox Press.

Gen. 3:19

Hal H. Hopson

29

We are dust; to dust we   will   re - turn.

Music © 1992 Westminster/John Knox Press.

Mark 11:9

Hal H. Hopson

30

Blessed is he who comes in the name of   the   Lord.

Music © 1992 Westminster/John Knox Press.

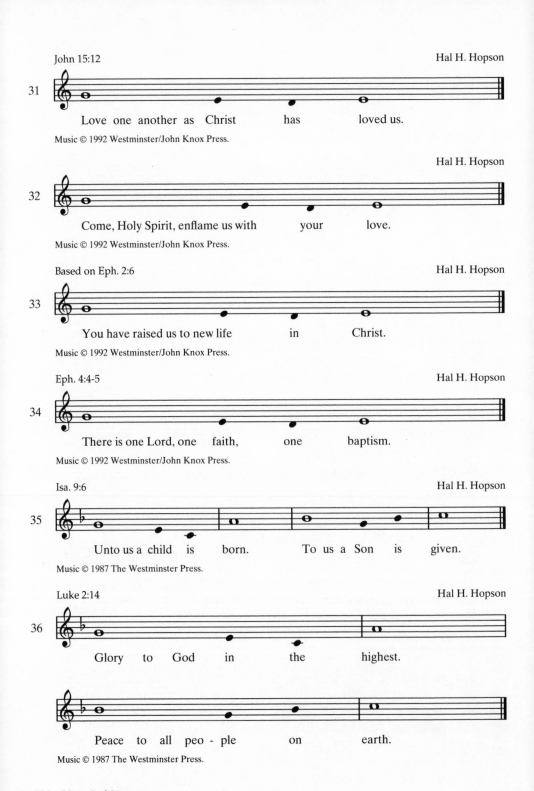

John 15:12

Hal H. Hopson

31

Love one another as Christ has loved us.

Music © 1992 Westminster/John Knox Press.

Hal H. Hopson

32

Come, Holy Spirit, enflame us with your love.

Music © 1992 Westminster/John Knox Press.

Based on Eph. 2:6

Hal H. Hopson

33

You have raised us to new life in Christ.

Music © 1992 Westminster/John Knox Press.

Eph. 4:4-5

Hal H. Hopson

34

There is one Lord, one faith, one baptism.

Music © 1992 Westminster/John Knox Press.

Isa. 9:6

Hal H. Hopson

35

Unto us a child is born. To us a Son is given.

Music © 1987 The Westminster Press.

Luke 2:14

Hal H. Hopson

36

Glory to God in the highest.

Peace to all peo - ple on earth.

Music © 1987 The Westminster Press.

St. Meinrad V
Based on Mark 1:11
Samuel Weber, O.S.B.

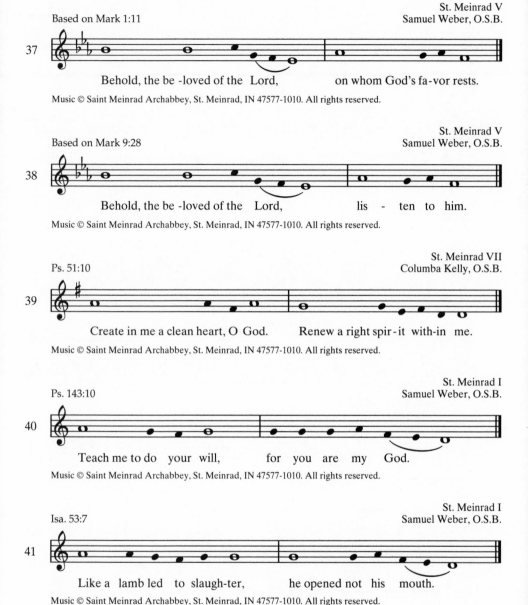

Behold, the be-loved of the Lord, on whom God's fa-vor rests.

St. Meinrad V
Based on Mark 9:28
Samuel Weber, O.S.B.

Behold, the be-loved of the Lord, lis - ten to him.

St. Meinrad VII
Ps. 51:10
Columba Kelly, O.S.B.

Create in me a clean heart, O God. Renew a right spir-it with-in me.

St. Meinrad I
Ps. 143:10
Samuel Weber, O.S.B.

Teach me to do your will, for you are my God.

St. Meinrad I
Isa. 53:7
Samuel Weber, O.S.B.

Like a lamb led to slaugh-ter, he opened not his mouth.

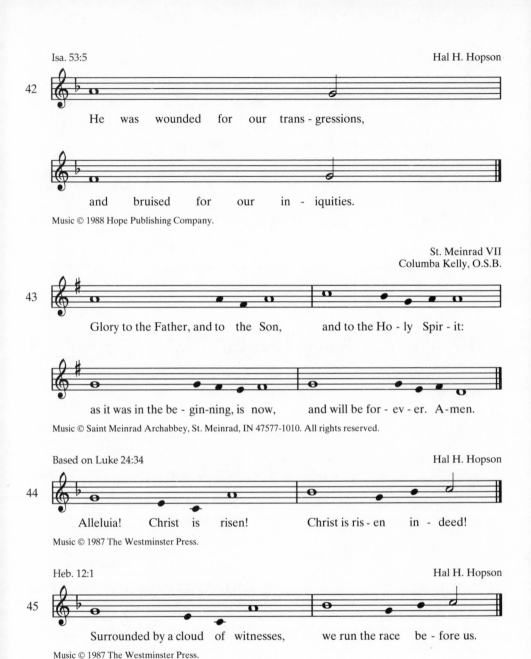

Isa. 53:5   Hal H. Hopson

42

He   was   wounded   for   our   trans - gressions,

and   bruised   for   our   in - iquities.

St. Meinrad VII
Columba Kelly, O.S.B.

43

Glory to the Father, and to   the   Son,   and to the Ho - ly   Spir - it:

as it was in the be - gin-ning, is   now,   and will be for - ev - er.   A-men.

Based on Luke 24:34   Hal H. Hopson

44

Alleluia!   Christ   is   risen!   Christ is ris - en   in - deed!

Heb. 12:1   Hal H. Hopson

45

Surrounded by a cloud   of   witnesses,   we run the race   be - fore us.

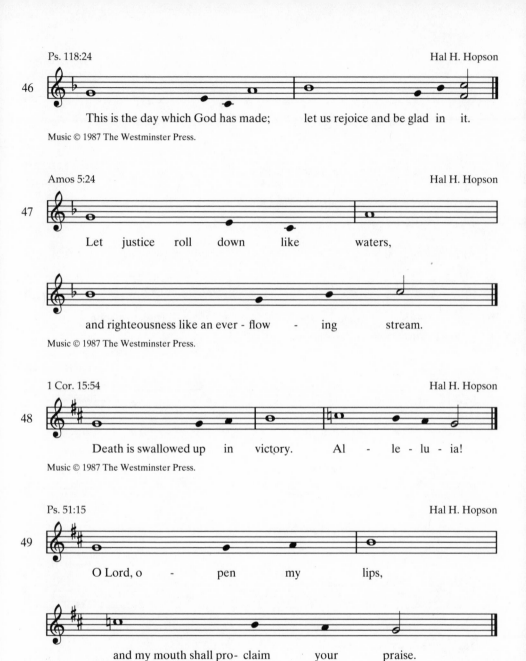

46. Ps. 118:24 — Hal H. Hopson

This is the day which God has made; let us rejoice and be glad in it.

Music © 1987 The Westminster Press.

47. Amos 5:24 — Hal H. Hopson

Let justice roll down like waters,

and righteousness like an ever - flow - ing stream.

Music © 1987 The Westminster Press.

48. 1 Cor. 15:54 — Hal H. Hopson

Death is swallowed up in victory. Al - le - lu - ia!

Music © 1987 The Westminster Press.

49. Ps. 51:15 — Hal H. Hopson

O Lord, o - pen my lips,

and my mouth shall pro- claim your praise.

Music © 1987 The Westminster Press.

Phil. 2:10–11

Hal H. Hopson

50

At the name of Jesus every knee   shall   bow,

and every tongue confess: Jesus Christ   is   Lord!

Music © 1988 The Westminster Press.

Based on Rev. 22:20

Hal H. Hopson

51

Lord,   come   soon.   Lord,   come   soon.

Music © 1988 Hope Publishing Company.

John 1:5

Hal H. Hopson

52

The   light   shines   in   the

dark - ness. Al - le - lu - ia. Al - le - lu - ia.

Music © 1988 Hope Publishing Company.

Ps. 130:1–2

Hal H. Hopson

53

Lord, I   call   to   you;   O   hear   my   cry.

Music © 1986 Hope Publishing Company.

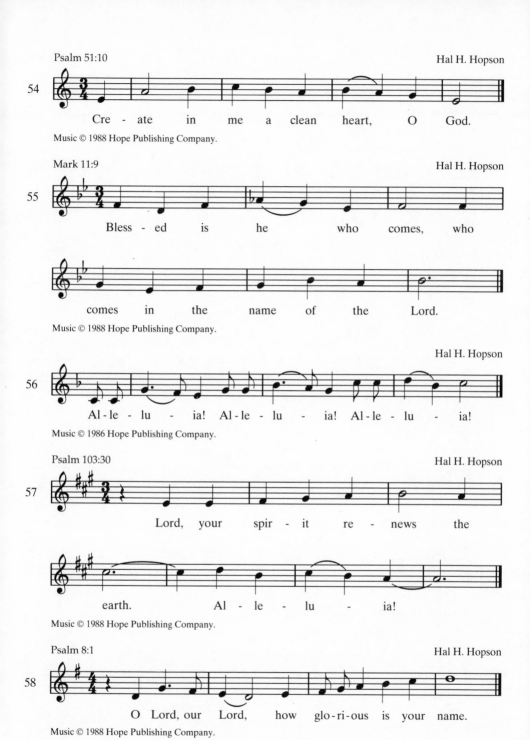

54 Psalm 51:10 — Hal H. Hopson

Cre - ate in me a clean heart, O God.

Music © 1988 Hope Publishing Company.

55 Mark 11:9 — Hal H. Hopson

Bless - ed is he who comes, who

comes in the name of the Lord.

Music © 1988 Hope Publishing Company.

56 — Hal H. Hopson

Al - le - lu - ia! Al - le - lu - ia! Al - le - lu - ia!

Music © 1986 Hope Publishing Company.

57 Psalm 103:30 — Hal H. Hopson

Lord, your spir - it re - news the

earth. Al - le - lu - ia!

Music © 1988 Hope Publishing Company.

58 Psalm 8:1 — Hal H. Hopson

O Lord, our Lord, how glo - ri - ous is your name.

Music © 1988 Hope Publishing Company.

59 Join all the saints to praise the Lord.

Al - le - lu - ia!

Music © 1988 Hope Publishing Company.

Psalm 118:24

60 This is the day which the Lord has made.

Let us re - joice! Let us re - joice! Al - le - lu - ia!

Music © 1988 Hope Publishing Company.

Psalm 67:3

61 Let the peo - ple praise you, O God. ____

____ Let all the peo - ple praise you.

Music © 1987 The Westminster Press.

Psalm 135:1

62 Praise the Lord. Praise the Lord. Praise the name of the Lord.

Music © 1987 The Westminster Press.

NOTES

NOTES

For reference numbers given at the end of liturgical texts, see Sources of the Liturgical Texts, pages 419–421.

Preface

1. "The Second Helvetic Confession," *The Constitution of the Presbyterian Church (U.S.A.)*, Part I, *Book of Confessions*, 5.226.

Introduction to the Liturgical Calendar

1. Peter C. Bower, *Handbook for the Common Lectionary* (Philadelphia: Westminster Press, 1987), pp. 19–21.

2. Thomas J. Talley, *The Origins of the Liturgical Year* (New York: Pueblo Publishing Co., 1986), pp. 231–238.

3. Peter C. Bower, "Editorial Introduction," *Reformed Liturgy & Music*, vol. 16, no. 4 (Fall 1982), p. 146.

4. *Didache* 14:1; Cyril C. Richardson, trans., *Early Christian Fathers*, The Library of Christian Classics, vol. I (Philadelphia: Westminster Press, 1963), p. 178.

5. *The First Apology of Justin, the Martyr*, 67; Cyril C. Richardson, trans., *Early Christian Fathers*, p. 287.

6. John E. Burkhart, "Why Sunday?" *Reformed Liturgy & Music*, vol. 18, no. 4 (Fall 1984), pp. 160–161.

7. Horace T. Allen, Jr., "Lord's Day—Lord's Supper," *Reformed Liturgy & Music*, vol. 18, no. 4 (Fall 1984), p. 165.

8. *The Epistle of Barnabas*, 15; *Early Christian Writings: The Apostolic Fathers* (Baltimore: Penguin Books, 1968), p. 215.

9. Easter Sunday is always the Sunday after the first full moon that occurs on or after the spring equinox on March 21. Therefore, Easter Sunday can occur no earlier than March 22 or later than April 25.

10. "Baptismal Homilies," in Edward Yarnold, *The Awe-Inspiring Rites of Initiations: Baptismal Homilies of the Fourth Century* (London: St. Paul's Publications, 1971).

11. William H. Willimon, "Letting Go Down Here," *The Christian Century*, March 5, 1986, pp. 231–232.

12. Brian Heldge, *A Triduum Sourcebook*, ed. Gabe Huck and Mary Ann Simcoe (Chicago: Liturgy Training Publications, 1983), pp. 77, 78.

13. Talley, *The Origins of the Liturgical Year*, pp. 57–61.

14. "The Scots Confession" in *The Constitution of the Presbyterian Church (U.S.A.)*, Part I, *Book of Confessions* (Louisville, Ky.: The General Assembly of the Presbyterian Church (U.S.A.), 3.13.

15. Talley, *The Origins of the Liturgical Year*, pp. 85–103.

16. From the hymn, "God Rest You Merry, Gentlemen," an eighteenth-century Christmas carol.

17. Adolf Adam, *The Liturgical Year* (New York: Pueblo Publishing Co., 1981), pp. 144–146.

18. These were examined closely by Bernard Botte in "Maranatha," *Noël, Epiphanie: retour du Christ, Lex Orandi* 40 (Paris, 1967), pp. 25–42.

19. Since the beginning of the ultimate fulfillment of God's saving purpose commences with the birth of Christ, it is easy to understand why Christmas should be considered as the beginning of the liturgical year. Advent actually is the open-ended waiting, hoping, and pleading for the coming of Christ in glory which occurs in the last days (the eschaton). As such, it is the rightful way to end the liturgical year.

20. From the nineteenth-century carol "Away in a Manger."

21. Joseph D. Small, 3rd, "Practical Aids to Lectionary Use," *Reformed Liturgy & Music* vol. 22, no. 1 (Winter 1988), p. 37.

22. The material on the Baptism of the Lord, the Transfiguration of the Lord, All Saints' Day (November 1), and Christ the King was previously published in the 1982–83 *Presbyterian Planning Calendar* in the essay "The Year of Our Lord," by Harold M. Daniels.

23. Harold M. Daniels, "Recent Changes in the Presbyterian Celebration of the Liturgical Year," *Reformed Liturgy & Music*, vol. 16, no. 4 (Fall 1982), pp. 155, 156.

Commentary on Liturgical Resources

1. *The Service for the Lord's Day*, Supplemental Liturgical Resource 1 (Philadelphia: Westminster Press, 1984).

2. *The Service for the Lord's Day*, pp. 155, 156; and each issue of the annual *Presbyterian Planning Calendar*.

3. Texts 183, 185, and 188.

4. Adrian Nocent, *The Liturgical Year, Volume One: Advent, Christmas, Epiphany* (Collegeville, Minn.: Liturgical Press, 1977), p. 163.

5. Other biblical or apocryphal allusions include the following: O Wisdom: Prov. 8:22–31; Sirach 24:3, 5; Wis. 8:1; Isa. 40:3–5. O Adonai: Ex. 3:1–15; 6:2, 3, 12, 13; 20:1–17; 3:2; 6:6. O Root: Isa: 11:1–10; Rom. 15:12; Isa. 5:15; Hab. 2:3; Heb. 10:37. O Key: Isa. 22:22 (cf. Rev. 3:7); Isa. 42:7; Ps. 107:14; Luke 1:79. O Radiant Dawn: Zech. 6:12; Luke 1:78; 2 Peter 1:19; Heb. 1:3; Mal. 4:2; Isa. 9:2;

Luke 1:78, 79. *O Ruler:* Hag. 2:8; Pss. 2, 72, 110; Gen. 49:10; 2 Sam. 7; Isa. 28:16; Eph. 2:14; Gen. 2:7. *O Emmanuel:* Isa. 7:14; 8:8; 33:22; Gen. 49:10.

6. *The Presbyterian Hymnal: Hymns, Psalms, and Spiritual Songs* (Louisville, Ky.: Westminster/John Knox Press, 1990).

7. Hal H. Hopson, *Psalm Refrains and Tones for the Common Lectionary* (Carol Stream, Ill.: Hope Publishing Co., 1988).

8. *Psalms and Canticles for Singing* (Louisville, Ky.: Westminster/John Knox Press, forthcoming in late 1992).

9. The Episcopal hymnal, *The Hymnal 1982* (New York: The Church Hymnal Corporation, 1985), provides a stanza for each of the seven antiphons. Singing this hymn in the traditional sequence of the antiphons will require reordering the stanzas as they appear in the hymnal as follows: 2, 4, 5, 6, 7, 3, 1.

10. *The Worshipbook—Services and Hymns* (Philadelphia: The Westminster Press, 1970, 1972).

11. See note 6 above.

12. Other refrains might be formed by adapting the appropriate portions of the settings of the "Holy, holy, holy Lord . . ." that are found in the *Lutheran Book of Worship* (Minneapolis: Augsburg Publishing House, 1978), pp. 69, 89, 110; *The Hymnal 1982* (New York: The Church Hymnal Corporation, 1985), nos. S117–S130; and in Joseph Roff, *Eucharistic Acclamations* (Chicago: G.I.A. Publications, 1980).

13. Perhaps the most usable resource providing the texts for the passion narratives from Matthew, Mark, and Luke (as well as the narrative in the Gospel of John) arranged for choral reading is: The National Liturgical Office, ed., *Passion Narratives for Holy Week* (Ottawa, Canada: Canadian Conference of Catholic Bishops, 1985). This resource provides suggestions for acclamations (p. 77) to be sung throughout the reading of the narrative. It may be ordered from the Canadian Conference of Catholic Bishops (address on page 426). The text arranged for choral reading may also be found in: Hoyt L. Hickman, Don E. Saliers, Laurence Hull Stookey, and James F. White, *Handbook of the Christian Year* (Nashville: Abingdon Press, 1986), pp. 135–152. The text is also available in an eight-page folder (5″ x 8″) suitable for including in a church bulletin: "The Passion of Our Lord According to Matthew [or Mark or Luke] for Congregational Reading" (Philadelphia: Fortress Press, 1975).

14. A musical setting of Lamentations 1:1–14 is included in Gabe Huck, *The Three Days: Parish Prayer in the Paschal Triduum* (Chicago: Liturgy Training Publications, 1981), pp. 103–106. (It may be ordered from Liturgy Training Publications, address on page 426.) This setting is a traditional chant which includes the successive letters of the Hebrew alphabet. In the Hebrew text, each verse begins with a successive letter in the Hebrew alphabet. In singing this text, it is traditional to sing the Hebrew letter of the alphabet with which that verse is associated.

15. See pp. 35ff.

16. Jacques Berthier, *Music from Taizé*, vol. I (vocal and instrumental editions) (Chicago: G.I.A. Publications, 1978, 1980, 1981). Order from G.I.A. (address on p. 426).

17. Perhaps the most usable resource providing the John 18:1—19:42 text (as well as the Matthew, Mark, and Luke texts for Passion/Palm Sunday)

arranged for choral reading is: Canadian Conference of Catholic Bishops, *Passion Narratives for Holy Week*, cited above in note 13. This resource provides suggestions for sung acclamations (p. 77). The text arranged for choral reading may also be found in Hickman, Saliers, Stookey, and White, *Handbook of the Christian Year* (see note 13), pp. 181–186. The text is also available in an eight-page folder (5" x 8") suitable for including in a church bulletin: "The Passion of Our Lord According to John for Congregational Reading" (Philadelphia: Fortress Press, 1975).

18. An alternative text for the bidding prayers in this resource may be found in the *Lutheran Book of Worship* (Minneapolis: Augsburg Publishing House, 1978), pp. 139–141; and the United Church of Christ *Book of Worship* (New York: United Church of Christ, Office for Church Life and Leadership, 1986), pp. 220–223.

19. An alternative text for the Solemn Reproaches may be found in the Taizé Community's daily prayer book: *Praise God* (New York: Oxford University Press, 1977), pp. 151–152.

20. Directions for making a paschal candle may be secured from the Theology and Worship Unit, Room 3408A, 100 Witherspoon St., Louisville, Ky.: 40202-1396.

21. A table of readings used in various traditions and periods of history is provided in Gabe Huck and Mary Ann Simcoe, eds., *A Triduum Sourcebook* (Chicago: Liturgy Training Publications), pp. 80–81. Order from Liturgy Training Publications (address on page 426).

22. The text may be found in Gabe Huck, *The Three Days: Parish Prayer in the Paschal Triduum* (Chicago: Liturgy Training Publications, 1981), pp. 80, 81. Order from Liturgy Training Publications (address on page 426).

23. The Consultation on Common Texts, *A Celebration of Baptism* (Nashville: Abingdon Press, 1988).

24. *Holy Baptism and Services for the Renewal of Baptism*, Supplemental Liturgical Resource 2 (Philadelphia: Westminster Press, 1985).

25. *The Funeral: A Service of Witness to the Resurrection*, Supplemental Liturgical Resource 4 (Philadelphia: Westminster Press, 1986).

26. See note 7 above.

27. See note 8 above.

SOURCES OF THE LITURGICAL TEXTS

The designation (alt.) indicates that the text was altered for this resource. The reference numbers given at the end of liturgical texts serve as a means of identification in the following lists of sources.
The hymnal designations used throughout the book are as follows:

HB   *The Hymnbook* (1955)
WB   *The Worshipbook* (1972)
PH   *The Presbyterian Hymnal* (1990)

Scripture References

All scripture quotations are from the *New Revised Standard Version of the Bible* (NRSV), except as noted. The following quotations are altered: Gen. 3:19; Deut. 7:9; Ps. 34:8; Ps. 118:1; Ps. 130:5; Isa. 2:4; Isa. 7:14b; Isa. 35:19; Isa. 58:7, 8; Isa. 61:1; Joel 1:1a; 2:28–29; Matt. 4:23; Matt. 17:5; Matt. 28:19a, 20b; Luke 1:49; Luke 3:4–6; Luke 4:18; Luke 8:15; Luke 10:25; Luke 21:36; John 6:63, 68; John 13:34; John 15:5; John 15:16; John 17:17; Acts 1:8; Rom. 5:5; 2 Cor. 5:19; Eph. 1:17, 18; Phil. 2:15, 16; Heb. 4:12; Heb. 4:14, 16; Heb. 12:1; 1 Peter 2:9; 2 Peter 3:13; Rev. 7:9–10.

The following quotations are from the *Revised Standard Version of the Bible* (RSV): Ps. 96:2–3 (alt.); Isa. 40:3; Isa. 40:6b–8; Isa. 40:9; Isa. 53:4; Isa. 53:7 (alt.); Isa. 60:1–3; Matt. 11:28; Matt. 16:16; Matt. 24:42, 44 (alt.); Matt. 26:45 (alt.); Mark 14:34 (alt.); Luke 2:10, 11; Luke 9:35; Luke 21:28 (alt.); John 1:14; John 6:35, 37 (alt.); Rom. 18:32 (alt.); 2 Cor. 8:9; 1 Thess. 5:23 (alt.); Phil. 1:9, 10 (alt.); Phil. 4:7.

1 Cor. 10:16–17 (alt.) is from *The New English Bible* (NEB).
Ezek. 36:26 is from *The Bible in Today's English Version* (TEV).
1 Cor. 5:7, 8 (alt.) is from the *King James Version of the Bible*.
The following are based on more than one version: Ps. 16:9, 10; Ps. 51:6–7 (NRSV, *Book of Common Prayer*, Grail); Ps. 105:1–5 (RSV and Gary Chamberlain, *The Psalms*); Matt. 23:9, 10 (RSV, NEB); Matt. 24:42, 44 (RSV, NRSV);

Acts 2:26, 27 *(Jerusalem Bible,* RSV, NRSV); Eph. 5:8, 10 (RSV, NRSV); Phil. 2:8, 9 (RSV, NRSV).

Isa. 38:10–20 (Canticle of Hezekiah) is from the *Book of Occasional Services* (Episcopal).

Prayers

The numbers that follow refer to the numbers at the end of each liturgical text.

The sources noted are the sources from which the texts in this resource were taken, or sources those resources cited. In many cases the particular text is not original with the source noted, since many liturgical texts that are widely shared are derived from a longer tradition and appear in a number of contemporary service books.

Written for this resource: 2, 3, 4, 11, 15, 16, 30, 31, 34, 35, 36, 43, 49, 55, 56, 57, 63, 68, 69, 70, 85, 92, 98, 105, 111, 114, 115, 131, 140, 141, 144, 145, 146, 186, 187, 188, 190, 191, 192.

From *Book of Alternative Services,* Anglican Church of Canada: 10 (alt.), 18, 24, 28, 32 (alt.), 37, 39, 42, 48, 50, 51, 61 (alt.), 64, 65, 71, 76, 77, 79, 86, 100, 109, 118, 121, 126, 129, 133, 134, 142, 147, 148, 149, 150, 154, 155, 157, 158 (alt.), 164, 166, 167 (alt.), 169 (alt.), 172, 173, 175, 177.

From *Alternative Collects, 1985,* The Anglican Church of Australia: 83 (alt.), 163 (alt.), 183.

From *The Book of Common Prayer,* Episcopal Church (U.S.A.): 54 (alt.), 59 (alt.), 62 (alt.), 82 (alt.), 96 (alt.), 101 (alt.), 107 (alt.), 108 (alt.), 123 (alt.), 128 (alt.), 143 (alt.), 176 (alt.), 178 (alt.), 179 (alt.), 181 (alt.), 189 (alt.).

From *The Book of Common Worship,* Presbyterian Church in the U.S.A., 1946: 13 (alt.), 112 (alt.), 116 (alt.).

From *Book of Worship,* United Church of Christ: 81, 84 (alt.), 104 (alt.).

From *Daily Prayer* (Supplemental Liturgical Resource 5): 12 (both litany and concluding petition), 137 (concluding collect).

From *Handbook of the Christian Year* (Nashville: Abingdon Press, 1986): 91 (alt.), 97 (alt.), 102, 106 (alt.).

From Horace T. Allen, Jr., *A Handbook for the Lectionary* (Philadelphia: Geneva Press, 1980): 6.

From *Holy Baptism and Services for the Renewal of Baptism* (Supplemental Liturgical Resource 2): 110 (based on).

From Italian Sacramentary, translated by Fr. Peter Scagnelli: 46 (alt.), 52 (alt.), 151 (alt.), 168 (alt.), 170, 174 (alt.).

From *Lutheran Book of Worship:* 9 (alt.), 41 (alt.), 72 (alt.), 75 (alt.), 78 (alt.), 80 (alt.), 88 (alt.), 95, 124, 135 (alt.), 136, 147 (alt.), 152 (alt.), 156, 160 (alt.), 161 (alt.), 182 (alt.).

The following are translations from the Latin Roman Missal as they appear in the *Lutheran Book of Worship:* 7, 23, 25 (alt.), 27 (alt.), 53 (alt.), 93 (alt.), 103 (alt.), 119, 127, 153 (alt.), 162.

From Report of the Special Joint Committee on the Worshipbook *(Minutes of the 186th General Assembly (1974) of the United Presbyterian Church in the U.S.A., Part I, Journal):* 67 (alt.), 185 (alt.).

From *The Roman Missal: The Sacramentary:* 99 (alt.), 122 (alt.).

From *Uniting in Worship,* Uniting Church in Australia: 40 (alt.), 44 (alt.), 73 (alt.), 74 (alt.), 159 (alt.), 171, 180 (alt.), 184 (alt.).

From *The Worshipbook:* 1 (based on), 5 (alt.), 8 (alt.), 14 (alt.), 17 (alt.), 19, 20, 21 (alt.), 22 (alt.), 26 (alt.), 29 (alt.), 33 (alt.), 38 (alt.), 45 (alt.), 47, 66, 87 (alt.), 89, 90 (alt.), 94 (alt.), 113, 117, 120 (alt.), 125 (alt.), 130 (alt.), 132 (alt.), 138 (alt.), 165 (alt.).

From liturgy used at the 192nd (1980) General Assembly of the United Presbyterian Church in the U.S.A.: 137, 139.

Source unknown: 58 (alt.), 60 (alt.)

Other Texts

The Festival of Lessons and Carols (pages 82–84) is adapted from the traditional service at King's College Chapel, Cambridge, England.

The Tenebrae (pages 152–158) is adapted from the Episcopal *Book of Occasional Services.*

The Greeting in the Maundy Thursday service (page 160) is from *The Book of Alternative Services* of the Anglican Church of Canada.

The Reaffirmation of Baptismal Vows is adapted from *Holy Baptism and Services for the Renewal of Baptism,* Supplemental Liturgical Resource 2.

The Declaration of Pardon in the Maundy Thursday service is from *The Service for the Lord's Day,* Supplemental Liturgical Resource 1, and is based on a declaration of pardon in the *Book of Common Worship* (1906, 1932, 1946).

"Lord, have mercy," the Apostles' Creed, the preface dialogue to the eucharistic prayers (and the adaptation for use with the prayers of thanks), "Holy, holy, holy Lord," the contemporary-language version of the Lord's Prayer, "Jesus, Lamb of God," and the Canticle of Zechariah are agreed ecumenical texts prepared by the English Language Liturgical Consultation (ELLC).

The acclamations in the eucharistic prayers are from *The Roman Missal: The Sacramentary.*

FOR FURTHER READING

General Texts

Adam, Adolf. *The Liturgical Year*. New York: Pueblo Publishing Co., 1981 (English translation).

Bosch, Paul. *Church Year Guide*. Minneapolis: Augsburg Publishing House, 1987.

Cobb, Peter G. "The History of the Christian Year." In *The Study of Liturgy*, edited by Chesyln Jones, Geoffrey Wainwright, and Edward Yarnold, pp. 403–419. New York: Oxford University Press, 1978.

Martimort, Aimé Georges, Irenée Henri Dalmais, and Pierre Jounel. *The Liturgy and Time*. Translated by Matthew J. O'Connell. Volume IV of *The Church at Prayer: An Introduction to the Liturgy*. Collegeville, Minn.: Liturgical Press, 1986.

McArthur, A. Allan. *The Evolution of the Christian Year*. Greenwich, Conn.: Seabury Press, 1953.

Reformed Liturgy & Music, vol. 25, no. 1 (Winter 1991). Theme: Liturgical Calendar.

Talley, Thomas. *The Origins of the Liturgical Year*. New York: Pueblo Publishing Co., 1986.

Wegman, Herman A. "Festivals and Celebrations Throughout the Year." *Christian Worship in East and West: A Study Guide to Liturgical History*, pp. 25–34, 98–107, 172–177, 225, 277–285. Translated by Gordon W. Lathrop. New York: Pueblo Publishing Co., 1985.

Time

Bouyer, Louis. "Sacred Time." In *Rite and Man*, pp. 189–205. Notre Dame, Ind.: Notre Dame Press, 1963.

Dix, Dom Gregory. "The Sanctification of Time." In *The Shape of the Liturgy*, pp. 303–396. London: A. & C. Black, 1945.

Eliade, Mircea. "The Regeneration of Time." In *Cosmos and History: The Myth of the Eternal Return*, pp. 49–92. New York: Harper & Row, Harper Torchbooks, 1954.

———. "Sacred Time and Myths." In *The Sacred & The Profane: The Nature of Religion*, pp. 68–115. New York: Harcourt Brace Jovanovich, 1957.

Hatchett, Marion J. *Sanctifying Life, Time, and Space*. New York: Seabury Press, 1976. (Read portions relevant to the "sanctification of time.")

Johnson, Lawrence J., ed. *The Church Gives Thanks and Remembers: Essays on the Liturgical Year*. Collegeville, Minn.: The Liturgical Press, 1984.

Micks, Marianne H. "Rhythm in the Calendar." In *The Future Present: The Phenomenon of Christian Worship*, pp. 35–53. New York: Seabury Press, 1970.

Schulz, Frieder. "Liturgical Time in the Traditions of the Post-Reformation Churches." In *Liturgical Time*, edited by Wiebe Vos and Geoffrey Wainwright, pp. 52–73. Rotterdam: Liturgical Ecumenical Center Trust, 1982.

Talley, Thomas. "Liturgical Time in the Ancient Church: The State of Research." In *Liturgical Time*, edited by Wiebe Vos and Geoffrey Wainwright, pp. 34–51. Rotterdam: Liturgical Ecumenical Center Trust, 1982.

White, James F. "The Language of Time." In *Introduction to Christian Worship*, pp. 44–75. Nashville: Abingdon Press, 1980.

History and Eschatology

Taft, Robert. "Historicism Revisited." In *Liturgical Time*, edited by Wiebe Vos and Geoffrey Wainwright, pp. 97–109. Rotterdam: Liturgical Ecumenical Center Trust, 1982.

Talley, Thomas J. "History and Eschatology in the Primitive Pascha." *Worship*, vol. 47 (1973), pp. 212–221.

Sunday

Allen, Horace T., Jr. "Lord's Day—Lord's Supper." *Reformed Liturgy & Music*, vol. 18, no. 4 (Fall 1984), pp. 162–166.

Burkhart, John E. "The Lord's Day." In *Worship: A Searching Examination of the Liturgical Experience*, pp. 53–70. Philadelphia: Westminster Press, 1982.

———. "Why Sunday?" *Reformed Liturgy & Music*, vol. 18, no. 4 (Fall 1984), pp. 159–161.

Maertens, Thierry. "Sabbath and Sunday." In *A Feast in Honor of Yahweh*, pp. 152–192. Notre Dame, Ind.: Fides Publishers, 1965.

Porter, H. Boone. *The Day of Light—The Biblical and Liturgical Meaning of Sunday*. Greenwich, Conn.: Seabury Press, 1960.

Rordorf, Willi. *Sunday: The History of the Day of Rest and Worship in the Earliest Centuries of the Christian Church*. Philadelphia: Westminster, 1968.

Paschal Cycle

Allen, Horace T., Jr. "Celebrating the Sunday before the Holy Week According to the New Calendar." *Reformed Liturgy & Music*, vol. 11, no. 4 (Fall 1977), pp. 7–17.

———. "Proclaiming the Pascha." *Reformed Liturgy & Music*, vol. 21, no. 4 (Fall 1987), pp. 246–247.

Baker, J. Robert, Evelyn Kaehler, and Peter Mazar, eds. Suzanne M. Novak (artist). *A Lenten Sourcebook: The Forty Days*, 2 vols. Chicago: Liturgy Training Publications, 1990.

Berger, Rupert, and Hans Hollerweger, eds. *Celebrating the Easter Vigil*. Translated by Matthew J. O'Connell. New York: Pueblo Publishing Co., 1983.

Crichton, J. D. *The Liturgy of Holy Week*. Dublin: Veritas, 1983.

Daniélou, Jean. "Easter." In *The Bible and the Liturgy*, pp. 262–286. Notre Dame, Ind.: Notre Dame Press, 1956.

———. "The Ascension." In *The Bible and the Liturgy*, pp. 287–302. Notre Dame, Ind.: Notre Dame Press, 1956.

———. "Pentecost." In *The Bible and the Liturgy*, pp. 303–318. Notre Dame, Ind.: Notre Dame Press, 1956.

Davies, J. Gordon. *Holy Week: A Short History*. Richmond: John Knox Press, 1963.

Gunstone, John. *The Feast of Pentecost*. London: Faith Press, 1967.

Hickman, Hoyt L., Dan E. Saliers, Laurence Hull Stookey, and James F. White. "Passion/Palm Sunday." *Handbook of the Christian Year*, pp. 125–152. Nashville: Abingdon Press, 1986.

———. "Holy Thursday Evening." *Handbook of the Christian Year*, pp. 160–170. Nashville: Abingdon Press, 1986.

———. "Good Friday." *Handbook of the Christian Year*, pp. 179–190. Nashville: Abingdon Press, 1986.

———. "Proclaiming the Paschal Mystery: An Introduction to the Seasons of Lent and Easter." In *Handbook of the Christian Year*, pp. 105–110. Nashville: Abingdon Press, 1986.

Huck, Gabe. *The Three Days: Parish Prayer in the Paschal Triduum*. Chicago: Liturgy Training Publications, 1981.

Huck, Gabe, Gail Ramshaw, and Gordon Lathrop, eds. Barbara Schmich (artist). *An Easter Sourcebook: The Fifty Days*. Chicago: Liturgy Training Publications, 1988.

Huck, Gabe, and Mary Ann Simcoe, eds. *A Triduum Sourcebook*. Chicago: Liturgy Training Publications, 1983.

Maertens, Thierry. "The Feast of the First Sheaf of Wheat or The Feast of Pentecost." In *A Feast in Honor of Yahweh*, pp. 98–151. Notre Dame, Ind.: Fides Publishers, 1965.

Pfatteicher, Philip H., and Carlos R. Messerli. "Celebrating the Cross and Resurrection." *Manual on the Liturgy: Lutheran Book of Worship*, pp. 305–338. Minneapolis: Augsburg Publishing House, 1979.

Reformed Liturgy & Music, vol. 24, no. 1 (Winter 1990). Theme: Easter Cycle.

Schmemann, Alexander. "Introduction: Lent: Journey to Pascha." In *Great Lent*, pp. 11–15. Tuckahoe, N.Y.: St. Vladimir's Seminary Press, 1974.

Senn, Frank C., "The Lord's Supper, Not the Passover Seder." *Worship*, vol. 60, no. 4 (1986), pp. 362–368.

Stevenson, Kenneth. *Jerusalem Revisited: The Liturgical Meaning of Holy Week*. Washington, D.C.: Pastoral Press, 1988.

———. "On Keeping Holy Week." *Theology*, vol. 89 (1986), pp. 32–38.

de Vaux, Roland. "The Ancient Feasts of Israel." In *Ancient Israel: Religious Institutions*, vol. 2, pp. 484–505. New York: McGraw-Hill Book Co., 1961.

Christmas Cycle

Bouyer, Louis. "The Mystery in the Liturgical Year: The Advent Liturgy, Christmas, and Epiphany." In *Liturgical Piety*, pp. 200–214. Notre Dame, Ind.: University of Notre Dame Press, 1954.

Buttrick, David G. "The Christmas Cycle." *Reformed Liturgy & Music*, vol. 21, no. 3 (Summer 1987), pp. 178–180.

Erickson, Craig Douglas. "Epiphany: Christmas Finale or *Postscriptum?*" *Reformed Liturgy & Music*, vol. 22, no. 3 (Summer 1988), pp. 149–152.

Hickman, Hoyt L., Don E. Saliers, Laurence Hull Stookey, and James F. White. "From Hope to Joy: Advent and Christmas/Epiphany" *Handbook of the Christian Year*, pp. 51–104. Nashville: Abingdon Press, 1986.

Jounel, Pierre. "The Christmas Season." *The Liturgy and Time*, translated by Matthew J. O'Connell, pp. 77–96. Volume IV of *The Church at Prayer: An Introduction to the Liturgy*. Collegeville, Minn.: Liturgical Press, 1986.

O'Gorman, Thomas J., ed. Tom Goddard (artist). *An Advent Sourcebook*. Chicago: Liturgy Training Publications, 1988.

Reformed Liturgy & Music, vol. 22, no. 3 (Summer 1988). Theme: "Christmas Cycle"

Simcoe, Mary Ann, ed. *A Christmas Sourcebook*. Chicago: Liturgy Training Publications, 1984.

Supplemental Liturgical Resources. The following soft-cover trial use resources have been prepared in anticipation of a new service book scheduled for publication in 1993. These may be ordered from the Presbyterian Publishing House (address on page 426).

> *Service for the Lord's Day*. Supplemental Liturgical Resource 1. Philadelphia: The Westminster Press, 1984.
>
> *Holy Baptism and Services for the Renewal of Baptism*. Supplemental Liturgical Resource 2. Philadelphia: The Westminster Press, 1985.
>
> *Christian Marriage*. Supplemental Liturgical Resource 3. Philadelphia: The Westminster Press, 1986.
>
> *The Funeral: A Service of Witness to the Resurrection*. Supplemental Liturgical Resource 4. Philadelphia: The Westminster Press, 1986.
>
> *Daily Prayer*. Supplemental Liturgical Resource 5. Philadelphia: The Westminster Press, 1987.
>
> *Services for Occasions of Pastoral Care*. Supplemental Liturgical Resource 6. Louisville: Westminster/John Knox Press, 1990.
>
> *Liturgical Year*. Supplemental Liturgical Resource 7. Louisville: Westminster/John Knox Press, 1992.

ADDRESSES

Canadian Conference of Catholic Bishops, Publications Service, 90 Parent Avenue, Ottawa, Ontario, K1N 7B1, Canada.

G.I.A. Publications, Inc., 7404 S. Mason Avenue, Chicago, IL 60638. Phone: 708-496-3800 (Fax 708-496-2130).

Liturgy Training Publications, 1800 North Hermitage Avenue, Chicago, IL 60622-1101. Phone: 312-486-7008, extension 24.

Presbyterian Publishing House, 100 Witherspoon Street, Louisville, KY 40202-1396. Phone: 1-800-227-2872.

ACKNOWLEDGMENTS

Material from the following sources is gratefully acknowledged and is used by permission. Adaptations are by permission of copyright holders. Every effort has been made to determine the ownership of all texts and music used in this resource and to make proper arrangements for their use. The publisher regrets any oversight that may have occurred and will gladly make proper acknowledgment in future editions if this is brought to the publisher's attention.

Scripture quotations from the Revised Standard Version of the Bible are copyrighted 1946, 1952, © 1971, 1973 by the Division of Christian Education of the National Council of the Churches of Christ in the U.S.A.

Scripture quotations from the New Revised Standard Version of the Bible are copyrighted © 1989 by the Division of Christian Education of the National Council of the Churches of Christ in the U.S.A. and are used by permission.

Scripture quotations from The Bible in Today's English Version are copyrighted © 1976 by the American Bible Society.

Scripture quotations from the New English Bible are copyrighted © 1961, 1970 by The Delegates of the Oxford University Press and The Syndics of the Cambridge University Press.

The Book of Alternative Services of the Anglican Church of Canada, © 1985 General Synod of the Anglican Church of Canada. Used by permission.

The Book of Common Worship, copyright, 1946, by The Board of Christian Education of the Presbyterian Church in the United States of America; renewed 1974. Used by permission of Westminster/John Knox Press.

Book of Occasional Services, © Church Pension Fund. Used by permission of The Church Hymnal Corporation.

Book of Worship United Church of Christ. Used by permission of the Office for Church Life and Leadership, United Church of Christ.

Daily Prayer (Supplemental Liturgical Resource 5). © 1987 The Westminster Press. Used by permission of Westminster/John Knox Press.

The General Synod, Anglican Church of Australia, for prayers 83 (page 143), 163 (page 246), and 183 (page 259). From *Alternative Collects 1985*. Copyright Anglican Church of Australia Trust Corporation. Published by the Anglican Information Office. Reproduced with permission.

A Handbook for the Lectionary, by Horace T. Allen, Jr. Copyright © 1980 The Geneva Press. Used by permission of Westminster/John Knox Press.

Handbook of the Christian Year, edited by Hoyt Hickman et al. Copyright © 1986 Abingdon Press. Altered and reprinted by permission.

Holy Baptism and Services for the Renewal of Baptism (Supplemental Liturgical Resource 2). Copyright © 1985 The Westminster Press. Used by permission of Westminster/John Knox Press.

International Commission on English in the Liturgy, for the English translation of the memorial acclamations and collects and for the Exsultet, from *The Roman Missal* © 1973, International Committee on English in the Liturgy, Inc. All rights reserved.

Liturgy Training Publications, for translations by Fr. Peter Scagnelli from the Italian Sacramentary.

Lutheran Book of Worship: Minister's Desk Edition, copyright © 1978. Used by permission of Augsburg Fortress.

Minutes of the General Assembly of the United Presbyterian Church in the U.S.A. (1974). Used by permission of the General Assembly, Presbyterian Church (U.S.A.)

Uniting in Worship, copyright © 1988, The Uniting Church in Australia Assembly Commission on Liturgy. Used by permission of the Joint Board of Christian Education, Melbourne, Australia.

The Worshipbook—Services and Hymns. Copyright © MCMLXX, MCMLXXII, The Westminster Press. Used by permission of Westminster/John Knox Press.